Traversing Gender

Traversing **Gender**
Understanding Transgender Realities
by Lee Harrington

MYSTIC
PRODUCTIONS LLC

Notice

Traversing Gender: Understanding Transgender Realities
© 2016 – Lee Harrington and Mystic Productions Press
www.TraversingGender.com

Published in the United States by Mystic Productions Press, LLC;
603 Tudor Rd. Anchorage, AK 99503 www.MysticProductionsPress.com
All text by Lee Harrington, except where otherwise noted
www.PassionAndSoul.com

Artwork by Andi Fogt www.AndiFogt.com
Interior and Exterior Layout by Rob River www.RobRiver.com
Image of Lee Harrington by Darrell Lynn www.KiltedPhotography.daportfolio.com

ISBN – 978-1-942733-81-2
Ebooks: MOBI – 978-1-942733-82-9
ePub – 978-1-942733-83-6
PDF – 978-1-942733-84-3

For those who died too young.

Traversing Gender: Understanding Transgender Realities
By Lee Harrington

Health 63

World at Large

What is Transgender?

When a child is born, instead of saying "it's a baby," we lift them up and declare "it's a boy" or "it's a girl." In an instant, a child's gender identity, orientation, life experiences, sexual behaviors and social interactions have been painted upon them by societal expectations and standards. The truth is, people are more complex than that.

For most people, the gender they were assigned at birth is the same as the gender that they identify with throughout their lives. For others, they are not a perfect match. They might not be a match at all.

Every person notices gender for the first time at different moments in their life. For some it occurs when you notice that boys and girls have different bodies. Perhaps it was when a parent took away a doll from you, or said that you should "man up." Others experience this when someone tried to dress them in frilly outfits, or said "that's not very ladylike."

Whether a person notices gender on a day to day basis, gender affects us in different ways. It affects what people wear. How we navigate culture. The expectations of our family, friends, and associates. This is because gender is embedded in the societies we live in. This includes how people perceive our gender, as well as the messages the world around us tells us about gender.

For transgender people, this is an even bigger issue. An estimated 700,000 transgender people live in the United States[1], with millions living worldwide[2]. By traversing their various experiences, we will help make the world a better place for transgender individuals. This will lead to the world being a better place for all of us, since gender affects every one of us.

This book is intended as an overview of diverse gender journeys, the many topics that affect transgender and gender nonconforming lives, and those of the people who care for and about them. It is an introduction to the topic, a road-map to the world of gender variant people. Creating this map, whether we are trans or otherwise, will build an awareness of gender, or the paths we already find ourselves on.

"Trans" is a shorthand for transgender. Trans means "across," "on the other side," or "beyond" in Latin; used commonly in terms like "transatlantic." Both transgender and trans have been used to create social cohesion for a movement towards equality, with the goal of bringing individuals of different gender journeys together. They are powerful and useful terms. They have simultaneously been considered reductive of the experiences of individuals and populations who do not identify with these words. This is important to consider because not everyone that is trans within a specific definition is necessarily trans according to their own definition. This is why transgender and gender nonconforming (TGNC) is often used as a broader net, including a wider range of people from diverse gender experience.

The term transgender is offered in contrast to those who are non-transgender, or academically speaking, cisgender. The prefix "cis" is the Latin term for "on the same side of," and refers to individuals whose gender is in alignment with the sex they were assigned at birth. There are those who use "cisgender" in a derogatory way or perceive it to be offensive. The term itself is not inherently offensive, simply a different adjective, similar to describing one person as brunette and another person as blonde. Being referred to as blonde is no better or worse than being brunette, it is simply an adjective to describe someone's hair. So it is with cis or trans, especially within the context of this book.

Transgender is also an umbrella term. For the context of this book, it includes all concepts of gender variances outside of having your gender or sex assigned at birth correspond with your gender experience, as discussed further in Chapter 1. Since transgender is sometimes used as a specific term to discuss people moving from one end of a binary to another, such as women who transition to being men, and men who transition to being women, the terms gender-nonconforming and gender variant will also be used throughout the book.

Gender identity is not a choice for most transgender people. Their gender is part of who they are, and it simply "is what it is." There are, however, select individuals who chose their gender, or express gender creativity, after examining their own personal truths. Just because there are exceptions, this does not mean that the "born this way"[3] experience is not real and true for the vast number of trans people.

There are many terms under the transgender umbrella:

- **Transsexual** (moving from one gender and/or body configuration to that of the opposite gender and/or body configuration)

- **Trans woman** (a woman who was assigned male at birth, who identifies as a woman)

- **Trans man** (a man who was assigned female at birth, who identifies as a man)

- **Two-Spirit** (a term used by certain North American indigenous populations for those who exist beyond the heterosexual, cisgender experience)

- **Third Gender** (a diverse category of individuals who are beyond or between binary genders worldwide)

- **Agender** (a person with no personal gender, or believes their bodily gender has little to do with their identity)

- **Genderqueer** (a person working beyond the concept of gender binaries)

- **Gender Fluid** (a person who flows back and forth between or among genders)

- … and many other forms of gender identity and expression!

These terms are often confused with the term "transgendered," which is slowly cycling out of common language, since the word "transgender" is most often an adjective not a verb. Thus, a "transgendered person" is like saying a "brunetted person." One cannot be "brunetted." The person in question would be referred to as a brunette person, and so it is with a trans person. While transgender is occasionally used as a noun (I am a transgender, we are transgenders), it is less common in current Western English-language vernacular. There are also those who use "transgendered" to refer to someone who has shifted from one gender to another, use of the word "transitioned" is more common.

For the context of this book, the words *trans, transgender* and *gender nonconforming (TGNC)* have been chosen for simplification of discussion for this complex topic. For those who do not identify with these labels, know that the use of it was not intended to cause harm or end the conversation. Instead, they are a way to start this rich dialogue. Other concepts, identities and labels will be shared throughout this text as counterpoint.

Learning about labels is important because labels are used in lots of different ways:

- As a tool for us to sort out our own brain (This person is trans)

- As a way we make decisions (They are trans, we should make sure they will be comfortable in this space)

- As a way to create a safer society (Trans individuals deserve respect)

- As terms we refer to people when they are not around (You know, the trans guy)

- As something we tell people they are (You are trans)

- As something we tell others we are (I am trans)

- As something we tell our peers as a way to identify as a group (We are all trans)

- As a way we think in our own head (Am I trans?)

When asking if someone is transgender, consider which labeling category you are asking about. When we say "labels don't matter," we are saying that a person's self-identity does not matter. If that person says labels don't matter, and you force a label on them, we are saying that their autonomy doesn't matter. Other people's self-labels are not about us; those labels are about them. Labels, like pronouns and preferred names, can be a delicate issue. In chapter 10 there are ideas concerning this concept, and navigating the topic.

This diverse collection of terminology can feel confusing at times for those attempting to learning it, while building trans awareness. This is the case whether you are trans or otherwise, which is why a glossary is included at the back of this book, along with a collection of resources for further support and learning.

Some people are expanding their awareness due to a generational or cultural upbringing that expect the concepts of sex, gender and gendered behavior to always "match" in a certain way. Others are transgender or gender nonconforming, and want to develop terms to explain their own personal experiences. An individual might be learning language and tools around trans issues to build awareness, compassion and allyship as we all journey together. It is also possible that some are curious about the whole "trans thing."

If you are trans or gender nonconforming and are looking for an in-depth guide to navigating all of the details of your journey, there are additional resources out there. There are great books available in the resources segment of this book, ranging from legal resources to health information, youth resources to movies about trans experience. If you are looking for something that takes you deeper into these topics, or learn best from personal stories, and read only one of these other books, consider the deliciously complex and accessible text *Trans Bodies, Trans Selves*[4].

This book is written with present day knowledge and discussion. The theories, concepts and information presented in this book will continue to shift over time. This also means that the concerns and fear around these topics will also shift, because through knowledge and awareness we all have a chance to learn and grow. To do so, there are three different goals for the book:

- To help those who are new to these concepts build an understanding of the lives of diverse trans experiences.

- Provide language, resources and awareness for those on various gender journeys for exploration, activism and moving forward on their personal paths.

- Enable individuals to become social, emotional, professional, and medical allies to transgender communities and in doing so, help make the world a better place, one life at a time.

Let's begin, shall we?

Journeys

No two transgender or gender nonconforming individuals follow the same path. They may have known and communicated their gender realities from a very young age, or transitioned in their later years. Their path may lead them into a space of being androgynous, or firmly transitioning from one binary gender to another.

Since there are such diverse gender journeys, the next three chapters of this book introduce us to many possible places people are traveling.

In Chapter 1 we review the concepts of sex and gender:
- basic terminology of sex, gender, identity, and orientation
- diversity of sex and biology
- concepts of gender-based behaviors and assumptions
- differences between gender identity and sexuality

In Chapter 2 we sift through various types of transgender journeys:
- transsexual, transgender, and binary gender transitions
- gender expression outside of a Western perspective
- expressions of gender beyond male and female
- conscious gender exploration

And in Chapter 3, we look into different time periods for transition:
- childhood and teen transitions
- adult transitions and interpersonal relationships
- transitioning later in life, and trans elder care
- alternate routes of transition

Chapter One

Sex, Gender, and Orientation

Sex, gender, orientation, sexual behavior, intimacy, relationships…

People sometimes assume that these things line up in a specific way. However, each of these are different and distinct concepts, and this is very important if we plan to understand transgender experiences. One way to break it down is as follows:

- Sex is the body we have
- Assigned gender is what we were told we were at birth
- Gendered behaviors are the actions we engage in
- Gender expression is how we communicate our gender
- Perceived gender is how other people see us
- Legal gender is what the government says we are
- Gender identity is how we see ourselves
- Orientation is who we are attracted to
- Sexual behavior is what we do with our bodies

Not every culture around the world categorizes these things in the same way, but this gives us a basic place to start the dialogue for the context of this book. So let's buckle in and look at these individual concepts to help us see where a lot of misunderstandings around transgender come from.

Sex

The concept of sex is based around the body we were born with. It is based on our biology. Sex is broken down into a few major categories: chromosomes; primary sex traits; and secondary sex traits.

Chromosomes

In school, many people are taught that there are only two chromosomal types: XX and XY. Girls are assumed to be XX, and boys are assumed to be XY. But there are a wide diversity of other chromosomal variances and intersex conditions.

Intersex conditions happen in one child out of 2000[1]. Most children are XX or XY, but others are XXY, X0 or XX0[2]. A child might have a mixture of two fertilized eggs, have a Mosaicism (patchwork of cells), or have a diversity of chromosomes within a single body[3]. People who were assigned female at birth might be XY, while people who were assigned male at birth might be XX.

Very few people ever have the opportunity to have, or know it is possible to have, their chromosomes tested. Most people don't know if their gender matches their chromosomes. Many of us are making assumptions about our bodies that might be challenged if we had access to all the information.

Primary Sex Traits

Primary sex traits include not just the chromosomes, but the gonads, anatomy of the internal genitalia, and the anatomy of the external genitalia. Early on in the development of a fetus, all genitals begin with a similar structure – if not in function[4]. Gonads, such as ovaries or testes, are responsible for holding and producing the eggs and sperm for producing future offspring. Female individuals have ovaries and males have testes; girls have vaginas and clitorises, and boys have penises and scrotums. For most XX and XY individuals, this specific type gonad to body configuration applies, but there are exceptions.

There are people who believe that females have estrogen and males have testosterone. This is not entirely accurate as everyone has estrogen and testosterone in their systems. Females traditionally have more estrogen while males have more testosterone, but variances in levels of productions for those hormones occur all the time.

Just as chromosomes are not as binary as they seem, neither are genitals. Everyone is different! This is sometimes due to birth differences, including phallus size, scrotum length, the degree to which the clitoris is exposed or the length and color of someone's labia. Other differences are from medical operations, such as a person who has had a hysterectomy (uterus removal, sometimes with ovary or cervix removal) or having the testes removed. It may also be due to culturally imposed standards, such as foreskin removal (circumcision) or clitoral nullification (female genital mutilation).

Secondary Sex Traits

Appearing usually at puberty, secondary sex traits are the body characteristics including breasts, body hair, menstrual cycles, fat distribution, and overall height. It is through these secondary sex traits and the cultural cues (such as the color a person wears, hairstyles, or scents worn) that we figure out  whether someone is a man or a woman when we see them on the street.

Just like shape and size of genitals, the diversity of secondary sex trait distribution varies wildly; not just by person, but by family, nationality or ethnic background. The belief that only men having large upper bodies and shoulder girdles creates a story that some women of Polynesian or African descent are "manly," or that only women have little body hair infers that various Asian men are somehow "girly." Women with facial hair get painted as less feminine, while men with mammary tissue get harassed for their body realities.

Secondary sex traits have certain patterns, but are not as all-inclusive or homogenous as depicted by mass-media. At different points in history specific physical displays of femininity and masculinity have been praised. Cultural standards vary as well, from the flat-chested flapper-girls of 1920s to Rubens' 1600s voluptuous ladies, lithe J-pop singers to curvaceous Nigerian fashionistas.

Intersex Conditions

An intersex person is born with the sexual anatomy, reproductive organs, or chromosome patterns that do not fit the typical definition of male or female. Being intersex is not about sexual orientation or gender identity[5]. It was sometimes referred to in historical contexts as being a hermaphrodite when a child had traits of both expected sexes, but this term is nowadays considered inappropriate and even offensive[6] to many – but not everyone. Intersex circles and activists point out that it is inaccurate, and refers to a story within Greek mythology[7].

In the case of some intersex children, there is a hesitation by medical professionals in determining whether male or female should be assigned, based on the presentation of their genitals. For 1 in 20,000, this ambiguity leads to a drawn out process[8]. This sometimes causes discomfort for both parents and medical professionals, due to a desire to have an expression of binary gender, as well as confusion for administrators who are not able to issue birth certificates until a gender is assigned.

With only male and female available as markers on birth certificates in the United States, it can alienate these children whose body do not match with the expectations of those assigned sexes. Over the years there have been many doctors who have attempted to "disambiguate" babies with ambiguous genitals, forcing them into one expected gender or another through operations[9]. There has been a push to develop the rights for intersex children to stop unnecessary surgeries[10], with some countries having already passed laws on the matter[11].

Intersex traits manifest at many different times during a person's life, such as during puberty, with the development of secondary sex traits. Boys grow breasts, and women develop extensive body hair. Other intersex conditions are only discovered when someone is trying to reproduce. They have different internal gonads than expected or variations in hormone levels and fertility.

Before we even examine gender, we see that sex itself is not as simple and binary as most have been taught to believe. People have argued that "biological sex" is something that makes a man a man, and a woman a woman. This is flawed logic, as it states that women have breasts (not all women do, and some men do), men have more body hair, and other gender fallacies. Arguments like "women have the ability to give birth" marginalizes women who are infertile while simultaneously harming intersex and trans people.

Assigned Gender

The gender you are given at birth based on biological sex is called an assigned gender. It is done at the doctor's best guess, determined by visible expressions of sex traits rather than internal configurations. This assignment can also take place before birth when a doctor or nurse says "you're going to have a boy" while looking at a sonogram. This confuses parents when they were told it would be a boy based on that guess, but they are handed a girl upon birth.

When a parent has been told "it's a boy" or "it's a girl," the difference of projection on that child happens almost immediately. Their room gets decorated differently, their clothes are different (or purchased anew if they were "wrong"), and whispers at night will tell the child of their parents' expectations for them. There are religious groups and communities where assignment affects what medical procedures are done to the child, from modifying their genitals to having their ears pierced.

Most often, assigned gender aligns with gender of rearing within a culture, though situations of "boys raised as girls"[12] and "girls raised as boys" do exist.

With only two expected genders of rearing, it makes things challenging for children who experience themselves as a mix of genders, don't experience themselves emotionally as boys or girls, or for parents who try to raise their children in a place beyond gender expectations. In recent years, there have been parents exploring non-gendered child rearing[13], and trans and gender nonconforming parents have become more public about their own experiences[14]. Even dialogues around whether toys should be labeled as "boys' toys" and "girls' toys"[15] have been part of an active dialogue in modern culture. In and of themselves, a doll is a doll and a truck is a truck. They do not inherently have a gender beyond the expectations of specifically societally-gendered behavior expectations.

Gendered Behaviors

Also known as gender roles and gender stereotypes, gendered behaviors are the assumptions attached to various actions a person takes. These behaviors include, but are not limited to:

- What people wear
- What careers someone has
- Who does the housework
- Who makes decisions in the home or at the office
- Types of schooling a person pursues
- Who rears children
- Communication styles
- Mannerisms
- Courtship and sexual styles
- Hobbies a person has
- Toys a child plays with
- Colors to like
- Who to be friends with
- Games that can be played
- How emotions are expressed

All of these are based on a cultural or sub-cultural context. The social construct of each culture dictates these details, learning them from our family, neighbors, media, schooling, religion and peers. It is picked up through what we see, what we are told, behaviors modeled, and how people respond to what we are doing. We see parents telling children to "man up," "be a good girl," or "I'd rather die than see my daughter do something like that." Television even depicts women who gain popularity through sexualizing their body, or boys getting power through force.

Children mirror what they see – often unconsciously. This means that children enforce the gendered behaviors they have seen, learned, or been taught, in extreme ways. Children become cruel enforcers of any gender norms they see or hear, even if they do not understand them. A child can also learn to be open minded to different or atypical gender behavior if they observe a permissive model in the world around them.

Part of this challenge of gendered behaviors also has to do with a story in our culture around what being "masculine" or "feminine" means. For example, when looking at who has power, we encourage women to "masculinize" themselves rather than empowering femininity or feminine attributes. Women in men's cut suits are described as powerful or sexy, but putting men in dresses is seen to be humiliating, or somehow makes them weak.

Men are belittled for liking glitter or wanting to raise children from home. This further creates a culture of marginalization and oppression against what is considered "feminine," in many cases even unconsciously amongst those who are battling for gender equality. Becoming aware of this issue also helps us understand why so many trans women (male to female transgender individuals) are seen to have given up their power through their transitioning. These concepts also give context to women who choose to dress or live as men to be able to provide for their families[16].

When we look at our own gendered behaviors, we become aware of what gender roles we have unconsciously followed in our life or imposed upon others. By doing so we get to choose which behaviors are ones we want to follow, and which ones are unhealthy for us personally.

These issues are even embedded in language, where people unconsciously say things like a person is "surprised they are doing a man's job" or that someone should "learn to wear the pants in their family." Statements of this sort marginalize people of any gender journey who fall outside of those cultural norms, whether they are transgender or not. When a person is transgender, these layers of response cause further conflict both internally and with the world they live in. They meet conflict with a gender change based on those cultural biases ("how could you want to become a woman, you are a great engineer") or face the risk of serious loss based on those same stories ("if you transition to being a man, you are no longer fit to be a mother to your children.")

Gender Expression

Sometimes referred to as gender performance, gender expression is the way that someone uses gendered behaviors to communicate their own gender. If we imagine gendered behaviors as the colors of paint we have, gender expression is the piece of artwork we create. People might follow the classical forms of presentation that their culture sets out, or craft something that is societally unexpected.

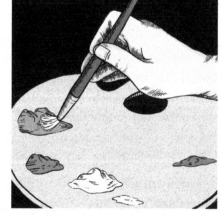

People use hairstyles, makeup, clothing, jewelry, grooming, how they move, name they choose, and style of speech to craft their expression. Beyond each culture, each subculture also has certain forms of gender expression. While wearing lipstick is considered an explicitly feminine expression in sports subculture, it is a gender-neutral performance in goth musical subculture. Cultural norms shift over time, such as the aesthetic of pop musicians being revolutionized by the *Beatles*. They presented a new style of masculine presentation that, at the time, was considered beyond the expectations of binary gender expression.

Different styles of expression display distinct approaches to femininity, masculinity or androgyny. Someone wearing a bikini is expressing a different performance of femininity than someone in a hijab. In and of themselves, neither a bikini nor a hijab are illicit or political in nature. Based on society's beliefs and approach to what it means to be a woman, they take on values. A person in the hijab might be seen by certain viewers as being devaluing because a woman's body is restricted or kept away; Others celebrate a person's choice to be private, saving themselves only for those they, are close to or share traits with. The person in the bikini can be seen as being devalued and sexualized as entertainment for the male gaze, or celebrated for the pride and joy she has in her body.

A transgender or gender nonconforming person can use gender expression as a way to communicate their gender through being aware of these points of cultural awareness. They may pad their hips, bind their chest, wear prosthetics, or tuck their genitals. An agender person might choose to dress in gender-neutral clothes, while someone who is very creatively gendered may choose to use a mix of every color of paint they have at their disposal. A gender fluid individual can choose different wardrobes and types of speech for different days, expressing what point they are at on the spectrum for the moment.

Each person also changes their gender expression based on the type of presentation they want to put forward. A person who chooses to wear shorts, as compared to wearing a suit, is choosing to consciously or unconsciously communicate a different face of themselves. Their gender expression may not even match their gender, with a cisgender woman choosing to wear a men's suit and don a mustache to explore what that performance is like for a while. This argues that the concept of a single gender binary – with the ultimate vision of womanhood on one end and the ultimate vision of manhood on the other end – is a myth. There is no single binary. Instead there is a diverse series of spectrums that we each traverse.

Perceived Gender

When someone encounters a baby in a stroller, it is incredibly common to ask the person pushing the pram, "are they a boy or girl?" Upon finding out their gender, people often unconsciously say statements such as "what a pretty girl" or "he seems so smart," instead of saying "what a lovely child" or "they seem so clever." Whenever we state these unconscious points of praise, we emphasize the gender norms to that child during their youth; a story that girls are supposed to be pretty and that boys are supposed to be smart. These early statements embed a story of what traits a child should strive towards; a shift in how we talk to our children is necessary to empower children of all genders[17].

Walking down the street, we scan the people around us to do a quick determination of gender, assigning stories, approachability, and threat founded on the genders we see around us. This is done based on the expected binary genders we were raised with, behaviors mirrored from others, and our personal experiences of joy and danger alike. Those who fall inside expected genders are considered "normal." People who do not match these expectations face potential ridicule, confusion, fear, discrimination, or violence. As awareness around gender diversity expands in television[18], movies[19], and on the news[20], culture develops more space for genders beyond the binary stereotypes.

When we project a gender upon someone, we are seeing a story of what that gender means to us. Each person carries stories about what being a man or woman "means," constructed through the lens of our history and upbringing. We consciously and unconsciously make decisions about how we behave towards them, layered with stereotypes based on race, age, physical abilities, accent, and style of dress. Whether or not our internal experience of what our own gender is, or how we experience our own gender; this is about the person perceiving us. Their perceptions are not about who we actually are.

When we look at this concept of perceived gender, it is important to acknowledge privilege experienced by those whose perceived gender matches their own experience of gender, or a societally acceptable gender binary. Privilege is a sociological term that refers to any special rights or status granted to a person or group in society based on a specific trait that is denied to people who do not share that trait. It is not a way to say that the person or groups are privileged to be male. It instead refers to the notion that by living in a culture that favors men in a variety of specific situations, men have not chosen, but simply are set up for a variety of specific advantages in most cultures.

Cisgender privilege is the concept that our culture unconsciously sets cisgender people at an advantage in many situations, and people outside of this perceived "norm" at a disadvantage. Transgender people who "pass" for being cisgender experience this privilege, whether they asked for it or not – a concept discussed further in chapter 9. Trans men become seen not only as more powerful, but also receive the flip-side of privilege where women cross the street to get away from them at night. Trans women who pass receive that flip-side of advantage by being treated as incapable people within specific professions, including being denied raises[21]. They are given privilege over those who do not pass, avoiding certain experiences of stigma, abuse, and overall loss of autonomy. Many cisgender people will not experience the issues discussed later in this book, which is form of advantage.

Legal Gender

The gender marker noted on someone's birth certificate, state identification, and passport are what denote a person's legal gender. Legal gender appears on airline travel documents, resumes and work history, social security, estates, and birth documents for a person's children. When our legal gender is noted in health insurance files, it determines what care is available. Paperwork stating someone is male for example, might not allow for receiving a pelvic exam; and a women's insurance company may not be able to approve testicular cancer care.

There are many other places where legal gender affects us in surprising little ways, which are discussed further in Chapter 8. It is important to note that changing legal gender is a complicated process, meaning that the perceived gender of a trans person might not match their legal gender. This causes potential problems every time someone hands their identification over when using a credit card or when having to interact with the police. When filling out legal paperwork it can be considered illegal to tell falsehoods, making denoting a "M or F" tricky when state identification and perceived gender show one gender and their birth certificate shows another.

Gender Identity

Who we experience ourselves to be is referred to as gender identity[22]. This is about self-identity and self-experience, rather than how other people see us. Many non-trans individuals do not even consider their gender identity because it has never come up for them. For transgender individuals, it comes up on a regular basis because their gender identity does not align with one or more of the concepts discussed already.

If gender identity, assigned gender, and perceived gender are the same, this concept is a new one for various cisgender individuals. That does not make a person "bad" for not knowing about the topic. When transgender concepts are brought up, they may have only ever heard about hormones, surgeries, or have misconceptions about "men pretending to be women." When a person is wanting their gender identity to align with their perceived and legal gender, it is not about pretending. It is about creating alignment; wanting who they see in the mirror to match the person they know themselves to be in their head and heart.

Gender identity manifests for cisgender people when exploring their own womanhood or manhood. For example, a person might have a gender identity as a butch (notably masculine presenting) woman or femme (notably feminine presenting) woman – having examined their womanhood and found an experience and presentation of masculinity or femininity within that experience of being a woman. That person still has a gender identity under the umbrella of woman, but has analyzed their gender and found their personal truths to still be that of their assigned gender.

Each layer of awareness reveals new information for a person's exploration of their own gender identity. No one else has the capacity to determine the gender identity of anyone else. It is a personal and internal experience. No identity has a greater intrinsic value than any other identity, though society awards greater privilege to some than others. A wide array of these identities and the paths associated with them are shared in chapter 2.

Orientation and Sexual Behavior

Who you are attracted to is referred to as orientation. Gender is about who you are. There is both sexual orientation (who we are erotically interested in), and romantic orientation (who we fall in love with). Whether homosexual (attracted to the same gender), heterosexual (attracted to the opposite gender), or otherwise... orientation is different than gender.

A transgender person might be bisexual, asexual, pansexual, queer, heteroflexible, homoflexible, same gender loving, curious or questioning. It is possible to be interested in a type of sexual play more than a specific gender, specific identity, or a body type – rather than what is between someone's legs. They experience a diversity of orientations, just like everyone else on the planet.

Their sexual behaviors also may or may not match their romantic orientation. For example, there are men who have sex with men who are very happily romantic with women. There are also individuals who are far more aligned to specific genders who will be their closest friends and confidants than who they choose to be in romantic or sexual partners, if they have any. This is cultural as well – heterosexual men in Saudi Arabia hold hands with one another because that is normal and holding hands with a woman would be considered scandalous.[23]

There are individuals, cultures and communities for whom orientation and gender are intertwined concepts. One example is when trans men have constructed their lives enmeshed in lesbian community. In transitioning, they may stay part of lesbian community because that is where their chosen family and history are based. A politically and sexually queer individual can also retain their queerness no matter where they are on the gender spectrum. There are also parts of the indigenous world before colonization that did not, or do not, draw the same strict lines around gender binaries – and these two concepts of orientation and gender are not delineated in the same way.

As Rev. Deborah Addington[24] states, "Gender identity and sexual practices are in relationship to one another, but why do we always bring sex into the conversation, either to legitimize or disprove something about gender?" Unfortunately, the legalities of orientation do affect people, as well as their gender expressions, worldwide[25]. In Louisiana, though it was made legal in the United States at large[26], it is still illegal to engage in all forms of oral sex and same-sex coupling, making the sex lives of transgender people potentially worthy of prison sentences[27]. In Iran, being transgender is legal, while being homosexual is not – it is punishable by death under the law.[28]

Outside of Iran, as of 2015, Singapore has up to a 2-year sentence for male homosexual acts, and requires medical intervention for transgender people to have heterosexual marriages.[29] Russia requires sterilization to be considered transgender, while "spreading gay propaganda," often through something as simple as being gay, has a prison sentence attached to it.[30] Meanwhile, extreme anti-gay sentiment is an issue that carries over to the transgender community in much of Southeastern Asia, about half of the African nations, and over half of the Middle East where being gay (as well as being legally transgender is not acknowledged) leads to extended prison sentences and worse.[31] What is considered heterosexual marriage in Iran is not legal in other countries. Such relationships are met with prison, fines, whipping, flogging, castration, torture or even death[32].

Beyond how a person identifies their own gender and orientation, gender affects by how their orientation interacts with the law of the land. Individual people do not believe that "transgender" is real or valid. For these individuals, a man who marries a trans woman is gay, and a woman married to a trans woman might be seen as heterosexual or, in a confusing double standard, as lesbian. This sets heterosexual men, who happen to fall in love with a woman who has a different medical history than other women, as being a different orientation than he experiences himself to be. This oppression of the partners of trans and gender nonconforming people is painful for all parties involved.

Chapter Two

Diversity of Transgender Journeys

There are a wide variety of transgender and gender nonconforming journeys, from transsexual to third gender, agender to gender fluid, and beyond. The terms and language of transgender discourse are evolving all the time.

Language worldwide for these diverse journeys and concepts vary. However, the various terminologies embraced in the United States have been taken on in other places; especially pushed online and through English-language media. This leads to a belief that only one set of language or terminologies is appropriate, and others are not. This can be useful for communication and helping allies understand the difference between affirming and offensive language, but isn't the only way to discuss these concepts.

Telling people of transgender experience that the terms they use to refer to themselves as is wrong can feel invalidating. There are people who walk diverse gender journeys who do not identify with, and even dislike, the concept of being transgender. They consider the word frustrating, or offensive. Asking people what terms mean to them, and why they use them, helps us understand their personal journey. This includes terms that we believe we know the definitions for, because no two people are identical in their path, even though there are trends in trans and gender nonconforming experience.

New terms are also being invented all of the time to express a diversity of personal experience. Terms are being re-discovered, re-claimed or brought to light from communities and cultures around the world. To help access these diverse concepts, for the course of this book, the term *trans* is being used

as the umbrella term for all of these journeys. This is not because the other terms being discussed are less valid, but because it is a term in use in current times. It is meant to access the entire umbrella, or the descriptor of trans as an adjective. It is hoped that those who do not use this term will continue to speak the terms of their own truth, making sure that their voices are heard in the world at large.

None of these journeys and identities are any more, or less, valid than any other, just as being transgender is not any more or less valid than being non-transgender. Trans and gender nonconforming communities are diverse, complex and unique, not monolithic or homogenous. This is one of the reasons that diverse language has emerged. It is also because so many diverse journeys exist. Pressure exists that state that every transgender journey needs to follow similar patterns or scripts. This is not true. No single book defines every person's individual views. The hope is that this one will share a wide variety of them.

To simplify this concept, consider people's taste in food. There are people that have a sweet tooth, and others do not understand eating highly sugary treats. A person may love spicy food, and regularly order food that confuses people who don't have the same palate. We understand that the other has different tastes, even if we cannot imagine having those preferences ourselves. So it is with gender.

This is not to infer that gender is a choice. Many individuals have had firm and consistent gender identities throughout their lives. Other trans people have had transient and shifting identities, or experiences that have moved from one to another across a lifetime[1]. Keep this in mind when discussing these journeys, as it helps us understand that there is more than one timeline for any one of the journeys listed. This concept is discussed further in Chapter 3.

In the media discourse, there is an assumption that transgender individuals are planning to move from one binary gender to another. Though it is a common and valid experience of gender journey, it is only one approach to trans experience, and excludes non-binary individuals. This assumption is based on images in the media where all trans people are presented as either male or female, becoming the other. This is the case whether the topic is looked at with grace, or from a comedic and derogatory perspective. It might also be because the expected genders in our culture are binary. Even terminology such as cisgender and transgender is seen in certain circles as reinforcing that binary[2], as it is a binary unto itself.

In this chapter we will be exploring the diversity of gender journeys under the umbrella concepts of transgender and gender nonconforming, and some that stand beyond these notions. These additional journeys are included because some people on those journeys consider themselves trans. Reading all of the journeys in this chapter is encouraged as concepts cross over between these arbitrary groupings. Even the examples of individuals who fall within one category or another may have multiple self-identities, use different definitions than the ones provided for their identity, or not identify as transgender or gender nonconforming at all.

At the end of each journey or concept listed, there are examples of people who are on, or have been on, that path. The hope with these examples is to show the wide diversity of people across the gender spectrum who are doing amazing work already, while providing opportunities for further exploration of these inspiring individuals.

Instead of duplicating materials, they flow from one into another, as there are also people who will use the terminology for one of these categories to define the experiences listed in another category. This is part of the ever-evolving language in this dialogue, and why it is important to ask the question "what does that mean to you?" when encountering the variety of terminology in trans and gender nonconforming discussions. Remember, as well, that there are individuals who shift between these various journeys over the course of their lifetime as they come to understand themselves in different ways.

Transsexual

The term of transsexual is one that many Western audiences have been introduced to in some way. It is a term that has been in media and medical discussions for a longer period of time than other gender terms. The umbrella of transgender issues was originally simplified in the 1940s in the United States[3] as the notions of transsexual and transvestite, with transvestite (now commonly referred to crossdressing) being seen only in its erotic context (as later discussed in this chapter). This model was based on the concepts introduced in the 1920s[4] by Dr. Magnus Hirschfeld.[5]

While talking, "transsexual" is confusing as it uses the suffix "sexual" which can infer a sexual orientation such as "homosexual," or "heterosexual." Even in activism, media, and community, the transgender and transsexual experiences in general are grouped as LGBT (Lesbian, Gay, Bisexual, and Transgender), when the other three are orientations. The T is grouped together with the LGB out of shared oppression, and a shared need for human rights. However, transsexual is not related to orientation in any way. The sex referenced in transsexual is referring to biological and assigned sex. There are those who are uncomfortable with the term because of this confusion by various parts of the population. In recent times, the acronym LGBT has been expanded to LGBTQQIAA (Lesbian, Gay, Bisexual, Transgender, Queer, Questioning, Intersex, Asexual, and Agender). Through this expansion, the T is no longer the only gender-based part of the acronym.

Within a medicalized context, people who are transsexual often experience a large degree of gender dysphoria, though that is not always the case. Gender dysphoria is the feeling that one's emotional and psychological identity as male or female are opposite to their birth sex. Gender dysphoria is a medical disorder, while body dysmorphia is a mental health disorder that can be diagnosed if a person's body-based dissonance and obsession with an incongruent form causes regular and ongoing emotional and psychological distress. This second experience does not happen for all transsexual individuals, and both are discussed further in chapter 7.

In the 1960s, sexologist and endocrinologist Harry Benjamin created a classification system for transsexuals and transvestites that he called the Sex Orientation Scale (SOS). Within the SOS, Benjamin broke down transgender individuals into six categories, based on their reasons for crossdressing and the urgency of their desire (if any) for sexual reassignment surgery.[6] Based on some of Benjamin's work, there are people who believe that to be a "true transsexual," a person needs to desire surgical procedures. Dr. Benjamin argued that some transsexual people might seek surgery, but did not require it to be at the highest end of his spectrum.[7] Benjamin also stated that the transsexual label included a wide array of gender variance; all things that under modern language are now defined as fitting under the transgender umbrella.

The transsexual experience often involves coming out to family and colleagues, transitioning gender on legal identification, and medical interventions such as hormone replacement therapies (HRT) or surgical procedures as tools for living as their experienced gender. Many of these systems are broken down within the work of the Standards of Care (SOC)[8] laid out by the World Professional Association for Transgender Health (WPATH)[9], which updates its approach to those standards every few years.

The SOC is not agreed upon by all transgender people, while others have found it useful. There are circles where the SOS has fallen out of fashion, with the argument that it is paternalistic and relies more on medical "gatekeepers" than a model oriented toward the individual's informed consent called ICATH (Informed Consent for Access to Trans Health)[10]. The concept of transsexual experience is broken down into two dialogues: FtM (Female to Male) and MtF (Male to Female), as discussed below. Keep in mind that a number of people who identify as MtF or FtM do not identify as transsexual. Additional notions on medicalized trans journeys are discussed in chapter 5, while issues around access to care will be discussed in chapter 9.

MtF, Trans Woman, and Transwoman

When people in the West think of the word "transgender," they most often think of trans women. This is because the media seems fascinated by individuals who were assigned male at birth and have transitioned to female. This includes the front covers of newspapers in 1952 that read "Ex-GI Becomes Blonde Beauty: Operations Transform Bronx Youth"[11] to the focused eye on a former Olympic medalist turned television personality[12]. It also unfortunately includes the obsession with the "shock reveal" of fictional trans women in movies such as *The Crying Game.* These stories and stereotypes are often awkwardly portrayed or outright false, but might be the stereotypes embedded in the minds of the people a trans woman discloses her truths to.

The experiences of trans women are incredibly diverse beyond what is portrayed in media, both positive and negative. Designated male at birth (DMAB), these individuals transition gender from male to female, thus using the shorthand MtF (male to female) or M2F to describe this experience. DMAB is succinct and accurate, compared to the confusing terminology of bio-male, as are AMAB (assigned male at birth) and MAAB (male assigned at birth). The concept that only cisgender women are bio-female does not represent the experience of individuals who experience that they were born with a medical defect or anomaly, needing corrective surgeries to live as their true gender as women. They have always experienced themselves as female, and thus their body is just another form of being female.

Some people use the language of having been "born in the wrong body" to express this experience. Others consider themselves having been "born a girl," but their parents and the doctor made a mistake. There are also people who appreciate the language of having been assigned male at birth, but they are in fact women[13]. None is any better of a descriptor of experience than another.

For a trans woman, there can be many points along the journey. They may be debating for themselves whether they are female. Perhaps they have become aware of their womanhood, and have not told anyone. Maybe they have told a therapist, a best friend, or anonymous individuals online, even if they have not told anyone else.

A person who has a "gender transition" is considered to be "transitioning" or "has transitioned," based on where they are on their journey. Though the language of transition is more common, it is also referred to as identity confirmation. If a person has told someone else about being MtF, that individual might be considered to be "in transition." Others believe that the terminology of transitioning begins as soon as they began an internal dialogue, or not until come out to their family, pursue legal transition options, or begin medical interventions.

"Transwoman" as a single word is often used interchangeably with "trans woman." There are also those who see them as separate concepts. One group uses "trans" as an adjective attached to the noun "woman," similar to "petite woman." It is part of their bodily experience, not their identity, as inferred in cases where transwoman as a single noun. This is important as there are also individuals for whom "transwoman" is their gender or identity, whole and unto itself.

Within certain populations, the terms translatina or translatin@ are used as a form of cultural expressions in combination with a gender journey[14]. The @ at the end providing a gender neutral or gender "other" space beyond the *a* or *o* gender-specific endings in Latin-based languages. This concept is also applied with such terms as chican@, filipin@ and latinx. Terms such as t-girl and gurl are used by select trans women to describe themselves, while the term *tranny* is seen by many transgender people to be a derogatory term, or one that should only be used between trans people and not by outsiders, as discussed further in Chapter 8.

There are many medical interventions and technologies used by various trans women, and are different from person to person. These may include hormone blockers, replacement therapy, prosthetics, cosmetic procedures, and medical surgeries, and are broken down further later in the book in Chapter 5. In common vernacular, an individual who has not undergone lower body surgical procedures is referred to as "pre-op," while a person who has done so uses the terminology "post-op." Other individuals choose never to surgically transition. The terminology that is often used is "non-op." This does not remove the authenticity of being a trans woman.

Trans women choose not to have medical procedures for a wide range of reasons, from health concerns that do not allow for surgery (such as blood clot disorders) to religious reasons or enjoying the flexibility of their current form. It is usually considered rude to ask a person you do not know whether they are pre-op or post-op, as you would not ask another person you have just met what is going on between their legs except in situations where that issue is appropriate. Others cannot transition due to a myriad of factors including access to medical specialists, finances, where they live, or whether they are a legal resident.

There are trans women of every body type, just as there are women of every body type. There are women who have deeper voices, or have a more distinct Adam's apple, while others have soft features and a higher pitch. Every trans person is affected by their hormones and other medical interventions in different ways, often based on their family history and their bodies before transition. Individuals can choose to take vocal training, while others change their exercise routine to build the form that they are desiring. Not all trans women will grow long hair or develop padding around their hips, especially if their ethnic makeup does not usually have such development, while others have genes, or contributing factors, to develop such traits.

Once an individual has transitioned, regardless of surgical choices, they may or may not use the terms of MtF, transwoman, or transgender woman when referring to themselves. They might refer to themselves simply as a woman, and the details of her past are only discussed in a medical context, or with their family – if at all. There are even MtF individuals who do not use the language of MtF at all, and instead refer to themselves as women who have a complex medical background, which is only important for their doctors to know.

The language that is used self-referentially is one of the challenges with getting demographic information on transgender people in general. Census forms do not provide spaces for transgender options, and even when being provided such options, not all transgender people list themselves under a transgender label when trans woman is their truth, rather than transwoman.

As noted in Chapter 1, gender identity and gendered behavior are different, which means that every trans woman will express herself in a unique fashion, just like every woman will. There are high-fashion models, classic soccer-moms, and those that work on oil rigs. There are trans women who play sports, attend high tea, or have to work multiple jobs to take care of their kids. None of these affect whether someone is a woman. For most trans women, the default pronoun for referring to them is as a woman and with the pronouns of she/her/hers.

Examples of MtF individuals who have received media exposure have included:

- **Activists:** Community and HIV advocate Dee Dee Chamberlee; Black Lives Matter advisor Elle Hearns; trans youth activist Jazz Jennings; Stonewall activist Marsha P. Johnson; founding executive director of the National Center for Transgender Equality Mara Keisling; community activist Miss Major; and civil rights pioneer Sylvia Rivera.

- **Artists:** Actress Alexandra Billings; violinist and vocalist Tona Brown; composer Wendy Carlos; playwright Jo Clifford; 70s punk musician

Jayne County; actress and activist Laverne Cox; Danish intersex artist Lili Elbe; performance artist Ali Forney; musician Laura Jane Grace; singer/songwriter Antony "Anohni" Hegarty; K-pop star and actress Harisu; musician Kokumo; Film maker and artist Tara Mateik; actress Stéphanie Michelini; Japanese pop idol Ataru Nakamura; actress Mya Taylor; directors Lana and Lily Wachowski (from "The Matrix"); and dancer and choreographer Jin Xing.

- **Athletes:** Bodybuilder Chris Tina Bruce; Olympic athlete and reality television star Caitlyn Jenner; and body builder Janae Marie Kroc.

- **Authors:** Author and educator Kate Bornstein; author and journalist Janet Mock; blogger and activist Monica Roberts (AKA the TransGriot); author and researcher Susan Stryker; and author and activist Riki Wilchins.

- **Military Personnel:** Navy SEAL Kristin Beck; World War II veteran and entertainer Christine Jorgensen; Australian Defense Force Lieutenant Colonel Cate McGregor; Army Lieutenant Colonel philanthropist Jennifer N. Pritzker; and Army veteran and activist Allyson Robinson

- **Models:** Model and activist April Ashley; model and Miss International Queen Sirapssorn Atthayakorn; model Carmen Carrerra; model Isis King; model Andreja Pejic; model Lea T; and Miss Universe contestant Jenna Talackova.

- **Politicians:** Indian politician Shabnam "Mausi" Baso; New Zealand parliamentarian Georgina Beyer; Polish parliamentarian Anna Grodzka; politician and electrocardiogram technician Adela Hernández; politician Kim Coco Iwamoto; politician Rtu Rassmussen; and Thai politician and pop star Yolanda "Nok" Suanyos.

- **Scientists:** Ophthalmologist and tennis player Reneé Richards; and biologist Joan Roughgarden.

- **...and more:** Video game innovator Dani Berry; Texas judge Phyllis Frye; talk show host Ai Haruna; judge Victoria Kowalski; attorney Alyson Meisleman; and journalist and children's author Ja'briel Walthour.

FtM, Trans Man, and Transman

Just as an MtF person is transitioning from male to female, a FtM individual is transitioning (or has transitioned) from female to male. Trans men have served a rich and varied role in United States history, from the influential 1950s jazz musician Billy Tipton to 1800s stagecoach driver Charley Plankhurst, who was

the first "woman" to vote for President in 1868. In current times, the media has become fascinated with the diversity of FtM experience from trans men competing for men's health magazines[15] to pregnant men appearing on Oprah[16].

FtM individuals use terminology such as F2M, transman, trans man, or for youth, trans boy. In certain communities, terms such as boi [17] and boy are used as well[18]; though these terms are used by other people who are not FtM or trans[19]. There are trans men who refer to themselves as men receiving medical care for a medical anomaly. No matter their perspective, individuals along this path are people who were designated female at birth (DFAB), as use of DFAB is more accurate than terminology that is out of date, such as bio-female, as are AFAB (assigned female at birth) and FAAB (female assigned at birth). For most trans men, the default for referring to them is as a man and with the pronouns of he/him/his.

At this time, there is less access to genital surgeries for trans men due to their expense, diversity of surgical approaches, and outcomes that may or may not fit the needs of those interested in them. The complexity of female to male bottom surgery is discussed more in Chapter 5. Thus, language for whether or not a trans man has had a breast reduction, double mastectomy, or torso reconstruction surgery is referenced when using "pre-op," "post-op," and "non-op," or alternately "pre-top," "post-top," and "non-top." Whether someone has had genital surgeries or not is referred to as having "bottom surgery." The topic of medical choices is incredibly personal, and it is usually considered rude to bring it up with anyone who you do not know, and has not given explicit permission, as stated previously concerning trans women.

Trans men may face fewer points of daily discrimination based on men in general receiving less daily abuse than women in large parts of the world, having been granted a de facto male privilege. Those who do not "pass" do not receive this temporary exemption, nor do those who are "outed."

Just as there are trans women who are taller, more muscular, have broader shoulders or larger feet face challenges blending into certain cultural expectations of femininity, so it is for trans men who are shorter, less muscular, thinner, or have higher pitched voices. Every trans individual is affected by hormones differently, often based on their familial history. Not all trans men will get chest hair or beards, especially if their family line does not have such traits, and they may get receding hairlines, often (but not always) determined by their genes. Remember – there is no way to instantly tell in all cases if a person is transgender. Body diversity of men in general is broad, thus it is broad for trans men as well. There are cisgender men who are shorter, less muscular, thinner and have higher pitched voices. And just as no two men will be the same when it comes to their careers, hobbies, family or friends, so it is for trans men, in turn.

Examples of FtM individuals who have received media exposure have included:

- **Activists:** Actor and activist Buck Angel; activist Thomas Beatie (known in the press at "the pregnant man"); singer and activist Chaz Bono; minister and activist Rev. Louis J. Mitchell; Ugandan activist Victor J. Mukasa; founder of Deaf Queer Resources Center (DQRC) Dragonsani "Drago" Renteria; activist Diego Sanchez; and gay and trans activist Lou Sullivan.

- **Artists:** Musician Alexander James Adams; Photographer Kael T. Block; gospel singer Willmer "Little Ax" Broadnax; singer Meryn Cadell; photographer Loren Cameron; choreographer Sean Dorsey; film maker Jake Graf, rapper and slam poet Katastrophe (aka Rocco Kayiatos); singer Lucas Silveria; Jazz musician Billy Lee Tipton; Spanish classical singer and painter Manuela Trasobares Haro; pianist and singer Geo Wyeth; poet Kit Yan; and documentarian Kortney Ryen Ziegler.

- **Athletes:** Basketball player Kye Allums; Japanese speedboat racer Hirosama Ando; German pole vaulter Balian Buschbaum; and German shot putter Andreas Krieger.

- **Attorneys:** Attorney Spencer Berstedt; attorney and professor Kylar Boadus; attorney Shannon Price Minter; and lawyer and academic Dean Spade.

- **Authors:** Editor and artist Morty Diamond artist and editor; author and educator Jamison Green, PhD.; author and professor Jack Halberstam (aka Judith Halberstam); academic and artist Dr. Jordy Jones; journalist and author Tiq Milan; author, artist and educator Ignacio G. Rivera; author and speaker Julia Serano; and author Max Wolf Valerio.

- **Judges:** Canadian judge Kael McKenzie.

- **Military Personnel:** Army Sgt. Shane Ortega; and documentarian and Navy sailor Landon Wilson.

- **Scientists:** Neurobiologist Ben Barres; sociologist and sexologist Aaron Devor; and physician Alan Hart (who developed tuberculosis detection technology).

- **...and more:** Model Laith Ashley, police officer Tony Baretto-Neto; hip-hop producer Black Cracker; academic Paisley Currah; entertainer Kritipat "Jimmy" Chotidhanitsakul, motivational speaker and model Aydian Dowling; comedian and actor Ian Harvie; health educator and social justice activist Yoseñio V. Lewis; International Mr. Leather 2010 Tyler McCormick; 1800s stagecoach driver Charley Parkhurst; and academic and educator Allucquére Rosanne "Sandy" Stone.

Two-Spirit

Two-spirit is the umbrella term used in modern times by some Native Americans and Canadian First Nations to describe a wide variety of gender variant people. Many two-spirit individuals are seen as having both male and female spirits in them, and there is diversity of types of gender and orientation variance expressed under two-spirit experience. This term has been adopted by many North American indigenous peoples to have access to a word beyond gay, lesbian, bisexual, transgender and other English language terms that do not necessarily reflect their experience.[20]

The term two-spirit emerged into popularity in 1990 during the inter-tribal Native American and First Nations gay/lesbian conference, from the direct translation of the Ojibwe term, *Nizh manidoowag*. Gatherings are held for two-spirit people that are private[21], as well as those that are open to the public[22]. There are North American indigenous populations that find the use of the term two-spirit by individuals who are not of their shared ethnic history to be inappropriate. For them, using the label is seen as stealing, or appropriating, their cultural heritage. Instead they encourage people to pursue terms from their own ethnic or cultural history. This is important to be aware of because there are non-indigenous individuals that use the term *two-spirit* because they believe it best describes their experience and who do not intend to cause offense.

There are individuals who find the term two-spirit reflective of their personal experiences, while others do not. Not all tribes use this terminology, and it is important to look at what the concepts of gender variance and diversity are within each individual tribe. With well over 560 federally recognized tribes in the United States alone[23] (with numerous unrecognized as well) – each tribe has its own history. Saying that all First Peoples use the term two-spirit is reductive in its approach to the diverse pre-colonization population of the North American continent. Though many have come to use the term today, it is not the only First People's term for non-binary gender expression.

Historically, two-spirit individuals filled a wide variety of roles depending on the tribe, from matchmaker to conveyors of oral tradition, makers of ritual regalia to doing specific ceremonial work or serving as medicine people. Because of this, being two-spirit is not only limited to a personal experience. It is also a role within community. They might have been called not only because of who they were attracted to or how they saw themselves, but how their tribe interacted with them. It is not about *doing* a role because someone happened to be two-spirit; they are *being* a role because of who they are. Because of this, both two-spirit and third gender journeys are different than other transgender paths that are based only on identity.

Western exposure to other cultures and ethnicities who fell beyond the two-gender system has happened as long as there has been colonization, and many Western binary perspectives found this hard to understand. Part of this confusion for an outside eye was because people were seen to be wearing clothes or doing work that was not always designated for their "appropriate" gender, or partnering with people other than classical heteronormative pairings. Western anthropologists, coming from their own cultural perspective, transformed the meaning of "men wearing women's clothes" into an act of degradation[24]. In some regions, individuals who fell outside of a binary gender-normative experience were killed by colonial forces as a way to eradicate local culture and customs[25].

As a way to categorize two-spirited and alternatively gender expressing individuals, they were referred to as "berdache" by anthropologists. This word has fallen out of favor and is considered to be inappropriate or offensive[26] given its French roots translating as "passive homosexual," "kept boy" or "male prostitute." In native tongues, two-spirit experience is reflected in a diversity of terms including Aranu'tiq (Yu'pik); Arnuutiq (Sugpiaq), AyagiiGuX (Unangam Tunuu), K'atxaan (Tlingit) Nádleehé (Navajo), Wí te (Lakota), Ninauposkitzipxpe (North Peigan Blackfoot), and Zapotec Muxe (Mexico). Notions of cross-gender identity appear in over 155 tribes across the first peoples of North America[27].

Examples of two-spirit individuals who have received media exposure have included:

- Politician Susan Allen (Rosebud Sioux); writer Beth Bryant (Mohawk/ Scottish-Irish); poet and activist Chrytos (Menominee); writer and educator Qwo-Lit Driskill (Cherokee, African, Irish, Lenape, Lumbee and Osage); Filmmaker Sydney Freeland (Navajo); activist and author Jewelle Gomez (Ionay/African-American); 19th century warrior and dancer Kuilix/Pend d'Orielle (Crow); public policy advocate and Miss Native American Transgender Arizona Trudie Jackson; author and community leader Sandy Leo Laframboise (Dancing Two Eagle Spirit; Algonquin/Cree-Métis); author, broadcaster and tribal representative Donna Loring (Penobscot); 19th century shaman and warrior Lozen (Apache); activist Heather Purser (Suquamish); musician Shawnee (aka She King); writer and artist Storme Webber (Aleut/Choctaw/African American); 19th century tribal ambassador We'wha (Zuni); and 19th century warrior and chief Woman Chief (Crow).

Third Gender

In various places around the world, imposing of binary gender system was used as a tool for imposing order. This imposed judgement was part of outside (or colonizing) perspectives on indigenous populations – populations that are currently rebuilding or slowly coming out of hiding in their countries. In other places, there is still profound oppression of systems that fall beyond female and male.

Dialogues around these diverse communities and concepts are sometimes grouped under the umbrella "third gender." Many of the genders listed below may not be considered genders per se. For example, some are religious constructs, such as the Machi who are shamans of the Mapuche of Chile, or the Bajasa who serve as spiritual intermediaries for Toradja Bare's people of Celebes. Confusion also arises from to English, or other languages, from the native tongue, or translations of cultural values within a given country. An example of this challenge is seen with the Muxes' annual pageant, the four-day long La Vela de las Auténticas Intrépidas Buscadoras del Peligró, which translates to *The Celebration of the Bold Seekers of Danger.*[28]

There are words for third gender realities that have become complicated to use, situations where the same word is an accurate term, while also being used as a slur. Examples include *hijra* in India, or *baklâ* in the Philippines. In Pakistan, the term *khawaja sara* has come into use to replace hijra without the same social stigma[29]. Around the world, third gender language, just like all transgender language, continues to shift.

Even cultures that are perceived as being very binary in their approach to gender in modern times have classical systems that were deeply nuanced. One example is that of Judaism which classically had six distinct genders[30]:

- *Zachar* (phallus/male)

- *Nekevah* (crevix/female)

- *Androgynos* (both male and female characteristics)

- *Tumtum* (indeterminate)

- *Ay'lonit* (female develops to male at puberty, who is infertile)

- *Saris* (male develops to female at puberty, or lacking penis)

Around the world, diverse third gender, third sex, or other gendered concepts include or have included:

- Acault (Myanmar); Akava'ine (Cook Islands Māori); Aravani (Tamil Nadu); Ashtime (Maale, Southern Ethiopia); Bianxìng (China); Bajasa (Celebes); Baklâ (Philippines); Bantut (Toasug/Philippines); Bayot (Cebuano/Philippines); Bissu (Indonesia); Biza'ah (Teotilán); Brotherboys (Australian Aboriginal); Burrnesha/Virjinesha (aka Sworn Virgins, Balkans); Calabai (Indonesia); Calalai (Indonesia); Ergi (Norse); Fa'afafine (Samoa); Fakaleiti (Tongan); Femminiello (Napoleonic France); Guevedoche (Dominican Republic); Hijra (India, Bangladesh and Pakistan); Kathoey (Thailand); Khawaja Sara (Pakistan); Lakin-on (Philippines); Machi (Mapuche of Chile); Māhū (Polynesia); Mahu Wahine (Hawai'ian); Maknyah (Malaysia); Mangaiko (Mbo of Democratic Republic of Congo); Mashoga (Kenya); Metis (Nepal); Mollies (England 18th Century); Mukhannathun (Middle East); Muxe (Mexico); Sādhin (India); Sekrata (Madagascar); Sistergirls (Australian Aboriginal); Takatāpui (Māori); Tomboy (ThailandTravestí/y (Brazil); Tritiya-prakriti (India); Uranian (England 19th Century); Waria (Indonesia); Whakawahine (Māori of New Zealand); X-Jendā (Japan); Xanith (Oman); and Yimpininni (Australian Aboriginal).

Many of these fall into other Western categories broken down in this chapter, do not consider themselves transgender, or don't experience themselves as gender nonconforming. Some third gender people consider modifications to their body to be part of their path, but do not consider it to be any sort of transition. They were third gender before, during, and after modifying their body. There are also individuals who are third gender who also choose to undergo medical transition, thus making them third gender as well as transgender.

Third gender has also become a popular term in and of itself, not just a way to group the diverse concepts above. In this new use, third gender is a person who is "somewhere beyond a binary," or "between binaries." This self-identity is framed in the cultural and linguistic paradigm of the Western world, and individuals from this new gender terminology pushed towards visibility of gender beyond the binary. Sometimes this has been done in conjunction with other third gender populations, and other times it has been done using these other populations as a way to validate their own truth.

There have been legal advances on an international level to have more than two genders available on by such groups as the International Intersex Forum[31]. For example, starting in 2003, Australian passports began offering an option of X in addition to F and M[32]. In Germany, birth certificates no longer required someone to choose a gender marker[33]. Meanwhile, India[34], Nepal[35], and New Zealand[36] have chosen to have three options available – male, female, and other. The legal ramifications of these systems have not been made clear when it comes to traveling or emmigrating to countries with only two gender markers.

Examples of third gendered individuals who have received media exposure have included:

- Baklâ author and activist b. binaohan; Pakistan khawaja sasa community leader Saima Butt; Pakistan politician Bindiyan Rana; Mexican muxe politician Amaranta Gómez Regalado; Nepalese former soldier and activist Bhakti Shah; Nepalese LGBT activist Aakanshya Timsina; Indian activist Laxmi Narayan Tripathi; Muay Thai boxer Nong Tum; trans Pin@y poet Kay Ulanday Barrett.

Genderqueer, Gender Variant, and Gender Fluid

People who are genderqueer, gender nonconforming, gender non-binary, gender expansive, or gender variant move in a space outside of the societally expected or assumed binary options. This may manifest in behavior, expression, or identity. These experiences show that gender is a spectrum where a person exists, rather than a world where male or female are the only options available. Instead of a solid line between cisgender and transgender, everyone exists in a blur somewhere between. Gender variant has also been used as a catch-all term for all gender categories beyond a binary assumption or approach to gender.

The terms used in this category shift wildly in definition. What one person calls genderqueer is what another person adamantly refers to as gender fluid, bigender, butch, or something else entirely. Keep this in mind when looking at the descriptions that follow. There are also those who layer these words on top of one other. For example, a transfeminine genderqueer individual is layering these words to convey that they are on a spectrum, identifying with femininity beyond the binary.

There are people who are designated male at birth that choose to transition their body, augmenting with hormones and breast implants, and identify as "she-male." This is far less common than those who identify as "trans woman." For most parts of the transgender community, the term she-male is considered out-of-date and highly offensive. Others self-identify with the term, considering themselves to be on the gender variant spectrum, rather than being a woman.

Genderqueer folks may set themselves outside the spectrum altogether. Their path is unique unto them, and whatever terms they use, they do not see themselves being a straight line between female and male at all. A person might choose to perform their gender variance in a certain way right now, and days, months, or years from now, shift to a different presentation of gender-variance, while still maintaining a gender variant identity. There are also transsexual individuals who began their journey in a genderqueer space and then later shift to a more binary presentation and identity, or vice versa.

There are people of all designations at birth who choose to be genderqueer, or experience themselves as being intrinsically genderqueer. Individuals who were designated male at birth sometimes have a more intense set of challenges than folks who were designated female at birth. This is because in many cultures, women who dress as men are seen as powerful, while men who dress as women are seen as weak. Outside of genderqueer-friendly space, the world at large is often not welcoming of people who crossdress, identify as trans women, or are perceived as trans women. This is important to know due to large number of hate crimes and homicides committed against these communities[37].

People who are genderqueer might have a single non-binary gender, while those who are gender fluid do not hold a single fixed point. Moving back and forth between their gender expressions like the tide, a gender fluid person might also use the terms nonbinary, gender flexible, or gender bending. Gender fluid individuals often have no set place along a spectrum. They express their gender in a specific way today, and may or may not express it the same way tomorrow. A trans woman can be gender fluid, wherein their base gender is as a woman, while shifting across the gender spectrum on any given day. Genderqueer transmen on the other hand have an identity as men that may not be what many people would consider a classically masculine.

Examples of genderqueer and gender variant individuals who have received media exposure have included:

- Genderqueer MtF rapper Heidi Barton Stink; author and queer disability activist Eli Clare; pop musician Miley Cyrus; intersex-born performance artist and writer Vaginal Davis; folk musician Chris Pureka; "post-gender" synthpop artist JD Samson; musician and author Rae Spoon; intersex author; and intersex artist Del La Grace Volcano.

Examples of non-binary and gender fluid individuals who have received media exposure have included:

- Indie pop musician Anjimile; musician k.d. lang; actor Tom Phelan; actor Ruby Rose; actor Richard O'Brien; musician and actor Kieran Strange; musician St. Vincent; and actor Tilda Swinton.

Agender, Gender Neutral, and Androgynous

People who are agender, gender neutral, ace, or non-gender are *neutrois*. This means they experience a genderless state or don't think of themselves as having a gender. This can be challenging for those who ask "are you a boy or a girl" and receive the answer "none of the above." Being forced to answer is sometimes invalidating for an agender individual. Living in a world that demands gender, for an agender person, can be confusing, frustrating, or painful. Thus, many agender people prefer gender-neutral pronouns such as they/them/theirs, ze/zim/zir, or being referred to only as their name. There are also genderqueer individuals who prefer these various pronouns, approaching them from a non-binary perspective, rather than being neutral in nature.

An agender person might have no personal expression (either physically or conceptually) of gender, or experience themselves in the spectrum of androgynous experience. Their own personal experience of a gender neutral state is about the agender person, not about the gender (or lack thereof) of anyone else. It is not meant to affront, even if it challenges the questioner's perspective on what gender should be – or that everyone should have a gender. This is an important point to remember for all people interacting with transgender people. A trans person's gender is not meant as an affront to anyone else.

Meanwhile, an androgynous individual is someone who does not fit neatly into the typical masculine and feminine gender roles of their society. They are a blending between male and female, or entirely genderless, while still experiencing themselves as having a gender. The term androgyny has also been used to refer to a variety of intersex conditions. Thus, terminology need to be discussed as to the difference between personal experience, gender expression, and physiology.

Examples of gender neutral individuals who have received media exposure have included:

- French surrealist photographer Claude Cahum; pop artist Grimes; rapper Angel Haze; singer-singwriter Elly Jackson; performer Jinkx Monsoon; and singer Shamir.

Examples of androgynous individuals who have received media exposure have included:

- Performance artist boychild; singer and actor David Bowie; rapper Casey; model Rain Dove; Culture Club lead singer Boy George; Japanese musician and kei artist Hizaki; performance artist Grace Jones; musician John "Diamond Rings" O'Regan; and singer Prince.

Bigender and Demigender

While a gender fluid individual has no single fixed point on the gender spectrum, a bigender, or intergender, person is someone who has two, or multiple, separate points of their gender experience that they alternate between. If gender were a linear spectrum to A to Z with A being female and Z being male, there are people who have combinations such as AZ, AZG, FW, or a string of every letter on the alphabet and beyond. Also known as dual gender, multigender, omnigender, pangender, polygender or mixed gender, each take on this multiple-choice answer comes with individual perspectives of what it means to use the term they have chosen. There are others who consider these concepts rolled into those of gender fluid, gender variant, or genderqueer.

A bigender person might be living one gender at the office, and another at home. They might have two specific ways that they perform their gender, based on who they are around or their own emotional experience on a given day. Their pronouns might be consistent every day, or their pronoun might shift based on what they are wearing.

Under this concept is the notion of being demigender. A demigender person expresses the idea of being partially, but not wholly, connected to a specific gender. Thus, a demigirl would be someone who identifies as a girl, but not wholly, and a demiboy would be an individual who identifies as a boy, but not wholly. As *The Who's* Pete Townshend once said "I know how it feels to be a woman because I am a woman, and I won't be classified just as a man."[38]

Examples of bigender, intergender and demigender individuals who have received media exposure have included:

- English comedian Eddie Izzard; Guitarist for *The Who* Pete Townshend; and singer-songwriter Steven Tyler[39].

Conscious Gender Exploration

Many people explore gender when trying on different clothes, play-acting as children, or when changing they avatar they use for online role-playing games. Most of the time though, non-transgender folk don't take a conscious look at the way they express gender. The major exception is for those who have done active work in feminist theory or battled with sexism head-on.

When we consciously explore gender, we look at how gender is expressed, and whether we want to embrace gender norms in society. Some examples

of exploration are the concepts of butch, stud, aggressive (ag), and femme. With their roots in the lesbian and gay communities, these terms actively explore different styles of masculinity and femininity. A femme individual has looked at their own feminine expression and through personal examination, has decided to consciously embrace it rather than do femininity out of habit, or because culture told them they "should" do it. Meanwhile, a butch, aggressive, or stud individual has done the same thing with concepts of masculinity.

Gender explorers may experiment for the course of one evening, or adventure for a lifetime. There are those that move back and forth between the variety of gender expressions available, or slowly modify their own core gender experience over time. Just because someone explores a gender presentation does not mean they have to maintain that gender permanently. Conscious journeyers may or may not also be transgender; with a trans woman able to be butch as much as she might be femme, or a two-spirit person able to try on the multiple types of "man" available in culture. Any given person will have their own preferences on pronouns. There are butch women who use the pronoun "she," to express being female, or "he," to express their masculine experience. There are also people for whom hearing a woman "dresses like a man," and uses the pronoun "he," that believe that makes the person in question a transman outright. This is not necessarily the case. Each human has their own unique experience of gender.

Being metrosexual, wherein a meticulous (usually heterosexual) man spends time and money to meticulously groom and present himself, is another way for men to explore their gender. It brings up questions as to what makes a man a man, and how a man "should" carry himself. Exploring gender does not inherently make someone transgender or interested in transitioning. In most cases, a femme man is a man, and a butch woman is a woman, staying within their cisgender experience. There are many cisgender people who spend time both consciously and unconsciously exploring their gender presentation.

Examples of femme, butch and conscious gender explorers who have received media exposure have included:

- Blues singer Gladys Bently; performance artist and author S. Bear Bergman; artist Lady Jaye Breyer; actress Lea DeLaria; queer/trans playwright/performer/comedian D'Lo; comedian Ellen DeGeneres; trans-feminist performance artist Joey Hateley; French swimmer Casey Legler; performance artist Bridge Markland; performance artist Sean Miley Moore; performance artist and musician Genisis P-Orridge; actress Portia de Rossi; author and activist Leslie Feinberg; actor Lee Joon-gi; comedian Elvira Kurt; artist Hans Scheirl; performance artist and vocalist Tobaron Waxman; and performance artist and filmmaker Wu Tsang.

Drag and Crossdressing

Crossdressing is the act of wearing clothes classically designated, by the culture you are part of, as being for the opposite sex. This may or may not involve shaving, wearing makeup, jewelry, footwear or donning wigs. Each culture and era has a slightly different take on what clothes and styles are associated with specific genders, and which clothes take on a level of taboo when worn by others.

The act of crossdressing is done for a wide variety of reasons. It might be a Halloween costume or a dare from friends. Crossdressing can make a political statement, or disguise someone's birth gender for safety reasons. People crossdress as an opportunity to explore gender paradigms, or to consider their self-identity. There are those who dress for a theatre performance, and others who simply enjoy the way the clothes fit. For some it is an erotic sensation, or they enjoy the fear of getting caught. It might be part of a daily lifestyle, or engaged in for emotional reasons. Though it seems like men who dress in women's clothes is more common, before the modern flexibility in what was appropriate for women to wear, female crossdressers were far more visible.

If done on a regular basis or for a core sense of self, crossdressing is sometimes referred to as transvestitism. Culture uses transvestite (TV) and crossdresser (CD) interchangeably at times, but transvestitism does not refer

to those who crossdress for an evening of fun or a lark, and it is often seen as an offensive or outdated term. The term transvestite was also originally associated specifically with crossdressing specifically for sexual stimulation, and is thus out of favor with folks who do not have an erotic attachment to their crossdressing.

Drag queens and drag kings are often performers that incorporate crossdressing as part of their transformation into a specific character. Referred in various circles as female or male impersonators, most drag performers are rarely trying to emulate how women or men actually dress. In fact, drag is often a caricature of the gender in question. There are even be female drag queens[40] and male drag kings. Performances on stage, or having a performative element to their persona, is normal for drag, and uncommon for crossdressing. When an individual is in drag, it is considered appropriate and polite to address them in the gender the are expressing in the moment, unless told otherwise. Meanwhile, when a person is crossdressing, the pronouns in use depend entirely upon what is wanted by the person in question.

There are those for whom crossdressing is a way to dip a toe into the possibility of transitioning, or to embrace that part of their gender without engaging in medical, legal, and social complexities. In general, there are two major approaches to the issue of whether crossdressers or individuals who do drag should be considered transgender. It boils down to whether or not you consider your personal crossdressing or drag to be about gender:

- I'm not transgender. This is about clothing being sexy or fun, not about my gender.

- Anything that involves expressing gender counts under the transgender umbrella. This is about gender; and therefore, I am transgender.

A third framework around crossdressing has evolved as well, that the clothes any person wears is by default, the clothes of their gender. This notion states that any given piece of clothing does not inherently have a gender, just as any given toy does not inherently have a gender. As comedian Eddie Izzard has said, "I don't wear women's clothes. Are women transvestites because they're wearing trousers? No. They just say they're wearing trousers. So I deny I'm wearing women's clothes. I just say I'm wearing clothes."[41] Under this framework, crossdressing does not really exist, only society's stigma against certain combinations of wardrobe and perceived gender.

The line between uses of terminology is also generational. There has been a shift in recent years towards people seeking out genderqueer and/or various transgender identities (including pursuing medical interventions) as compared to identifying as a crossdresser. Crossdressing as an activity is still very popular, and pursued by people from every generation and assigned gender.

Examples of crossdressing individuals who have received media exposure have included:

• German-American actress Marlene Dietrich; FBI director J. Edgar Hoover; English Turner Prize winning artist Grayson Perry; singer Iggy Pop; actor Jaden Smith; and Willie Mae "Big Mama" Thorton.

Examples of drag performers who have received media exposure have included:

• Singer and performer Jackie Beat; actor and dancer William Belli; Cher impersonator Chad Michaels; actor and performance artist Divine (Harris Glenn Milstead); Australian social anthropologist, journalist, and performance icon Dame Edna Everage (Barry Humphries); fashion icon RuPaul (Andre Charles); performer and recording artist Sharon Needles (Aaron Coady); soul singer Sylvester (Sylvester James Jr.); and Austrian recording artist and fashion icon Conchita Wurst (Thomas "Tom" Neuwirth).

Intersex... not Trans, but...

As mentioned in Chapter 1, intersex is someone's sex, rather than their gender. An intersex person is born with variation in sex characteristics including genitals, gonads, or chromosomes that are not distinctly female or male. Intersex people live as men, women, two-spirit, third gender, genderqueer, agender, or intersex.

There are intersex individuals who were raised as women who have later transitioned into living as men later in life, and vice versa, thus being transgender intersex people. There are also third gender and genderqueer individuals who use intersex as a way to describe their gender rather than the original use for the word.

The intersex and transgender communities have overlapping concerns on a social and political level and thus, at times, work with one another. Whether fighting for the ability to change gender markers, be legally married, or have access to medical care – the crossover exists. In addition, intersex and transgender populations both challenge the cultural assumption of only two genders.

There are transgender activists who use the existence of intersex people as a way to "prove" the validity of gender diversity. Other transgender individuals choose to identify as intersex, even if they are not necessarily biologically intersex. This becomes confusing, and is seen in some cases as invalidating, or as a form of exploitation of intersex experience.

It is very important not to conflate the issues of these two groups with one another. The intersex community has been fighting for the right to have healthy children not be operated on to "normalize" them, for example. Intersex-specific struggles are different from those of the transgender communities. Transgender people can, and should, act as active allies to the intersex community. One way to do so is by learning about intersex issues, or getting involved with activism on Intersex Awareness Day (October 26th) and Intersex Day of Remembrance, also known as Intersex Day of Solidarity (November 8th)[42].

Examples of intersex individuals who have received media exposure have included:

- Jazz musician and activist Eden Atwood; Australian politician Tony Briffa; Argentinian law activist Mauro Cabral; British aristocrat and author Lady Colin Campbell; author and activist Dan Christian Chattas; Chinese activist Hiker Chiu; English model Caroline Cossey; Welsh opera singer Lisa Lee Dark; psychologist Tiger Devore; Dutch athlete Foekje Dillema; Vietnamese general Lê Văn Duyệt; Scottish nobleman Sir Ewan Forbes; South African anti-apartheid activist Sally Gross; professor and author Morgan Holmes; Costa Rican author and activist Natasha Jiménez; Ugandan activist Julius Kaggwa; and composer and keyboardist Dee Palmer (formerly David Palmer of Jethro Tull).

Chapter Two

Time Periods of Transition

Just as each transition is a unique journey, so is the time in a person's life when they embark on that journey. Some knew as a small child that they needed to begin their transition. Others choose not to transition until they are near the end of life, or were called to do so as passionate teens. There whose journeys start during a busy part of their career, or who dance the path of raising children while in transition. For others, gender awareness comes in waves, with multiple points of consciousness coming over time as they come to know themselves better.

These different periods of life also affect what people, and circumstances a person will be interacting with at the time of their transition. Teachers, parents, and other kids on the playground? First crushes, sports teams, and grandparents? Spouses, kids, and co-workers? Military comrades, school reunions, and local community members? Each time period comes with its own opportunities and challenges, including chances for the people around them to provide support.

Trans Kids

There are children who at a very young age have pinpointed that they were born in the wrong body or know that they are a different gender than they were assigned at birth. Perhaps they look at their body and find it different looking than other people of the gender they see themselves as, finding themselves sad or confused. They may be puzzled or angry when referred to as a gender they don't identify as. These children are considered transgender youth.

Some experience themselves as not liking "girl activities" or "boy activities" which is about gender expression in our culture. There are also children who are gender-nonconforming, genderqueer, gender fluid, or do not fit the "born in the wrong body" model.

Transgender children have been able to clearly identify what gender they are, and have had a stability of gender identity, for an extended period of time. A lot of kids play with costumes or fluctuate for fun. Trans boys and trans girls fall outside of that notion of going through a "phase." Though there are people that believe trans kids will grow up to be gay, studies have actually shown otherwise, with children maintaining their gender consistently later in life[1]. Insistence, persistence, and pervasive certainty are the markers considered by medical professionals when deciding if a child should receive medical support for their journey[2].

Giving a child the space to state that clarity, without pressure, is important. Pushing any person into making a decision about their gender is inappropriate, as is demanding that it is only a phase. Neither leaves a chance for that person to be authentic. After all, a child is a person, even if they are one who is still learning and growing. Only the person who lives in that body – whether they are a child or an adult – has the ability to answer that question with time, exploration, and examination.

For transgender children, there are many for whom having their name changed, or dressing in the attire of their gender, is helpful for their sense of self. Others operate in one gender name and expression at school and another at home. Some live as a single gender everywhere. For those that pinpoint their gender from a young age, and experience distress, there is now support available that can help[3]. Through these resources including those listed in the back of this book, they and their parents are able to navigate the options available, so that everyone works as a team to figure out what is best for trans and gender nonconforming youth. Some options will not be viable or appropriate for every child. After all, each child is unique, and there is no one-size-fits-all for trans youth.

Children early in life are looking for stability and security. Knowing that they are still cared for in being who they are no matter what choices they make regarding their identity is important. When trans and gender nonconforming kids hear anti-trans jokes at the holiday meal table, they may believe that sharing their own truth will lead to being ridiculed as well. Making safe space for all people helps kids feel okay disclosing their truths to a loving parent.

Finding allies with the adults that a child interacts with is key. These include:

- Teachers who will refer to trans kids as their appropriate name and pronoun in the classroom

- School administrators who help find them gender-neutral bathrooms and devise policies for gender-flexible school uniforms[4]

- Coaches who will support the kid as they are introduced to their new sports team

- Babysitters who will show love and kindness to this unique child

- Pediatricians who will work with other medical professionals to help the trans or gender nonconforming youth get the full, and potentially complex, care they deserve

This is in contrast to pediatricians who do not believe in transgender issues or administrators that belittle the children for their expression. Professionals who have a negative perspectives affect parents and children alike. Having advocates who will speak up for their child is important because in most cases, a person under eighteen will need all of the support their parents[5] and other adults can give since they are still financial and legal dependents. Having people at home and in their educational environments who will keep them safe and supported is key.

Children early in life are also mirrors that reflect and mimic all of the words and behaviors they hear. This includes reinforcing gender-based stories and bullying behavior that children on playgrounds will have picked up at home and brought to school with them. Kids can be cruel, if not shown other

ways to behave. 78% of gender nonconforming students report having been harassed for their gender, including 35% having experienced physical assault, and 12% having endured sexual violence[6].

Creating systems to introduce a child's new name and gender is important, as is space for kids and other parents with questions to turn to a knowledgeable adult if they are confused. Some parents even move their trans kids to a new school after transition to help avoid these issues – with a plan in place for how to answer questions, if they arise. There are wide numbers of trans youth who have socially transitioned that experience much better mental health outcomes[7], which means that creating safe spaces to do so, no matter the approach, is important.

Gender neutral, genderqueer, gender fluid, or agender children may have different experiences. Some want to dress in a diverse collection of wardrobe, style themselves in specific way, or don't want to play in specifically gendered spaces. There are children that have a lack of interest or confusion around concepts of gender, or an interest in doing every option available. Others are confused about why they can't join both the girls' and boys' soccer teams.

At the end of the day – for any child – the core goal is mental well-being and overall physical health in a safe, supportive environment[8]. This is true whether they are trans or otherwise. Supportive families go a long way to help with this; along with every team member above. Creating a supporting home environment, treating the child with respect, and having a parent with the courage to find the resources they need to support that child are important[9]. Support networks are also being constructed for trans youth through camps for LGBT youth[10], LGBT organizations hosting youth-specific programming[11], and online safe spaces. Tracks of education concerning trans-youth at transgender conferences[12] and online opportunities for learning[13] are also coming into being.

Anything that helps children experience a sense of normalcy builds that sense of well-being. Access to books for children that show other trans and gender nonconforming experiences will show a child that they are not alone, and there are a number now in print[14]. Allowing them to live a childhood without having every moment of their life be focused around their gender also creates that sense of normalcy. This ranges from consistent gender-supportive parenting, including complex family arrangements, to promoting a foster care system that validates the needs of trans and gender nonconforming youth.

Every caretaker and family member needs support in turn. Exploring trans issues for a parent might be a new topic for them, and can seem scary and uncertain for trans youth and adult alike[15]. The same is true for a child's siblings, who will need support during these changes that affect their life as well. Groups like Parents, Families, Friends, and Allies Unites with LGBTQ People (PFLAG)[16] have meetings in every state in the United States, with over 350 chapters in the country to offer peer support[17]. There are also many peer-based resources online including those listed in the resource section of this book. Finding knowledgeable therapists and doctors, as well as attending conferences with classes and forums on trans children's issues, are both tools to alleviate some of that stress. Friends, allies, and fellow journeyers, all help make the parents of trans kids be more successful in providing excellence for their child.

Trans Teens

Living in an ever-shifting world beyond childhood and before their emancipation in the adult world, those who transition during their teen years have additional struggles from trans kids. Every person in this age group faces challenges around peers, bullies, parents, school, sports, and puberty. For a trans teen, these issues are amplified.

Peer groups are important in the lives of youth. High-schoolers tend to use those around them as the mirror for the evolution of an adult self. These include people around them in school, sports teams or their neighborhood, as well as those in their specific clique, gang, or spiritual community. The peers  of a trans or gender nonconforming teen will react differently to the news of a transition based on the teen's "role" in school, from quarterback to actor, academic to outsider. This is based on the group's pre-awareness of trans issues, and how embedded gender – in general – is for that peer group. For example, single-gender sports team members may have different responses than those in mixed gender artistic circles. These issues are also affected by whether a student is in a large town[18], small one[19], and the relative conservatism of their community. You never know though, some conservative communities can be incredibly inclusive, and many communities can be changed through passionate allies.

Friends and other teens might respond with full support and a smooth shift in use of names and pronouns, or begin excluding the trans teen from their social group. This fear of exclusion can affect teens. Bullying is a serious issue for all people in this age group, and gender differences are a way in which teens are known to be abusive to one another. From in-person assault to online bullying, there are teens who have felt so attacked and alone that they have committed suicide.[20] There are now groups trying to educate against such bullies[21], while providing support for trans teens. Their vision needs to be implemented on a broader scale. Part of this comes from administrators making bullying against anyone punishable by school rules, and even more by empowering trans and gender nonconforming teens, and their allies, to do peer-to-peer activism[22] and enact change[23] themselves[24].

These emotional and physical attacks sometimes come from their own families. Forms of abuse – emotional, verbal, physical, and sexual assaults – can lead to the trans teen running away. There are also teens that get kicked out of their home for their gender variance[25]. Of the 1.6[26] homeless youth in the United States, anywhere from 20[27] to 40%[28] are gay or transgender. Teens on the streets are assaulted; become sex workers based on necessity; acquired drug addictions, and more.[29] Creating, funding, and supporting spaces for those who have been kicked out or leave home is currently a serious issue[30].

Even with full support of family and friends, trans teens face the puberty experience. As secondary sex traits manifest, kids who previously had more gender-neutral bodies may face gender dysphoria that they did not previously struggle with. Flat chests become breasts, shoulders begin to bulk up, and outsiders cast further stories around how they "should" operate in their perceived gender.

Those who have not yet completed development may consider going on hormone blockers to delay the puberty experience[31], as discussed further in chapter 5. Because of the permanent body modifications and effects of hormone replacement therapies (HRT) such as potential fertility concerns discussed in that chapter as well, the issue of HRT for teens is a contested one. There have been teens who have undergone certain surgical procedures as well – though it is uncommon[32].

Trans and gender nonconforming experiences are also layered with questions around orientation. Crushes on people that are the same sex as their designation at birth can be perceived as gay attraction, which may not be the personal experience for the trans youth. Teens will be exploring what parts of their journey is about gender, and what is based on orientation, based on the information they have available to them at that time. Rising libido due to puberty can lead to confusing experiences as well, where sexual interactions do not match sexual desires.

Clothing and dress codes become confusing as well. What to wear to school, and what is socially expected in general, is an issue for all teens. For trans teens, questions of which set of wardrobe they should wear can be tricky. This interweaves with access to single-gender spaces such as bathrooms and locker rooms, and single-gender schools. Applying for women's and men's only colleges, or staying as students at gender-specific schools, has become an issue for teens and officials alike. Joyously, trans and gender nonconforming teens being embraced in their full self helps set them up for life success, entering into adulthood from a place of confidence and support from the people in their life. With college athletics now having trans policies in place[33], and many colleges trans-affirming systems[34], we can see evolution progressing in a supportive direction.

Trans Adults

In general, trans adults have advantages over trans youth because they can speak and act on their own desires for care. Adults that are transitioning have full and complex lives that need to be taken into account. Perhaps they have spouses, children, careers, or are involved in military service. The coming out and transition process will affect every relationship they have, from long-term friends who thought they knew them well, to parents who may or may not be surprised when they are told. Parents and friends may have also been part of a person's coming out multiple times, perhaps as a lesbian, then as a trans man.

Even if a trans person has known their identity for a long time and struggled with sharing it, it is new information for a parent, child or spouse. This can elicit feelings of confusion, uncertainty, fear, loss, and even anger or betrayal. A loved one who wants to support the journey of a trans or gender nonconforming person can also be struggling with their own emotions around the issue.

Partners and spouses also struggle with their own identity. Changes in terminology, legality of relationships, and what to tell others come into play. The question of "what does that make me" is fairly common [35], especially in relationships that were previously experienced as being heterosexual[36]. Some partners do not have challenges with their partner's transition; instead facing uncertainty concerning how to operate in a world at large that might judge them, or see either of them in a new light. This applies to homosexual relationships as well, such as when a femme lesbian no longer is "seen" as visibly queer when a butch lover transitions.

Facing these issues together helps all parties learn, expand and grow in some cases, deepening their connection through overcoming shared challenges. Not every relationship or friendship will remain in a person's life during, or after, transition. Some end in going different paths, with separation or divorce both amicable and not, and others reconnect after time apart to process. The way a relationship works changes – whether it is a sexual relationship shifting to a platonic one, or a platonic friendship turning into a once previously unconsidered romance.

People with children will need to keep in mind the age of the kids they have. Speaking to them in a language they will understand helps children understand what is happening. There are kids that worry they did something wrong, making their mom not be a mom anymore; while others simply want to know if they are still allowed to call their MtF (male to female) parent their dad. Each child is different, and navigating their journeys from an individual place is important. It will also need to be determined how kids should tell (or are asked not to tell) other children, the schools they go to, and the people they interact with. This is a struggle for some kids and a delightful adventure for others.

For those with living parents, changes in gender are also met with mixed responses. Some parents feel hurt by having their son or daughter "taken away from them." Others are fine until they realize that the name they chose for their child will no longer be the same. There are parents who suspected something was different all along and want to support their child, however possible. A parent may also respond negatively based on personal or religious convictions.

Adults in transition may be doing so on the job. Human Resources (HR) departments are often consulted first, so that a plan is created to address the issue with managers and co-workers alike. Systems for transition may already be in place – which soothes the process – and finding examples online to present to management and HR can be helpful for companies that have not dealt with the issue before[37]. Just like all people, there are co-workers who will respond differently than others, and may abrasive, or incredibly supportive.

There are workplaces that become hard to work in during transition, especially in careers that are dominated by specific genders. Transgender and gender nonconforming people experience misunderstandings, hiring bias, on-the-job discrimination, and wage inequities[38]. There are unclear legal protections for trans people, who are sometimes denied personal medical leave. There is a push for anti-discrimination laws to be extended to transgender people on a national level, with a lot of work still to be done. Luckily there are steps already being made to work on these issues as trans people and their allies fight for workplace rights[39].

These issues are also at play for those in military service. At least 12 countries worldwide allow for open service from transgender soldiers and officers[40], but in the United States, open service is still not within the military code of conduct. Though "Don't Ask Don't Tell" has been repealed, an estimated 15,000 service people are still forced to lie about their gender, or live as their gender at their own risk of expulsion or discrimination[41]. This policy changes in May 2016 due to a plan at the Pentagon lifting the outdated ban[42]. Either way, a trans person will be working with many of the same concerns as transitioning in the workplace, with the added benefits and challenges of government bureaucracies. Veterans services for trans service people are already in place[43], with continued need for evolving legal systems around gender as mentioned in chapter 8.

Transitioning Later in Life

There are a variety of reasons that people choose to transition later in life. Perhaps they denied their gender due to religious-based condemnation. They may have received emotional or physical abuse when they tried to share their truth, or were told to keep it a secret by a loved one. Some trans people wanted to just "be normal," denying their identity and experience for as long as they could, hoping their feelings would go away. Others struggled with their own internalized transphobia, where their mind told them that they were wrong, evil or bad for feeling how they did.

Beyond fear, there are those who decided to take the time to weight out their self-identity and make sure they truly wanted their path before changing their life and their body. The threat of loss is real for many people considering transition. Concerns rise about interactions with family, friends, social groups or children. For some trans individuals, they explored their gender early on and decided not to pursue their path until their kids were fully grown, their partner had passed away, or they had fewer obligations.

There are also trans individuals who slowly developed their identity over the course of their life and did not even consider various forms of gender variance until they were in their sixties, seventies, eighties and nineties. People may not have had an awareness of non-binary options until recent times, embracing a genderqueer or demigender self-identity once told about the notions. Joyful expression also manifests latent considerations, once a person's loved one happens to say they would love them, no matter who they are, or how they present themselves. There are no age limits on exploring identity, expressing your core self, or making changes in life[44].

Trans Aging

The issues of sexuality and aging are already considered taboo in parts of our culture; gender and aging is rarely discussed. This is an issue because all people age. Trans care needs to be looked from a lifelong lens, as compared to many of the resources available that tend to focus on people who are currently going through the transition processes. Resources and systems[45] have only recently been developing[46] for this very important, and ever growing, population. Awareness of these systems, along with active collaboration with trans people who are currently aging that are able to speak their needs[47], is necessary for change.

There are many who are later in life that transitioned when they were young. Just because someone transitioned 40 years ago does not mean that they are aware of the current data or resources pertaining to their journey.

The technology and information about gender and transition has advanced dramatically over the years, and new information is gained all the time. They also may not have awareness around non-binary gender options. There are elders that do not have access to information available online or are unaware of information that is trans-elder specific[48]. Gaps in medical data are also an issue, including how lifelong use of hormones in trans individuals affects the body, and how past transgender surgical procedures age along with a person.

Just as with individuals with disabilities mentioned in chapter 9, older trans people may have to go off of hormones due to other medication they need. Perhaps that receive physical assistance from caretakers that don't respect their gender journey. When gaining access to retirement homes, trans people risk the possibility of being housed with those of their assigned gender, or having their gender history outed by the staff. Given that care facilities and retirement homes are small communities, this has the potential to be socially damaging, leading to various forms of abuse from other adults and providers in that community. This is all assuming that transgender people find places to live, as there are currently no anti-discrimination laws in place for retirement facilities[49]. Trans and gender nonconforming facilities are beginning to open in a number of larger cities[50], giving hope for additional housing options appearing in the future.

Those without biological family, or who have been disowned by their family, will not have the same support networks, or connections with other elders they can be honest with. They will need to make their advanced health care directives, financial documents, and wills clear, as it may not be their direct family that they need to reach out to, and their presentation may not match their legal identification, social security, or retirement funds. There are individuals who choose not to disclose their transgender history when receiving various forms of home-based or facility care. Those that have been living without disclosing their trans history for decades might not seek care because they do not want to disclose that history. This can cause illnesses and or even death from preventable issues[51].

71% of older trans adults also report having contemplated suicide or ending life early, compared to under 4% for the general population[52]. Creating social networks for trans elders helps support these individuals; feeling alone contributes to suicidal ideation or thoughts. There are, after all, many trans adults who are living loving and supported lived. Groups like Services and Advocacy for Gay, Lesbian, Bisexual and Transgender Elders (SAGE) are working to develop expanded resources and support for transgender elders, bringing them the care they need and deserve[53].

Ebb and Flow

Not every gender journey follows a linear pattern. There are those who begin gender transition, return to their assigned gender, and then go on back to their transition over time. Others shift from a genderqueer space to an

agender space over time. Some people complete a medical transition, and then many years later decide to transition back to their assigned gender.

When exploring gender, there are also people who ebb and flow. Just because someone explores gender variance as a conscious explorer, it does not mean that they will necessarily undertake social or medical transition. Unlike gender exploration being a "phase," this concept is about someone dipping their toe into the waters of their own identity, confirming where they will want to take themselves in the future. Having a phase of exploration is also part of conscious gender exploration, with people who flow in the long term, short term, or for curiosity sometimes choosing to identify with being transgender.

Just because someone changes the direction of gender journey does not mean that previous parts of the journey were bad, wrong, or a mistake. People make best decisions for themselves based on their knowledge and self-awareness at the time. Though there are people with specific paths for a lifetime, others are authentically female at one point in their life, authentically male at another point, and authentically gender fluid later on.

Private or Limited Transitions

There are transgender people who are called to express their gender identity only in specific situations or around specific people. This includes trans women who only manifest that part of their personality at specific gatherings, conscious gender explorers who go by a different name at home, or trans men who express their male identity in the bedroom. Online options also exist for trans people who walk their life at large as their assigned gender, while establishing a different gendered self on the internet.

Limited transitions may be a temporary choice for people who undertake social or medical transitions later in life. For others though, it is a good plan for them throughout their life. Crossdressers may be happy to wear their clothes at home, without it meaning that the person is interested in having it be part of their larger world. This is important to consider, as assumptions should not be made that all gender journeys follow the same path, no matter when people happen to undertake their adventures.

Chapters Four–Seven

Health

There are a diverse number of things that affect a person's health. The Biopsychosocial Model (aka BPS) theorizes that biological, psychological, and social factors all play a specific role in human functioning[1]. The health of a trans person is not simply affected by what hormones they might be taking, but is best understood by examining all of the things that affect a person's success. Psychological issues entail thoughts, emotions, and behaviors while social issues include economic, environmental, inter-personal, and cultural factors. In hoping to understand transgender realities, it is key to examine how best to support every individual in their social, physical, and mental health, and by extension of those three issues, their sexual health as well.

The following four chapters break this model down as it applies to transgender people and their journeys.

In Chapter 4 we examine the notions of social health:
- social support systems
- gendered group experience
- gender archetypes
- living in a culture at large that can be toxic to trans individuals

In Chapter 5 we will look at various concerns around medical health:
- receiving routine medical care
- support from the general medical community
- various tools and techniques for presentation
- receiving trans-specific care such as hormones and surgeries

In Chapter 6 mental health concepts and concerns will be explored:
- the reasons individuals pursue mental health care
- the concepts of gender dysphoria and body dysmorphia
- standards of care for making authentic personal choices
- non-medical mental health systems

Finally, in Chapter 7 we address issues around sexual health:
- sexual pleasure
- disclosure of body variances
- making affirming choices in sex
- fertility and STDs

Chapter Four

Social Health

The complex health of an individual is affected by our social systems, interactions, and connections. The culture we live in ripples through our daily lives, sending messages about what is considered "normal" and healthy by society. Traversing this landscape, not to mention living and thriving in it, is of importance to be able to build one part of our healthy being.

Support Systems

Satisfying personal relationships with others, positive social networks, and existing as an interpersonally connected individual in the world, all help create space for being a socially healthy individual. A social network is any place two or more people regularly interact, and share a sense of unity and common identity. They are also places they receive emotional support, assistance, information, satisfaction, advice, engagement, or a sense of belonging. Examples of social networks include:

- Activist groups

- Community organizations

- Co-workers

- Drinking establishment peers

- Family of choice

- Family of upbringing

- Fraternities and sororities

- Gangs

- Gyms

- Hobby groups

- Housemates

- Musical communities

- Neighbors

- Peer discussion groups

- Political organizations

- Recovery groups

- Religious communities

- Schoolmates

- Shared fandom

- Sports teams

- Teachers

- …and more

These groups are found both in-person and online. A trans or gender variant person might interact with their networks on a daily basis, or on sporadic occasions. They might have a diverse web of networks, or have a core one they are embedded in.

When disclosing their transition to the people in their support networks, a trans person has choices in the methodology they use. Some will choose to sit each person down separately to discuss their life changes, while others announce their journey online with a long post. Choices get made as to which people or groups need to find out first, and which people even need to be told. There are explicit disclosures that share every detail of the person's journey to this decision, and other situations where a person shifts over time, never directly discussing what is going on unless the other person brings it up. Each comes with their pros and cons, and needs to be carefully considered for the best success of maintaining that network, as well as what the trans person has the capacity to handle.

Returning to a presentation of the gender from their past when appearing at family gatherings or maintaining use of a former name in certain work, legal, or social situations, where they may or may not have disclosed, is a valid choice. This may be based on religious beliefs, cultural constructs, legal issues, or concern around loss of a given network. Alternating between forms of presentation is similar in certain ways to individuals who have a punk rock aesthetic in their life at large, while dressing in very conservative wardrobe when at work.

Not every relationship with an individual or network will respond positively to a person's transition. There are those who embrace the person's truth with full acceptance, while others will want information and time to acclimate. There are those who will respond with verbal aggression or expressions of denial. Allies may show enthusiasm for a friend's new direction, or share that they are not surprised at all. From rage  to love, silence to huge hugs, fear to curiosity, humans have a diverse variety of responses. How their friends and family respond will help decide who will best support them overall during transition, and which people will need to be brought back into their life over time, if ever.

There are people who will have more knowledge about transgender issues, and for others this is a new topic altogether. Even for people with an awareness of the gender diversity, it is different for their daughter to come out as male than to know about a personality in the media. Interactions with fraternity brothers and sorority sisters also shift once transition has been disclosed.

When and how a trans person discloses is also based on physical and emotional safety. Just because a person has disclosed to one person does not mean that they are ready for everyone to know. Violence of all sorts is a real concern for many trans and gender nonconforming people, ranging from verbal abuse to sexual assault and murder. It is reasonable that trans individuals are reticent to share their truths, even with certain close friends and family.

Choosing to disconnect from people in our lives is hard, but is understandable when a person's family, friends, or co-workers have consciously, or unconsciously, hurt them. Whether this is trans teens being physically kicked out of their homes, or trans people later in life being informed they are no longer welcome in their congregation, this can be traumatic and deeply damaging to the well-being of a person.

There are also people who choose never to disclose their desires to transition because they were directly informed that if they transition, or consider transition, they will no longer be welcome. Often the threat is less direct: with friends or family displaying anti-trans behavior or language towards a celebrity or a passer-by. An extrapolation gets made – from a place of fear – that those same family or friends will show similar responses if the person discloses their truths.

During transition, the people around a trans person are changing and moving as well. Not everyone will be able to provide support, as they need time to work though their own responses and emotions. This transition can include mis-gendering, mis-naming, grief, social stumbles, fear, uncertainty, a need to learn more information, or a desire to be helped by the trans or gender nonconforming person to learn about what led to this decision. They are usually not intending to cause harm, but it might be painful to hear a person's own friend consistently using a former name, even if they apologize. This is different from a family member who *refuses* to use their name and behavior, even years later, outing their own sibling or child every place they go. The friend who is apologizing is likely trying to learn how to become an ally, even if they have not figured out how to be one just yet.

Part of transition involves stepping away from those that are harmful. There are trans folks who practice handling negative responses from friends and strangers alike, coming up with simple responses to their stumbles or challenges. Building internal stability and strength, through therapy and tools available later in chapter 7, also assist in transition. This time period of helping their social network shift may take a lot of work, or be incredibly simple. The people who seemed like they would handle it well might need time, and the stranger at work could turn out to be incredibly supportive, becoming a new friend.

It is possible to gain new social networks before, during and after transition. Whether trans specific or peers from their new gender presentation, these new support networks increase options for building self-esteem and helping the trans or gender nonconforming person not feel alone. A new workplace, friends, or family can come out of the woodwork to support in ways that were not there before, taking on a stronger role in the person's life. Pieces of old social networks might end up much deeper through the shared experience of the transition period, and knowing both the past and current parts of self from a place of loving integration. A distant aunt becomes a close confidant, or a passing friend shifts into being a dear one.

There are people who gain support networks through attending educational conferences about transgender issues[1], sharing trans information with others[2], or through becoming involved in various form of trans activism[3]. In-person spaces for trans youth[4] create unique social networks between those who would not have met otherwise. Creating new support networks is another way to fill a need for a group of individuals, such as the need for more support networks for trans elders[5]. There are also groups of people sharing positive stories about being trans[6], empowering others while finding the joy in their own experience.

With social networks, the key is to remember that they exist, and are there to be used in times of need. There are trans and gender nonconforming folks who feel deeply alienated, and forget they have anyone to turn to, whether that is an established connection or a stranger in a chat group. To support complete and complex health, turning to those networks in times of challenge creates a net to catch a person during those hard times. Social health does not mean having or using large social networks. It means having a supportive and healthy communities, friendships, and connections in general. Even if a trans person has one individual online that they have never met but whom they can talk with, it sets up a situation where they are not alone in their journey.

Learning Gender Cultures

Though we may have grown up in the same over-culture, a transgender individual may not have been privy to the experiences of the gender they were not raised as. Trans men might not know the norms of how to behave in the men's locker room beyond what they have seen in media, and trans women may not know how to navigate a bachelorette party. From salons and roller-derby rinks to sports bars and basketball courts, women and men are expected to behave in these spaces very differently based on their gender[7]. There are also family-specific gendered gathering rules that need acclimating to, such as women congregating in the kitchen, or men hanging out to watch sports.

There are exceptions of girls who were "raised as boys" or for households where everyone was part of everything; even there, the person previously did not get to experience single-gender locker rooms.

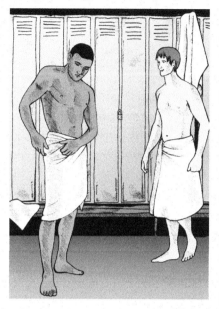

Men and women have different social cues, some of which are subtle. Many of these behaviors were never formally taught to children. Instead they learned them by bearing witness to the people around them of the same gender. Examples include how much people casually touch, how they acknowledge each other, the amount of eye contact people give, and how much emotional expression is common in given spaces. Though each person gets to decide whether to be part of those norms, understanding those norms allows for navigation within the gender of their presentation.

Adjustments to a new gender presentation can come with energy, enthusiasm, nervousness, or fear. Think of it as the teen years, when a person was trying to first figure out how to "be" around adults. Teens sometimes stumble as they learn their way. On top of learning a new gender system, a trans person is coming with years of experience living under a different system. In learning, they will also be working against the media portrayals of how people behave, rather than first-hand knowledge.

There are trans people who seek out mentors in their new gender to help navigate these spaces. Gender mentors of this sort are cisgender people whose path in life mirrors the path they are on that are happy to help without judgement, or an ulterior motive; quietly offering insights and feedback. Jocks who help jocks understand locker rooms, geeks who go with other geeks to science-fiction conferences, and models who attend photo shoots with other models. Other trans people connect with mentors who are other trans people that are further along in their transition journey; finding individuals who are on similar paths to help them along, rather than people on very different journeys that do not understanding the nuances. FtM jocks who help FtM jocks understand locker rooms, genderqueer geeks who go with other genderqueer geeks to science-fiction conferences, and MtF models who attend photo shoots with other MtF models.

Some of the fear around learning and integrating into these systems and spaces is reasonable. Newly transitioned trans people have been rejected physically or energetically from spaces for bringing the behaviors they learned in gender of rearing. There are also people, and groups, that exclude trans and gender nonconforming people who do not "pass" in their new gender. Trans women especially have been vilified, compared to sexual predators for trying to simply use the restroom. For this reason, there are trans women who choose not to use public restrooms at all, unless absolutely necessary, out of fear for having the cops called, or worse.

Beyond how others treat a trans or gender nonconforming person, it is also possible for that person will need a mourning period concerning access to their old spaces, and how they used to interact within gender-based cultures. Just because a person knows their gender to be true, does not mean they won't miss the way they operated in the world under their previous expression. This concept is further explored in the chapter on mental health.

Gender Archetypes and Stereotypes

It is common to encounter the vast stories and stereotypes attached to the gender a person is transitioning to. Not only wardrobe, but behavioral styles, careers, and lifestyles are brought into question. Having a stranger question whether you are "really a man" because you like pastel colors, or "really a woman" because you dislike high heels is demeaning and can feel hurtful. This concept is also embedded in the perceived gender norms of behavior; trans women who work as engineers, and trans men who are stay-at-home fathers, not being considered "real." None of these

things have to do with gender identity, as mentioned in chapter 1. Yet, when a close friend or family member questions a transition due to mismatches in gendered stereotypes, it can lead to self-doubt, or other emotional responses.

These kinds of responses are hurtful to people of all gender experiences. People from all genders like pastels, flat shoes, engineering, or being a stay-at-home parent. Unfortunately, these stereotypes create situations in which a trans person is questioned even more than a cisgender person about these issues. Health and wellbeing are impacted by these projections, as well as the models of gender provided within any given culture.

Various tropes and archetypes in culture are sometimes used by trans people to express their gender during transition. In Western society, this unfortunately includes certain unhealthy models. These models are shown in media and society though displays manhood involving drinking, anger and misogynist behavior; and womanhood including eating disorders, cattiness, and weakness. It affects what trans people unconsciously process as the ways they should express themselves.

An underlying question for many people is "what kind of person do you want to be" in their new expression of gender. There is a need for more diverse expressions of "manhood" and "womanhood," "girlhood" and "boyhood" for everyone in culture. Right now there is a story that to become a man or a woman you must act, talk, walk, and dress a certain way. The belief that people of certain genders have to behave in specific ways invalidates people as a whole, trans and non-trans alike.

This becomes a call for healthy gender expressions to be modeled for all children. Parents as well as other adults need to model and encourage everyone to be their best, healthiest, self. We get to move beyond our current culture that belittles girls for pursuing intellectual passions, or boys for expressing emotions; a culture that conflates masculinity with abusive behavior, and femininity with victimhood. Examining these issues creates an opportunity to craft a world where people of any gender expression to explore everything they are passionate about, engage with their emotions, and express themselves fully; a world transformed for our children to live without abuse, regardless of our path in life.

Cultural Toxicity

Social and mental health alike can be hard to maintain in a world that is often toxic for trans and gender variant individuals. Transgender issues are made fun of on television[8] as a way to get laughs. This is a form of what is referred to as "transphobia." Less commonly called transprejudice; transphobia is hostility or fear towards or concerning transgender or gender nonconforming people. It is similar to racism and sexism, where a person might be prejudice against someone, devalue, dehumanize, or treat a person poorly based entirely on having a specific trait.

Transphobic behaviors and attitudes can be unconscious or conscious. It manifests in the world of medicine, where 19% of trans people have reported being denied care due to their transgender or gender nonconforming status[9]. In manifests in work environments when jokes about a transgender employee are passed around the office, or a trans person is passed over for jobs and promotions [10]. Trans kids are ignored on the playground, or get bullied so much that they might commit suicide[11]. All of these are forms of transphobia. Transphobia happens all over the place, even in certain gay and lesbian groups and communities[12].

People in transphobic cultures receive an implied permission that it is okay to commit violence against trans people because they are not "normal." This concept is based on cisnormativity – the assumption that being cisgender is the only appropriate way to be. It can even be embedded in a trans person's unconscious mind, that they are not normal and somehow deserve such hatred. Cisnormative culture, combined with transphobia, gives rise to bullies and abusers perpetuating psychological, verbal, physical, and sexual abuse.

By creating visibility for the people behind statistics, a humanity is being returned to the trans experience. When trans are given a chance share their journey with their friends and the world, they slowly shift culture for the better. Movies and television that show complex and positive transgender and gender nonconforming characters help the tide begin to shift. This slowly expands the worldview of "normal," moving beyond cisgender existence being the only valid life experience, and the only one deemed worthy of living a full and healthy life. This evolution and revolution of understanding has already begun. But for now, being aware of this cultural toxicity is still important for the safety and wellbeing of every trans person, and those that love them.

Just as racism affects the people who are friends, family, loved ones and even acquaintances of those receiving such prejudice, transphobia ripples out to everyone as well. Transphobia manifests in the mocking of partners of trans people, parents of trans kids being vilified, and friends who try to stand up for a gender nonconforming friend being physically assaulted. Embedded transphobia in culture also leads to general discomfort with issues of gender differences. This affects everyone who lives outside of societally expected gender archetypes; men who wear nail polish; women who have no interest in children; and anyone who consciously, or unconsciously, live beyond what is considered "acceptable" in the world around them. Becoming aware of the internalized transphobia each of us carries is a way we have the capacity to contribute to stronger social, mental, and physical health for ourselves and others.

All people deserve social health. Social health helps build connection, communication, trust, self-identity, and self-esteem. This is as true for people who are transgender as it is for anyone else, though there may be of oppression that face trans people in acquiring the tools they need. It is supported through mutual respect, trust, compassion, reciprocity, and acceptance of each other.

Chapter Five

Medical Health

As part of the Biopsychosocial Model (BPS), we move into medical health and care. Though the dialogue around trans health care is often focused on hormones and surgeries, diverse medical care issues are complicated through being transgender. For this reason, we will be looking at general medical care and support from medical communities before turning to care that is specially related to gender transition and affirmation. The author is not a medical provider. Personal research and dialogue with qualified providers is always encouraged.

General Medical Care

Every person, no matter their gender, needs to be an advocate for their own health and healthcare. This is especially true for transgender individuals. There are many medical providers who have never had any dialogue in a professional or personal, setting about transgender people, let alone met anyone from the trans population. This is especially true outside of larger metropolitan areas.

Before examining trans-specific issues and care, it is important to remember that every transgender person is first and foremost a person. Like every other person, they will get the flu, experience twisted ankles, and need general medical care. However, many transgender people are turned away, don't find accessible care, or choose not to pursue care because of how people treat them or have treated them in the past. Poor treatment ranges from continuous mis-gendering of their patients, to outright discrimination. Examples include being shamed, being outed, belittled for their gender, experiencing denial of care, and outright physical abuse.

Advocating for health and healthcare can feel daunting for anyone. Layers of previous mistreatment make it especially hard for trans folk. This even applies to basic care. In the case of the flu, asking a trans man to take off his shirt for listening to his breathing can become an emotional, and physical, ordeal. Removing a chest binder or having to hear the nurse's passing curiosity about

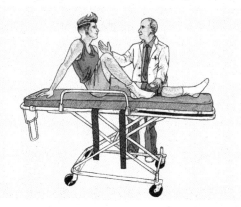

their mastectomy scars turns a routine visit into a challenge.

There are doctors that assume that if they don't know about trans-specific health, they won't be able to help that person at all. This does not make the practitioner a bad person, just an unaware one. In the example of the flu, there are no serious

differences between how influenza affects men and women and so there is no special knowledge needed to prescribe basic medications to a transgender person. Helping providers become aware of such simple things breaks down barriers to care.

Knowing about a trans person's physiological differences is important in certain kinds of care. When dealing with abdominal pain and concerns, it is important for a doctor to know if a trans man still has ovaries and a uterus, or that a trans woman has a prostate. Medication affects the drugs someone can be given, and hormones affect muscle mass or tissue density. When a doctor asks, "What medications are you on," this includes non-prescription medications such as self-acquired estrogen and testosterone. It is important for every person to share any physical realities that might affect the care they are getting to enable the best possible outcomes. Without awareness of a patient's medical history, providers will not know what issues to look out for.

The complexity of intake forms has the potential to be stressful for anyone. Especially so when health insurance forms, legal names and genders, preferred name and presentation do not all match up with societal expectation. A seemingly simple "M" or "F" is not always so simple. Having an intake coordinator or administrator disclose past gender and name information about a person in a small town affects the life of that individual. When a medical provider or administrator adds their own personal beliefs, judgement or verbal abuse to intake or care, it stops a person from seeking and receiving much needed aid. Every person deserves quality healthcare, whether we are aligned with gender expectation, or otherwise.

Support from Medical Communities

Part of access to – and the success of – medical care comes from the providers themselves. Having doctors, nurses, emergency medical providers,

pharmacists, and administrators who understand that there are gender expressions beyond male and female opens up dialogues beyond a binary perspective. Trans-aware providers create change one life at a time. Trans-aware and supportive communities create change for the world at large.

Though there might be a curiosity about transgender journeys, providers need to remember that their patient's current care is focused on their current medical situation. If the patient in care is the first trans woman, trans man, genderqueer, third gender or other-gendered individual a provider has ever met, it can be exciting to talk with them about that journey. There are people who are happy to share, while others find it incredibly invasive, inappropriate, or painful. If it has been ascertained that someone is happy to share, has given their full consent, and it does not distract from care, this could be a great place to learn. If there is the slightest case of doubt, or a person was shy to bring up their trans status, or someone is reticent, it is best to err on the side of not using their status as a provider to create a learning opportunity.

Many of the things that help trans patients, help all patients. For example, having individuals list their preferred name on intake forms allows for the person legally named William to list that they prefer to be called Bill, or Betty. By using the preferred name for an individual, they receive better care; building deeper trust through being seen as the person they are, not the name legally assigned to them at birth.

This can be done with pronouns as well, by simply having a box that lists he, she, and they, in addition to a blank space. When in doubt on gender, mirroring their own language goes a long way. If they call themselves he, use he. If they use they, use they. If in doubt, using their preferred name works as well. This mirroring concept applies to the people around the patient as well. Instead of projecting our assumptions of what a relationship is, asking what terms they use (friend, spouse, sister, brother, partner), by what pronoun to use with those individuals – and then using those terms – goes a long way.

Intake forms can also be modified to remove "female only" and "male only" sections, *or* by adding "not applicable" next to the options for dates of last period, number of pregnancies, mammogram, or prostate health concerns. If there seems like a mismatch of legal and medical information and presentation, the person should be called over to quietly discuss any details. Though this is the case for everyone's information, making sure to keep these details quiet and confidential is especially important for trans people. Questions about

unexpected name or gender combinations should never be done except intimately, as it leads to potential issues of safety or discrimination by those who heard it in waiting rooms – in small towns and large cities alike.

The concept of privacy and respect is important throughout all parts of care for trans individuals. When asking a person to disclose their medical concerns and information, spaces away from other patients and providers allows for that privacy. It's great for shy people too! If a person shares the details of their life, receiving that information professionally and non-judgmentally encourages a patient to share more, rather than self-edit. Self-editing affects receiving full details about that patient's case. Once a person is in care, make sure not to call out a patient's personal information from across the room, whether it is covered by HIPPA (Health Information Privacy Protection Act) or not.

Even when out of earshot, it is important to continue to respect patients. Non-judgmental responses and effective care using preferred names and pronouns models the tone for other care providers to do the same. Other patients occasionally overhear general discussion of patients on their floor of a hospital, especially in open air, or curtained cubicle environments. Seeing care providers offer respectful dialogue shows the other patients not just how to best respond to that specific trans person, but trans people in general. Simple respect comes in the littlest of ways, such as asking whether each person wants a bedpan or a urinal, rather than asking for information about everyone's genitals.

Subtle corporate activism is also starting to happen, shifting to gender-neutralizing administrative options. Doing so allows a doctor to choose procedures such as "prostate exam" without having the file have to be listed as "male." This is important as many basic procedures are not available if they are not available in electronic medical files, and care facilities can claim that a kind of care is not an option if it isn't in a database. With databases that have such issues, health insurance coverage and databases allow for the loophole of changing the gender on the paperwork, without a change in legal gender. This is a way for corporate and administrative activists to change lives.

The issue of access is an important one, as trans women need both breast exams and prostate exams, and trans men need pap smears as well as testosterone injections. Breaking down the gender stories on certain types of care can also help eliminate the biases around who should receive that care. There are women who receive testosterone injections, men who have intersex conditions that have vestigial ovaries that need removed, and men who have breast cancer. 1 in 1,000 men have a lifetime risk of breast cancer[1] and aren't screened or aware that they can contract it. Though this is much smaller compared to the 12% of the North American female population that contracts breast cancer, it should still be kept in mind. This lack of awareness affects trans women who believe they can't get it, trans men who believe that after cosmetic torso reconstruction that their entire risk is gone, and those who won't receive appropriate treatment due to gender bias around need and care. Trans people need to keep in mind both the medical concerns from their assigned gender as well as their medically transitioned gender, as no quality scientific research has been done at this time, and only anecdotal stories have been shared.

There are now staff trainers in North America who are available for building awareness for medical providers. Arranging for such training helps transform entire care facilities into trans-friendly spaces. Specialized trainings are also available for providers looking to become trans-capable not just trans-aware, including many of the events listed in the resources section of this book. Continued advocacy by medical professionals can also effect real change beyond their facilities. Work being done within the insurance field, or at the political level affecting the world of insurance, greatly affects the success of medical care for trans people at large.

For those who want to learn about trans-specific care models as providers, there are more and more programs slowly developing. There are also online projects that are showing basic protocols for care[2] for providers that do not have access to specialized trainings based in other states or countries, and help lines for providers who need help with specific issues[34]. These resources can also be passed onto their providers from trans patients.

The various tools offered in chapter 10 for building allyship are also encouraged for medical providers. These tools for success, as well as the ones listed above, help not just the person receiving care. They also aid the health care providers in being effective in their own work. Knowing what questions to ask, and how to navigate the basic concepts of transgender issues can lessen frustration and hurt feelings. Everyone gets the chance to work as a team. Though universal changes are needed in general health care, each provider and support person in the medical field has the ability to enable quality care and effect change at their level through respect, awareness, and doing what they can as allies.

Gender Transitioning and Affirming Care

Beyond general care, trans bodies may be different, and have specific care needs. The concept of "may" is important because transgender does not have to necessitate a medicalized reality. This includes both Western medicine, and mental health systems. Not seeking medicalized care can be due to diverse personal choices. It may also be due to lack of access to care. For those who desire medicalized care, it can be hard to access due to finances, location, or quality of options available. Other people have had care until they lost health coverage, or had a change in their health care programs.

Some insurance policies cover trans-specific care[5]; others do not. Even within health plans that cover hormones or hormone blockers, they won't necessarily cover upper or lower body surgeries. They are consider to be elective procedures under certain plans, though there are some steps that are possible to fight for various forms of coverage[6] for people whose care has been denied. A push is happening from within certain segments of the insurance world to cover trans care because doing so is a financially smart, and ethically appropriate, move[7]. Medicare in the United States technically covers surgeries, approving them on a case-by-case basis.[8]

There are providers that are unfriendly to their trans patients. Others are trans-friendly, but have no familiarity with trans-specific care, let alone had any trans-specific training. Though friendliness and empathy are a great first step, many medical providers learn on the job. Luckily, there are resources for them to access when issues or questions arise[910]. Trans people should not have to settle for care out of a sense that "someone will fix them." All patients deserve quality care.

To help create that quality care, there are now online projects that are showing basic protocols[11] of care for providers that do not have access to specialized trainings based in other states or countries, and help lines for providers who need help with specific issues[1213]. These resources can also be passed onto their providers from trans patients.

Trans medicalization is often provided as a reaffirmation of the binary model. Providers who are trained in transgender care from a model of all individuals being MtF of FtM may not have any awareness of the needs for genderqueer, two-spirit, or third-gendered patients. Even within FtM and MtF populations, the diversity of approaches to care are deeply individual choices, based on the bodily autonomy of each person. Providers are constantly learning about these options. Basic protocols of care are still a good place to start the dialogue, as they apply to many trans individuals, and spur on ideas for others. This requires an open mind and collaborative spirit between all parties.

Beyond local care, there are trans people who choose to pursue medical travel, or "medical holidays," to get the care that they need. Usually done in the context of surgical procedures, this sometimes involves traveling out of country. Keep in mind that seeking care with doctors who do not share their primary language, comes with its own risks in certain cases, and great success in others.

Medical holidays are sometimes chosen due to their costs or accessibility, especially for individuals who do not have health insurance or are paying for surgery out of pocket. Others chose to use known medical teams that they have seen the results of from diverse sources, both from word of mouth and presentation-based knowledge of overseas medical providers. These visual presentations of past cases serve as a portfolio, showing the approach and aesthetic of that surgeon. Hearing the experiences of others can also pass on challenges experienced with specific providers.

When traveling out of country for care, bringing a support person or support team can be helpful. Though it adds costs, having someone there who provides initial assistance during times of impaired mobility or to be your medical advocate can make a world of difference, especially if there are any unpredicted outcomes. Having a special person there with you to share moments of joy is also wonderful for various individuals.

Clothing and Prosthetics

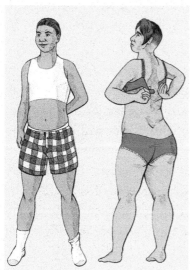

There are non-trans people who experience a mismatch between who they expect when their eyes are closed, as compared to looking in the mirror, around weight issues. They might have put on pounds, and look in the mirror and are unhappy and choose to lose that weight. Though bodies are beautiful at all sizes, and fat-shaming is its own issue in culture, imagine that sensation expanded to the whole of your life and body. This sense of having your body and mind being intensely discordant is referred to as body dysphoria – or when pertaining to gender specifically, gender dysphoria[14]. Being able to transform that feeling through modifying clothing, prosthetics, and makeup are basic tools for trans and gender nonconforming people.

When examining gender affirming healthcare, things that seem as "simple" as changes in clothing or adornment still affects health needs. Wearing binders, a tool designed for men with gynomastia (breast growth for people assigned male at birth), and men who prefer to streamline their midsection aesthetically, are a common tool for trans men and various gender variant individuals. Beyond the undergarment that compresses and streamlines the entire torso, there are others who use wide bandages, cling film, heavy tape over fabric, or very tight tank tops and tee shirts. Some flatten their breast tissue down towards their belly, while others tuck out towards their armpits.

Use of binders and compression shirts becomes challenging for people with large amounts of upper body tissue to create a "classic men's torso," due to the finished look achieved by the binder. Trying to achieve this "classic look" also invalidates men of all sizes, trans and otherwise. Binders are a useful tool for many people though, allowing them to operate more happily in the world at large through this non-medical intervention. Anecdotally, they can increase challenges for individuals with asthma or other breathing issues. They are also an expensive item to invest in for people on a budget, though there are various programs online helping people who have financial challenges. Beyond binding, wearing baggy clothes is a tool for some trans men, to cover their hips. They may also unconsciously gain weight or slouch to hide their upper chest tissue by blending it into their belly. Both have effects on overall health.

The act of going into the clothing store and buying clothes of an affirming gender is radical and profound experience for some trans folks. It can also be incredibly scary, especially for trans women. People who are designated male at birth that enter into the women's department, or dressing room, are sometimes read as potential aggressors. This leads to the shame and terror wherein trans women and genderqueer individuals quickly buy the first thing they see that might work. Others ask an ally to shop for them, or once in a while, acquire things covertly. Shopping on the internet, especially on websites that cater to larger sizes of bodies, has been empowering for some trans women who now have access to their needs without the same degree of fear or danger. There are also communities that have clothing stores owned by, or friendly to, members of the LGBT community, that provide safe shopping experiences for trans and gender nonconforming individuals.

One common way that individuals who were born with external genitalia wanting to experience their life otherwise is what is called "tucking." This technique involves pushing the testicles carefully up into the pelvic cavity, or pushed back between the thighs along with the phallus. External genitalia are sometimes held in place with medical tape, or the entire region is held in place with a gaff, which are effectively double-strength underpants created specifically for this purpose[15]. Through creating a streamline effect for the front of the body, a trans woman might experience less dysphoria from seeing something "wrong" with her body, or feel happiness from looking down and seeing it look "right." There are also folks who use padded underpants, girdles, padded bras and other fashion underpinnings, in combination with tucking, to help create their further desired body shape.

This degree of strictness can cause compression issues and skin irritation from sweat, or allergic reactions to extended use of medical tape on sensitive parts of the body. When people use duct tape instead of medical tape, the chances of irritation and damage to the skin increase, especially if they do not take tape off gently under warm water. Getting in and out of tight clothing or needing to "untuck," also adds to the likelihood that trans women will not use bathrooms while out and about – an issue already at play for safety reasons for trans women. Avoidance of the bathroom on an ongoing basis cases increased chances of urinary tract infections[16], and yet, being a woman with a bulge, or who fall outside the expected aesthetics of women in culture, increases risks of transphobic violence.

Prosthetics are another common technology used for gender affirmation. Examples include prosthetic cock, balls, and breasts. These prosthetics are worn underneath clothing, by both trans and non-trans individuals, to augment their bodies for medical or cosmetic reasons. Lower body prosthetics are affirming for some trans people, with the weight and shape of them in their underpants leading to an experience of feeling "complete." These tools vary in material, including silicone, "mystery rubber," and a sock balled up and put in the front of the underwear, though other creative ideas exist. Of the silicone models, there are models that are designed as medical-grade prosthetics and use high-end craftsmanship to be usable for long-term wear. Even those come with notices to be taken off once in a while lest long-term skin rashes evolve. Heavy sweat is common during physical exercise, and skin rashes sometimes evolve. Various adhesives are also used, which poses concerns for those with latex allergies, encouraging the use of medical grade adhesives. There is concern by some trans men of having them fall out at inopportune times, or not be able to wear them swimming, except in the cases of select models. There are versions built that are "STP"–stand to pee, that allow access to the social "norms" shared in the men's room or bedroom. Others are created for sexual activity, or a blend of the two.

These same concerns apply to upper-body prosthetics. Worn against the body all day, individuals occasionally develop allergies and rashes. This is especially true for those who do not have funds or access for medical-grade prosthetics. While others pad with socks, there are also many trans women whose estrogen-based breast tissue growth allows them to use padded bras as a way to emphasize their breasts, just like many women in society.

Although these efforts don't seem like they are worth it, they truly are for most trans and gender nonconforming people. Operating in the world at large as the gender they are is not just a desire, but a need. And it is not just about culture – it is about seeing yourself in the mirror in the way you see yourself with your eyes closed. Trans and gender variant people do not pass just to be seen by others as their gender. They do it for themselves.

Makeup modifies the look and facial shape for trans people, using tools like foundation, lipstick, and blush. Trans women choose haircuts, hair dying, braids, wigs, and weaves as common tools to present themselves in a gender-affirming way. Trans men shave off their facial fuzz, use light layers of mascara on the eyebrows or mustache, and find various affirming haircuts, dreadlocks, or braiding styles.

There are wide swaths of trans and gender nonconforming people who do not use any of these, and their choices do not make them less trans. There are, after all, women who wear "men's clothes," and men who express themselves in a feminine, cross-dressing, or drag manner. Neither should not be told they are not women, men, or whatever their true self is.

Hormone Therapies

Though there are diverse non-invasive choices for body transformation, there are others who need or choose, to pursue hormonal options to transform their bodies.

Hormone Blockers

Hormone blockers are medications that are used to treat central precocious puberty (CPP), pushing back the time in which a pre-teen or teen begins to experience the full body transformations of puberty. This allows teens and parents alike to reflect on choices around transitioning. Part of pediatric medical care, these blockers are normally used for children who have puberty that starts young. These medications are not an option for teens who have already reached adult levels of sex hormones in their body.

Unlike various hormones that cause permanent body modifications, going off blockers allows for puberty to proceed as normal, under a delayed schedule. Blockers may affect bone density, creating the need for supplements and regular testing. There are certain parts of the population who have extenuating factors, making hormone blockers not a viable option for their care. In addition, there are various opinions on how long blockers are used, affecting those children who hit the point of pubescent development where blockers would need to be started at an early age[17].

Hormone Replacement Therapies

Most often discussed in the context of post-menopausal women, hormone replacement therapies (HRT) is any use of outside hormones to supplement a lack of hormones in the body, or to supplement one hormone in the body with another. For transgender people, the most common forms of HRT are the use of estrogen, progesterone, and testosterone blockers for trans women, and testosterone for trans men. Though they cannot undo the development of

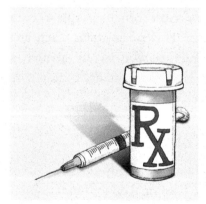

the sex traits brought on in puberty, they can develop additional secondary sex traits related to the gender of their preferred presentation or identity.

As HRT causes permanent body modifications, the current Standard of Care requires psychological counseling, and prefers for the individual to have lived, or experienced themselves, as their personal gender for a period of time[18]. There has also been a push by some groups for informed consent, making sure patients understand the risks they are undertaking before beginning HRT[19]. This includes medical providers and activists who have pushed for the concept of informed consent as a format rather than the WPATH Standards of Care[20]. Not all individuals or medical providers follow the above models, especially due to access to care, or relevant training. Not every medical practitioner is aware of the risks involved. This is why it is important for providers to develop trans-specific knowledge, as compared to simply being trans-aware. There are online resources now available for providers who prescribe medication[21]. Sadly, there are large numbers of endocrinologists who are unwilling to work with trans patients[22]. No matter who they see, patients are also encouraged to do their own research to help make sure their provider has the information needed for their care.

When undertaking HRT, there are a diversity of effects caused by the medications. Certain effects are temporary, while others are permanent. There is a push by many transgender individuals to start on high dosages to see results on a quicker timeline, though sudden shifts in hormones is not healthy for all people. The outcome of HRT is also individual per person. HRT does not manifest the body of a person's dreams; it manifests the person's own body. Often based on familial history, no two bodies will be the same.

This variety of outcomes is important to consider as well for genderqueer individuals who choose to take various forms of HRT. Medical communities in the various trans fields are still evolving on this topic, as original usages of these medications for transition were based on a binary model. There are trans-specific care providers who will only work with binary transitions at this time, while others are opening up to the diversity of gender experiences.

The effects of taking estrogen can include[23]:

- Decrease of facial and body hair
- Slowing in balding pattern
- Decrease in oily skin and acne
- Softer skin
- Change in body scents
- Decreased strength and muscle mass
- Fat shifting from the abdomen, to buttocks, thighs, and hips
- Enlarged nipples
- Breast growth
- Shrinkage of testicles
- Loss of erection and ejaculation
- Facial structure shifts
- Decrease in sex drive

These shifts can come with challenges, or complications, including[24]:

- Hypertension
- Nausea and vomiting
- Weight gain
- Skin darkening
- Migraines
- Gallbladder or liver disease
- Lipid abnormalities
- Hypothyroidism
- Blood clots (especially for those on oral estrogen or over 40)

Mood issues can also be involved with all forms of HRT. Changes that come with estrogen HRT include increased emotional sensitivity, anxiety, and depression. These challenges are furthered by individuals who already live with depression or anxiety. Having outside viewers such as a psychiatrist and peers – as well as observing one's self – is key for this reason. Depending on the medication involved, there are also recommended tests for the full health of individuals on HRT.

For those interested in testosterone, the effects of taking this hormone can include[25]:

- Deeper voice
- Growth of facial and body hair
- Oilier and rougher skin
- Change in body scents
- Increased muscle mass
- Fat shifting from the buttocks, thighs, and hips, to the abdomen
- Cessation of periods
- Increased red blood cells
- Clitoral enlargement and migration
- Facial structure shifts
- Shifts in energy level and appetite
- Shifts in sex drive

These shifts can come with challenges, or complications, including:

- Hypertension
- Injection site pain
- Acne
- Hair loss
- Back pain
- Headaches
- Fatigue
- Insomnia
- Upper respiratory infections

In the case of testosterone, mood swings, irritability, and short tempers are not uncommon. HRT also destabilizes some individuals with bipolar or other psychiatric disorders[26]. Though these are not uncommon, they are also not universal, with various trans men having positive shifts in mood, or no shift at all. Like with individuals on estrogen, individuals on all HRT should make sure to watch out for physical and mood complications. Developing ways to manage mood shifts helps maintain equilibrium during these changes in body and mind alike[27], and having outlets to process these changes. Challenges in health should be discussed with care providers, because dosages can be changed, and different types of HRT are available.

There are permanent, and temporary, body modifications caused by HRT. Because both voice and body frame shifts are permanent, they should be taken into consideration with the same degree as any other large, permanent, body modification, such as a tattoo. Though stopping HRT usually returns skin texture and mood to their previous condition, what returns or changes by stopping HRT is inconsistent. Though a person might transition back, or onto another presentation, they will never fully return to their past presentation.

In addition to visual presentation, hormonal changes affect fertility levels and can cause potential sterility. In considering HRT, there are people who choose to store sperm and eggs in advance if they desire to have children later in life. This effect is inconsistent though, and there have been numerous trans men who have given birth after going off of HRT, or whose HRT did not suppress their fertility at all. HRT should never be treated as a form of birth control.

With a wide variety of counter-indications for each form of HRT, there are individuals who are not able to take hormonal therapies, even if they desire it. These range from pre-existing conditions to drug interactions, and should not be taken lightly. Much is unknown about long-term use of hormone replacement therapies in trans people. As more and more people are taking HRT over the long-term, having only sparse anecdotal information is a concern for trans people and health care providers alike.

Whether discussing blockers or hormone replacement therapies, healthcare plans may or may not cover them. There are doctors who get them covered by saying that a patient has low testosterone or estrogen levels for their given gender, if their patient has already transitioned their gender legally. For trans men who have had a hysterectomy, the loophole might also be used that testosterone is another form of hormone replacement therapy rather than estrogen, and is not outside of previous care models.

Not everyone has healthcare access or insurance. This makes HRT access a socioeconomic issue. Less affluent trans people are disenfranchised, and it is important to understand that the ability to "just go to your doctor" is not a reality for everyone. In a 2013-2014 census survey in US, up to 20% of people in some states did not have health insurance coverage[28]. This affects trans people as well, and is amplified when providers won't prescribe desired HRT, or those medications are not covered by the care that is available.

Having less access to these routes of care has been known to lead to self-medication. The sources of medication are not always consistent, and may or may not contain what the bottle says it does. Re-using or sharing needles can lead to infections and the spread of blood-borne pathogens such as hepatitis C and HIV[29]. Lack of oversight through hormonal testing sometimes leads to unhealthy or inconsistent levels of testosterone or estrogen in the body. This amplifies the chances of side effects. Vilifying trans people who undertake this route to HRT does not help anyone. Instead, creating safe access to needle exchanges, testing, medical oversight and medication are actions that can be undertaken to help those in need.

There are also trans and gender nonconforming people who choose to approach changing their bodies through naturopathic and dietary systems. Whether because of health concerns, religion, desire for gender fluidity, or their own cultural context, hormones may not serve their personal path.

These options are anecdotally said to have varying degrees of success and costs associated with them. They range from specific vitamin combinations to dietary restrictions applied to eating, or avoiding, foods that have an association with the production of testosterone or estrogen.

Surgical Procedures

Ranging from mildly invasive body modifications to complex surgeries requiring multiple years to complete, different trans people might or might not choose to undergo these various options. There is no single specific "progression" for all individuals. It is a deeply personal choice, and each person should assess their needs, wants, and desires, before making any decisions. One common route for many MtF and FtM individuals is to begin their journey with clothing changes and prosthetics before undertaking HRT, then undertaking various surgeries. There are others who choose to have upper body surgeries and changes in wardrobe without ever undergoing HRT. Other routes exist as well. It is important for all individuals considering surgical procedures to do research on the surgeries they are considering, including the diverse outcomes and possible complications, before choosing any medical changes to their body.

"Cosmetic" Surgeries and Procedures

Though various procedures are considered only skin-deep (or just below the surface), their effects reach far deeper on an emotional level. Gender re-affirming medical options allow for a trans person to look in the mirror and see a body more in alignment with their internal image of themselves.

They are sometimes also chosen to help the outside viewer see the person within that same alignment.

Body shaving and waxing help remove body hair from legs, pubic region, arms, torso or face, and are common options for trans women. Others choose to undergo multiple sessions of electrolysis or laser hair removal as a longer lasting approach for those who are candidates for it.

As individuals who are designated male at birth are more likely to have a prominent Adam's apple, various trans women choose to undergo chondrolaryngoplasty, also known as tracheal shaving. Other facial feminizing surgeries (FFS) exist for having the nose or cheeks modified to produce specific aesthetics, or have Botox or collagen injections. There are also trans people who choose to have tattoos and piercings. This includes everything from tattooed eyeliner to full back pieces, earrings to genital adornment. In all of these cases, seeing a provider who is licensed in their field is important, as there are illegal providers who could do serious harm[30].

Upper Body Modifications

Taking estrogen can help individuals grow mammary tissue. For those who have a desire for further augmentation, there are also surgical options. Some choose to have breast augmentation options without taking estrogen due to medical concerns around hormones, or out of a desire to retain full function of their

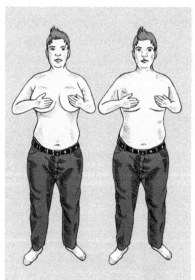

penis and fertility. A trans woman, or trans feminine individual, has choices around the size of their breasts during such procedures, with each person making their decision from a very personal place. Common options include saline or silicone implants – with the choice of implants varying from person to person.

For people who cannot afford breast implants, there are people who inject silicone. Injections are sometimes done alone, or at "plumping" or "pumping" parties, were trans women undergo injections together. Because the silicone is not contained, and some are low-quality silicone, it can be toxic and cause a variety of issues from site injections infections or organ damage, and even lead to death[31].

Doing smaller volumes at a time seems to – anecdotally – reduce risks, though in all cases, seeking medical attention in case of any complications (such as nausea, vomiting, chest pain, racing heartbeat, fever, dizziness, confusion, shortness of breath, or redness and swelling) is always advised. Others go to un-licensed individuals who offer steep discounts. Whether seeking care at home or overseas, if a price for any sort of care seems too good to be true, it might be just that. Seeing qualified medical providers with good reputations for care can reduce chances of complications for care in general.

For trans men, and individuals seeking a flatter chest, there are also various torso reconstruction surgeries or "top surgeries." These range from breast reductions from those desiring to minimize the size of their breasts, to full double mastectomies where the breasts themselves are removed. For small-breasted individuals, there are select reconstructions that use a "keyhole" method, where the extra tissue is removed through the area around the nipples. Double mastectomies are done by cancer centers, cosmetic surgeons, and the two working together, with chest surgeries occasionally covered by insurance as a form of preventative care for cancer. There are surgeries that retain the nipples, while others graft them back in place.

There are individuals who choose to have top surgery before beginning testosterone. This is sometimes done to enter into an androgynous state, or to flatten the chest before building muscle mass when the hormones hit the body. Body weight and size of the tissue already present affects individuals of every gender planning on undergoing surgeries, and not every surgeon has the same approach to these surgeries in general. Examining the outcomes from a diversity of surgeons will give an idea of what type of chest they tend to craft, in the same way that looking at the portfolios of tattoo artists can give an idea of how they do their artistry. Scar-reduction creams and gels help many people who have surgeries in general reduce the chance of scars, which should especially be kept in mind for individuals who tend to develop keloids (raised scars).

Thinking of tattoos, there are those who modify their upper bodies by having tattoos of nipples put on if their surgeries did not or were unable to preserve their natural nipples. Not everyone has ideal outcomes, and it is not uncommon for nerve damage, or slight asymmetry, to occur in the context of surgical procedures. Remember that no human body is symmetrical, and most cisgender women have one breast that is larger than the other, while cisgender men can have one nipple higher than the other. There are also individuals who choose to affirm their gender by having tattoos that express their femininity, masculinity, personal identity, or mark a rite of passage.

Beyond breast and chest options, liposuction and tummy tucks are done by people to remove fat or transfer it to other parts of the body. People may also undertake specific exercise regimens, with trans men hoping to bulk up their chest and shoulders working with weights, and people hoping to feminize doing more lean muscle work. All of these options work in combination with overall health, with those supported in their social health more likely to have success during the healing process by having people help them recover after surgeries. This is important because there is sometimes extended healing time for surgeries, and having physical and emotional support can go a long way towards a good outcome. The same is said of mental health, wherein an individual who is coming from a solid, internally supported place is more likely to heal well.

Lower Body Surgeries

Often referred to as Gender Reaffirming Surgeries (GRS) Sex Reassignment Surgeries (SRS), or Gender-Confirming Surgeries (GCS), these procedures were previously called Sex Change Operations. The last term has fallen out of popularity, as it is inaccurate due to the fact that a person's chromosomal sex is not changed, as discussed in chapter 1. SRS is still used as there is a reassignment of the alignment between sex and gender, but GRS will be used in this chapter due to the notion of reaffirmation. Reaffirmation applies to both those who knew their gender journey early on in life, as well as those who have shifted in their gender experience over time.

When asking trans people about their journey, people have been known to ask whether someone has had "the surgery." They are usually referring to GRS, which reduces trans people's "realness" to down whether or not their genitals match the expectations they have from a specific cisnormative experience. Not only does this simplify trans people down to their genitals, it also infers that trans men are not real unless they have large functioning penises, while simultaneously invalidating cisgender men who have small penises, or erectile dysfunction. The same logic states that trans women are not women because they cannot breed, harms cisgender women who are infertile, as does the argument of not being able to have vaginal sex is hurtful to cisgender women who live with vaginismus, where penetration of the vagina is painful.

It is considered rude to ask people about their genitals. This applies whether they are transgender or otherwise. As much as there may be a curiosity, unless there is a medical reason or a pending sexual encounter, there is usually little reason to do so. This is comparable to randomly asking someone whether they are circumcised or not. Individuals make choices due to the ways they want to have sex, the degree of their gender dysphoria, or body dysmorphia, and the geographic region in which they are based. Perhaps concerns around outcome, approval from mental health providers, or the joy of waking up in their desired form will fuel their decision. They may stem from desire for how they look in the mirror, their access to specific restrooms, or how they will feel in their clothing. Choices might come from interactions with partners, information on various operations available, or the costs associated. The issue of GRS is deeply personal, and the reasons to undertake these choices or not is similarly personal, and range from a solid and unwavering need, or an interest that shifts over time.

For trans women and individuals designated male at birth, GRS can include removal of current tissue present through an orchiectomy (testicle removal), or a penectomy (penis removal), though few penectomies are done in Western medicine without the construction of a new genital configuration. This is because the penile tissue is usually used for vaginoplasty (construction of a vagina), followed by labiaplasty (labia construction). GRS for trans women are often done in 1-2 surgeries, with prices varying.

For trans men and individuals designated female at birth, GRS can include removal of internal tissue, such as a hysterectomy (removal of the uterus, that may or may not include removal of the ovaries or cervix), or vaginectomy (removal of the vaginal cavity). Vaginectomies are usually done in conjunction with some change in the phallic construction, including metoidioplasty (loosening of the testosterone-enlarged clitoris/phallus from the labia) or phalloplasty (using tissue from another part of the body to enlarge and elongate the current tissue, often using pumps or implants for erection). Both can involve urethral reroute, reduction of the tissue around the pubic mound, and testicular implants. Wide varieties of FtM procedures exist, including metoidioplasties done without a vaginectomy, and different types of phalloplasties. GRS for trans men takes anywhere from 1 surgery (simple metoidioplasty) to 6 or more, and range from half to 8 times that of MtF surgeries[32].

Concerns around any surgeries clearly apply. No matter how simple a surgery is any use of anesthesia comes with potentially serious risks. Surgeries also come with possibilities around infection and other medical complications. Doing pre, and post, surgical care is important for these reasons, making sure to work with our medical[33], mental and social support systems to create a space for optimal outcome.

There are also many trans people who have no interest in GRS, happy with the lower bodies that they have. This does not invalidate their experience as being transgender, or being male, female, or any other gender for that matter. Being cautious of how we phrase dialogues around GRS is important for that reason, because people who enjoy their lower bodies have just as much right to live their life in peace.

Butt lifts and buttock augmentation are also lower-body surgical procedures, and they often get left out of the lower-body discussion. This is due to the focus around gender being directly being associated with a person's genitals. Buttock implants as well as fat re-distribution in the rear and thighs are common desires, especially amongst cultural groups that prize lower body curves.

Trans people come to the medical parts of their gender journey from diverse places. Before gender even comes into play, there might be issues including physical disabilities, heart or thyroid conditions, diabetes, auto-immune disorders, food and medication allergies, environmental sensitivities, and asthma. These conditions and realities may be counter-indicative to the options a person is interested in pursuing, and could put them at serious risk.

At the end of the day, every person must make medical choices for their best body realities, journey in life, and gender experience. It is not the choice of any other person, whether it is their social circle, partners, parents, children or even their medical providers. Medical providers, however, still get to make a call as to whether they will approve or perform procedures based on their own expertise or comfort. Unfortunately, medical providers continue denying care to trans and gender nonconforming individuals[34], even though it is illegal to do so in the United States[35].

Empowering trans and gender nonconforming people to make their own informed decisions is very important for this reason. People in the medical field also need to be empowered to provide quality medical care, whether it is for general medicine, or around trans-specific issues.

Chapter Six

Sexual Health

One of the challenges that faces transgender populations is that of sexual health. This interacts with the Biopsychosocial Model (BPS) because sexual health is part of the whole person, a blended space that incorporates medical, mental, and social health. This chapter is a collection of issues concerning sex and sexuality, ranging from disclosure – which is often a social health issue, to fertility – which concerns medical health.

We live in a world where even cisgender populations do not always receive adequate sexual education about their bodies. Trans people have to traverse issues including and beyond those that face cisgender people; such as dysphoria, body invalidation, and fear around how others will react to them. There are also individuals who have vilified or denied the existence of their own genital areas due to a variety of social and religious reasons. This makes dialogues about sex tricky.

Sexual health arises early for trans kids. They may ask why they do not have a penis, or why they are an outie rather than an innie like the rest of the girls. Think ahead of time, and coordinate with your pediatrician to have consistent answers. This can help a child understand that they are still beautiful, and that being different doesn't make them "less than" compared to others of their gender. It gives adults a chance to teach children that masturbation isn't bad; it is simply something to do in private, as they discover their bodies. Sharing that people engage in diverse sexual activity, and have different orientations, helps normalize how they are seen by others, and how they see themselves.

When bodies change, there are people who have shame or shyness in discussing what is going on with their body. When there is gender dysphoria, or a self-identity that does not match their bodily expression, asking questions about sexual health concerning the risk factors of their specific body may take more work. Asking friends or providers might work, but only if they have accurate information around what affects their specific body layout.

Even for those who know how to work with their body for meeting their safer sex needs – may not know how to explain their body in self-affirming ways – or in ways that are understood by their partner. There are people who rationally know this, only to have a hard time about it as they interact with genitals they don't personally identify with. Others don't know how to tell their partners about how their body is different than others. Lesbian trans women may not know how to dialogue about their flaccid phallus touching their partner's genitals, or a trans man know how to talk about his fluids to a lover.

One of the challenges around discussing sexual health is that what people call "sex" varies wildly. Sex can extend to sexual and sensual interactions for some people. Depending on how you define sex, it can include or exclude kissing, oral to genital interaction, genital touch, use of vibrators and sex toys, or different types of genital to genital contact, to be what they call[1] sex[2]. This makes it difficult to discuss issues around trans sex specifically. The types of sex trans people have could appear different compared to heterosexual, cisgender, penis-in-vagina, intercourse.

The same goes with how different trans people use sexual terminology. A trans man might refer to a prosthetic as his "cock," or a trans woman refer to her single available lower hole as her "pussy," while a care provider may make different assumptions as to what those terms mean. Terms like "front hole," "strapless," "bonus hole," "clit on a stick," "t-penis," or "bio-dildo," also become part of various trans-specific genital discussions that don't come up in other sexual dialogues. These diverse terms or approaches to the classical terminology available, can help create gender affirming language for lower body dialogues.

Pleasure

Part of perusing sex is the exploration of pleasure. A person will have different types of sensual and sexual activities that they enjoy before, during, or after transition. Their desire for sex may increase, decrease, or remain neutral. Their orientation might remain consistent, or shift. A person could experience an increase in tactility leading to desiring more hugs or cuddling, having their bodies caressed and massaged, or spending time enjoying long kissing sessions. Others find deep pleasure in autoerotic touch, and others with embracing an asexual or celibate period in their life.

The types of activities that provide pleasure are different for each person. Remembering this is important, because even if a lover has been with other trans men, that does not mean that what those men wanted will be what this

trans man will want. Just because one trans woman enjoys a type of activity does not mean that another will. Everyone will find pleasure in different types of sexuality, sensuality, and in life at large.

Trans and gender variant people needing to be encouraged to speak up for receiving the touch that they desire. Varieties of sexual connection do not have to include specific types of genital contact, orgasm or nudity. It may include soft sensations, intense sensations, caressing, massage, licking, sucking, biting, stroking, penetration of available holes, and stimulation of various erectile tissues. Sexual interactions include mutual masturbation, dildos, prosthetics, strap-ons, masturbation sleeves, pumping, extenders, nitrile or latex gloves, and lube. The lights can be on or off, involve body positions that affirm gender experience, sharing erotic fantasies, or use dirty talking of all sorts. There is no "right way" to have sex, or engage with their genitals.

With that in mind, encouraging all parties to speak up helps everyone receive the touch that they desire. How will we know what our partners want without asking them, and exploring with each other? There is a myth around sex that a partner should "know" what the other one wants. This is rarely as successful as having a regular stream of verbal, and non-verbal, communication going back and forth throughout an encounter.

Consent is important for all people. No one can tell you what to do with your body but you. Something as simple as not forcing anyone, children included, to be hugged unless they want to be, empowers people by knowing that their body is theirs, and that they should not take away that choice from others either.[3] Age-appropriate lessons in consent start the lessons in sexual health early.

There is a difference between not saying no, and saying yes[4]. Exploring what each partner desires can help build connection. It also makes for hotter sex. Some transgender and gender nonconforming people like describing what they want done with their bodies, while others don't like to use descriptor words. Instead, they have the ability to guide a lover's hands while kissing. Exploring together, with yesses, smiles, moans, and head nods, builds a sexual lexicon for playing in the future as well.

If a trans person is still learning their transforming body, it is an opportunity to try new things. This may involve finding new favorites, or discovering that their body liked something yesterday, but is not interested in that activity today. This is true for non-transgender people as well, especially as bodies change over the course of a life. Our tastes shift, and some days our bodies might crave different types of touch. Be understanding with yourself and each other. Who knows, you may just find a new favorite thing along the way.

For lovers who are used to pleasuring, or being pleasured by, specific types of genitals, someone's gender variant genitals may not be what they have experience with. There are people who want those genitals sucked, stroked, kissed, licked, grabbed, fondled, penetrated, caressed, or not directly interacted with at all. A strap-on for a trans man may not directly contact his genitals, but still experience profound pleasure from having someone play with it, just as can some trans women are when playing with their prosthetic breasts. Terminology can also contribute to pleasure, dirty talking about their "cock," "pussy," "hole," or other words that get them turned on, whether or not they match the assumption of what their body looks like. After all, whether cis or trans, each person's body looks different when nude.

Other people find it useful to not use words or explanations when exploring their form. Diving into sensations, without having judgement about those sensations, gives a broad opportunity for pleasure. Sometimes the stories each person has around how they "should" give or receive gets in the way of actually enjoying themselves. One partner might choose to give while the other receives, they can take turns, or engage with each other at the same time. This also happens when enjoying solo sexual and sensual touch. Closing one's eyes and just feeling, rather than painting a story about the body enjoying those feelings, allows for learning about what a person wants.

Afterwards, there are people who find that processing with a person about what you liked helps make next time even better. By sharing what parts were hot ("I loved it when…"), and what a person wants more of ("I wish we could have done that part all night long"), makes it more likely to actually happen. There may have been things that weren't enjoyable that can be replaced with new ideas ("Instead of kissing for a long time, next time let's wrestle instead"). Debriefing and in general looking at our desires outside of the heat of moment sometimes increases chances for knowing what we will want next time. Oftentimes, this is not done with a partner, but through self-reflection. Consider what you enjoyed, and how to make it even better in the future.

If your body has changed since last time you tried an activity, you could also learn that you can't do as much of something. Or perhaps you can now do much more. Finding your body at the point it is now leads to higher likelihood of pleasure, rather than comparing the body to where it used to be. Being here, and in the now, combined with awareness of desires and awareness of limits and boundaries, creates the possibility to make for delicious encounters.

Disclosure

Just as we get to make our own personal choices around who, and how, we share that we have chosen to transition, the same choices apply with sexual encounters. Examples of when to share information include:

- Before a first date. This includes only dating from within circles of trans aware communities, sharing information when socializing in general, or wearing clothing that denotes trans experience.

- After a few dates. In cases where a journey is part of medical history, having built trust with a person can lead to the comfort with which to disclose these details.

- While undressing. Letting a person know right beforehand, or while taking a piece of clothing off, so they know before seeing a different body type than they might have assumed.

- Letting them find out. Once undressed, people will see the body before them.

- Do not tell them. Not everyone feels a need to disclose their medical history of surgery and hormones.

Some people refer to this concept as *disclosure*. There are other individuals who do not use the term as they perceive it infers secrecy that needs disclosed, and not doing so is a form of deception[5]. For this book, disclosure is meant in the context of opening up about something personal.

These choices vary based on whether a sexual encounter is part of a long-term relationship or a single encounter or "hookup." Another decisive factor is based on safety concerns, as verbal or physical violence has occurred in situations when a person did not disclose in advance, and to some when a lover

finds out in the moment. Not disclosing one's trans status has also led to legal disputes[6]. People make decisions based on the venue where they met their lover, the part of the world where they live, as well as assumptions of wants and preferences made on previous knowledge and desires.

What people chose to disclose also varies. It might be their body reality ("I have a slightly different lower body than other men/women"), their history ("I used to be a gal/guy"), what they are interested in ("I prefer to just keep my clothes on" or "Having you massage me is wonderful"), or how they want the encounter to go ("I love making out before we get heavy" or "Let's play with the lights off").

Upon disclosure, there will be diverse responses from partners, lovers, and would-be hookups. Continued enthusiasm for connection; joy for being trusted with intimate information; fascination with a new adventure; uncertainty on how to navigate gender while still being interested; discomfort with the information; and outright rejection. All are all possible. It is hard to know which response might come. That can be scary for many trans and gender nonconforming people.

Outright rejection, especially on the part of someone who you have known for a while, can feel deeply personal. This is especially true when someone's reaction includes slurs or other offensive statements. Even if the statements are aimed *at* a trans person, they are rarely *about* the trans person. Fears around what someone else might think of them for being with a trans person, not knowing how to navigate the situation, and wondering what else they haven't been told, are not uncommon. Taking a breath and knowing that they are having their own process can help. For people who have responded poorly, having the strength to apologize, and process why it happened, can also make a difference.

In the case of people who are uncertain on how to navigate the new information, remember that you are exploring a lover. Every new lover is different. No two men like the same types of touch. No two women enjoy the same sexual activities. So it is with a trans person. Explore. Give positive feedback to each other when something feels good. Remember, when you stumble, make it part of the dance.

Making Affirming Choices

People make their sexual choices based on a variety of inputs. It may be the enthusiasm of exploring their body, or feeling acknowledged by others for their true gender. Perhaps drugs, alcohol, or coercion were involved. People have been known to get excited in the "heat of the moment," or forget that their bodies need to be healthy outside of their sexual encounters. Some feel profound pleasure in their sex life with others, with themselves, or being happily asexual.

Having been perceived as a different gender for part of their lives, there are trans people who experience a hunger for being "seen" as themselves. The first time a partnership or sexual encounter takes place where someone experiences them in their gender can feel not just affirming, but fulfilling as well. This can come from a delicious place, with true and deep connections made. As good as it may feel, it does not mean a trans or gender nonconforming person should have to make unhealthy choices based on their desire to be "seen."

No matter the reasons a choice is made, making those choices as self-affirming as possible sets a person up for better physical and mental health. Having safer sex supplies on hand, thinking ahead of time about where personal lines are, and sticking to your boundaries helps make quality decisions when such moments arise. So does knowing that no matter what has happened in the past, or is happening currently, moving towards a life that affirms a trans person in general can begin at any time.

"Teen" Rediscovery

Early on in many gender journeys, HRT can cause changes to the human brain, and how people think[7]. The last time many people experienced the rush of new hormones into the system was during their teen years. It was also the last time their body went through major transformations around secondary

sex traits and how they interacted with their genitals. This feels like a second puberty for some trans people, and leads to the same issues around making spontaneous sexual decisions that come up during teen exploits.

Because hormones are being introduced there is an opportunity to get to know the body all over again, both pleasurable and non-pleasurable ways. Styles of masturbation may shift, as well as types of sensual and sexual touch a person is interested in. Previous assumptions and habits around sex sometimes change, leading established partners to modify their sexual play; finding new ways to engage with one another. For people who have enjoyed their previous forms of sex, this can seem scary until they find their new equilibrium.

There are also people, amidst this shift, who choose to explore with new sexual activities or partners. Trans women who previously dated women might be interested in exploring with straight men. Trans men who played predominantly with women sometimes engage in play with cisgender men. This would allow the trans woman to try a different aspect of heterosexuality, or the trans man a different side of homosexual encounters.

Trans Admirers

There are people who want to have a sexual encounter based upon the fact that a trans person has a trans body. They are interested in a specific type of body, rather than a specific person. Others have an attraction or orientation towards trans men, trans women, or genderqueer people, and only date people who have that body type. This is not unlike people who only date blondes. There are also people that only date blondes, but want to find a blonde in the end that they truly like, and are a match.

There are those who have a romantic or sexual orientation only towards trans individuals. Just as there are people who are heterosexual men who date only women, there are people who are attracted to genderqueer individuals as a gender-based orientation. This is a real and valid orientation. Others have had the last few people they dated being trans women, even if they don't have a specific orientation to trans women rather than women as a whole.

Each trans person will have personal feelings on these concepts, and should evaluate whether attraction to their specific body type or gender experience is okay with them. Many people have specific types that they are attracted to, from people who like folks with round hips, or people who have tattoos, but not every round-hipped or tattooed person is comfortable with being sought after for that reason. This is important when dating online, as trans specific dating sites attract people who are interested in trans specific bodies, and are on those websites only for that reason.

There are people who find this dehumanizing, or disrespectful. This is especially true if a potential lover say they like to be with "freaks" or uses other potentially derogatory language. There are trans people who enjoy being fetishized for their body, seeking such passions consensually. At the end of the day, all trans people are individual humans, and respecting a person for being more than a body type or commodity is important.

Whatever gender someone identifies as; it is important for potential lovers to remember that when they are engaged sexually with a trans or gender nonconforming individual that that are the same gender they were before sex began. If a woman used the pronoun *she* before you played, and she was treated as their gender during conversation and romance, that should not change during a sexual encounter. This is true no matter what they looked like nude. That applies after sex as well, where a man should remain being called he. It should not matter whether he has had various gender reaffirming surgeries or not. Being a trans fetishist does not exclude this, unless the person in question has explicitly stated otherwise.

Drug and Alcohol Use

An issue in our modern culture at large, drugs and alcohol are known to affect decisions around safer sex and personal care[8]. There are trans people who use alcohol or drugs as a form of self-medication for depression, anxiety, as a form of escapism, or just for entertainment. The other effect of drugs and alcohol use might be a tuning out concerns around what happens to their body. People don't always remember or follow their personal boundaries, limits, or ethics when drunk or high.

Unfortunately, drugs and alcohol can also be related to incidents of sexual molestation and rape. Whether it is people who are drunk who have their bodies forcibly used while they are asleep, or people who have date rape drugs slipped to them, sexual assault is a real and staggering issue as discussed below.

Rape, Abuse, and Coercion

Consent is an important conversation for all people. The sheer number of people in the United States alone that report having been raped or molested is huge[9]. The statistics for transgender populations who have been raped or molested is even higher, with a staggering 64% of trans people in the United

States[10], and 70% in Canada[11], having reported that they had been sexually assaulted in their lifetime. This makes consent in sexual health also being something that needs addressed to help people maintain their mental and medical health.

Sexual assault is not the "fault" of the person attacked or assaulted. This kind of logic argues that they "should have" outed themselves before a date, that they "shouldn't have" gone down that street that "should have" fought back, that they "shouldn't have" worn an outfit like that. These statements cause further psychological violence against the person who has already been assaulted, rather than supporting them.

When reporting rape, some trans people are met with scorn, or non-affirming actions, by those they are reporting to. Furthermore, there are large numbers of trans women who report having been attacked by police or other people of power, which makes reporting these attacks challenging[12].

Anyone who does not pass, or who is "discovered" as trans can face these issues. This includes the murder of Midwestern youth Brandon Teena, whose death was the topic of the movie *Boys Don't Cry*, and other trans men who are raped[13] when their assigned sex comes to light. "Corrective rape" is another form of hate crime that has been perpetuated on various trans, gender nonconforming, and lesbian individuals over the years, wherein people who are designated female at birth are sexually assaulted by men to help "cure" them of their identity[14].

Beyond assault, coercion is also an issue in our culture. Taking trans people who are touch hungry into sexual acts goes against their body autonomy as well. Saying that if someone were "a real man" or "a real woman" that they would engage in specific acts is a form of coercion, as is the threat of removing love or affection is specific acts are not engaged in.

Emotional blackmail may lead to poor choices by that individual who is trying to keep a partner. When a lover causes hurt by saying things like "no one else will want YOU", or "you can't even make up your mind about what you are," they are creating an environment where the trans partner will be in extreme mental and emotional duress. This may manifest as a desperate desire to please the abusive partner in the hopes of approval and validation. Being kept in a worthless emotional state by a lover is emotional abuse[15].

Touch starvation may also be at play. This concept refers to a person who has been without physical connection, either casually or sexually, for a period of time. This feeling can begin to impact their physical, emotional, or mental health. For trans people that experience being touch-starved, there is sometimes a hunger, or desperation, to receive that touch. Some accept any touch they get that is affirming to their identity, even it causes harm. Receiving the types of touch that are needed, given with full consent, acquiescing or coping, will affect long term physical and emotional health. Keep in mind that personal responsibility is important, even if the choices are understandably hard, or may be situationally dubious.

We need to work towards supporting people in living the life that helps them thrive, rather than being pressured into the life, behaviors, and activities others want them to live. In the world at large, change is also made on this issue by training people from a young age that they should not overpower or coerce others[16]. Doing so will build a culture where people are taught to respect others who do not have the ability to consent[17], no matter their gender.

Coercion, abuse, and rape are serious issues for trans people whether through drugs, alcohol, manipulation, peer violence, stranger assault, domestic abuse, or other reasons altogether. Far too many transgender people have experienced sexual assault and consent violation. Resources are available to both hopefully prevent incidents, and for trans survivors if and when they occur[18].

Fertility

Trans and gender nonconforming people have children. Access to reproductive care for men who were designated female at birth who choose to reproduce is important. The notion that a guy wants to bear his own children is sometimes tricky for obstetricians and gynecologists at first, but it helps

allow for these men to maintain their full and complex mental, medical and social health during the process. This is true whether the discussion needs to be about the importance of going off of testosterone for the health of an unborn child, or setting up a birth plan for supporting the parent.

These issues are also key for women who fertilize their partners. Being honest about estrogen and its effects on sperm is just as important as the legal issues around the non-carrying parent's appearance on a birth certificate. There is also evolving technology on uterus transplants[19] for infertile women that may allow for trans women to be able to give birth in the future[20].

During planning, ask all parents what terms they want used concerning their parental roles, as trans men or trans women may want to be referred to as mother, father, or another term entirely. In recent years, gender diverse parents have come up with unique terminology to reflect their unique experiences in parenting. The seahorse has even been taken up as an empowering symbol of men who have chosen to give birth[21].

Gender also comes up in the world of fertility for trans men and transmasculine individuals who need to seek out the services of abortion clinics. The act of walking into spaces of all sorts that help with reproductive health are usually constructed to be welcoming to women, with patients and providers alike not always being understanding of men who might need such care. Training providers who handle all sides of sexual and reproductive health is important to helping trans and gender nonconforming people. This will help providers focus on their skills while building trust and honoring a patient's needs.

Sexually Transmitted Diseases and Infections

The dialogue around sexually transmitted diseases (STDs) and infections (STIs) can already be a loaded, and sometimes judgmental, issue. This becomes a further ordeal for people with gender dysphoria or body dysmorphia, discussed further in chapter 7. Such situations can evoke problems for a person allowing themselves – let alone others – discuss or examine that region of their body. If providers do not have an awareness of trans bodies, they may not know how to discuss the individual risks a person is exposed to. Post-op and non-op trans people might have different risks, for example.

Questions like "how many men have you had sex with" becomes blurry when you have sex with genderqueer or agender people. Unless there are clearer questions, providers are unlikely to get the information they are looking for. Having people doing testing ask about specific behaviors, rather than genders is often more helpful when trying to assess risk factors. People who have sex with large numbers of individuals they know and use condoms with, for example, may be at lower risk for STDs than individuals who have sex with fewer people, but have unprotected sex with strangers. Testing all people for all STDs is another option, as HIV and hepatitis C don't only spread between "high risk" individuals.

Pre-op or non-op trans men face challenges if they prefer to penetrate with their testosterone-enhanced phalluses, but aren't able to use condoms in the same way that other men do[22]. Tools such as the "female condom," or cutting the fingers off of a latex or nitrile glove, then cutting open the far side of the glove, to use the thumb for protected oral sex, with the rest of the glove providing coverage for their front-hole opening[23]. Trans men may also enjoy receiving penetration, and unaware providers might recommend hormonal-based options such as "the pill," or sub-dermal implants. Unfortunately, these

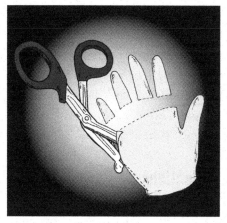

tools either neutralize the testosterone in the body, or are simply ineffective as a tool for fertility suppression.

Hormone replacement therapy alone does not stop fertility concerns, no matter which HRT someone might be taking. This is important for trans women to consider who enjoy giving penetration, remembering that condoms and other tools are a great option, as with being tested regularly.

Frequent testing becomes more important if a person, or their partner(s), plays unprotected. Body dysphoria[24] can also create challenges for safer sex, and creativity is important. Non-op trans women may find that using a dental dam over their erect tissue will prevent fluid transmission during oral interactions, while still supporting their gender, while a condom could trigger emotional distress.

During dialogues around safer sex[25], remember that it is called "safer" for a reason. Each person, trans or otherwise, will make their own choices around what tools and systems they will use to protect their body and those of the people they are engaged in various forms of play with. From barrier protection; being involved with only one person after being tested; engaging in non-penetrative sex; and choosing the types of play they feel comfortable with. Safer sex is a spectrum.

Whether enjoying penetration from a giving or receiving perspective[26], even carrying condoms can be tricky for some trans women. Over the years there have been cities that have used they carrying of multiple condoms as a way to "prove" that someone is a sex worker[27], making some trans women wary of having any. These "condom laws" are highly dangerous as it discourages people from protecting themselves. Trans women have a higher HIV rate than the rest of the population, with trans women of color even further disproportionately affected[28].

Given that there is a complex relationship between sex work, the need for money or a roof overhead, and trans issues, any barrier between safer sex and trans people affects these percentages as well. 19% of trans people have reported experiencing homelessness and 16% of have said they had been compelled to work in underground economies for income, such as doing sex work or selling drugs[29]. These issues are fueled by poverty and income disparities, which combines issues of social health and sexual health in turn. When this is combined with the sexual assault of trans people in general and trans women especially, the issues around sexual health extend beyond the gender dysphoria that may affect trans and gender diverse people.

This is why caring for the bodies that we have is all the more important. "If you have it, check it," has become part of the mantra in sex education as a whole, no matter your gender journey. As trans women have prostates, it needs checked for cancer and other concerns. If a trans man has a cervix, continuing to receive pap smears is also important. Creating spaces for receiving quality care, such as having gender-affirming language from providers when offering sexual health – especially continuing to use appropriate pronouns before, during and after procedures – helps trans and gender nonconforming folk want to actually receive care. It is also important to encourage all trans people to receive quality sexual education, and share information translated[30] to their experience[31].

Chapter Seven

Mental Health

Many conversations around trans issues begin with the concepts of mental health and emotional wellbeing. Within a Biopsychosocial Model, we see how that these topics are interwoven with social, medical, and sexual health. Just like other medical professionals, therapists and other mental health providers vary widely in their beliefs and approaches around transgender issues. Mental health professionals may have little exposure to LGBT information, let alone the diverse gender journeys that various trans people are on. Clients often end up teaching their therapists while "on the job," while other mental health providers have learned ad hoc over the years based on personal experience, or discussions with peers.

There are mental health professionals who have specific training on trans mental health. Their training and awareness may be up to date, or might have been undertaken decades ago when things were approached differently than current standards. Within those with specific training, each provider will come with their own experience, and beliefs. They may not know how to separate their personal experiences from providing for their patients, while others are excellent at the work they do.

This is especially important as there are mental health providers who do not believe that transgender is a "real" experience. Their approach is that all gender journeys outside societal norms are forms of mental illness, disagreeing with the *DSM-V*[1] (Diagnostic and Statistical Manual of Mental Disorders Manual), and – as a result of this belief – treat transgender people poorly.

Even those who are up-to-date within the current systems of the American Psychology Association and the American Psychiatric Association, may not understand journeys outside of binary MtF and FtM models. Finding out what training or background a provider comes from concerning the concepts of gender and mental health is helpful for establishing if they are a good fit for the assistance any given person is seeking.

Reasons for Care

Trans people are complex individuals who are more than their gender experience. They seek out mental health care for a variety of reasons, many that have little to do with their gender. Their concerns might revolve around relationships, career stresses, various life stresses and traumas, eating disorders, or post-traumatic stress disorder (PTSD). Their gender may not be first and foremost amongst their current issues, especially for people who go into

inpatient care. Receiving care for the potentially debilitating issues that took them into that care in the first place is incredibly important, and might or might not require therapy, medication, or other external support structures.

For people interested in examining their uncertainties around gender, undergoing any sort of transition might not be their desired outcome. Others are certain of their path, and have had a consistent and persistent awareness of their gender for a long time. It is this ongoing consistency that is considered a "cue" for the Western medical path when approving care for those who seek medical transitioning.

People who are seeking most procedures concerning gender-based body modification are asked to provide proof that they have undertaken psychological assessment and care pertaining to their transition. This includes everything from receiving access to HRT (hormone replacement therapy) to surgical options. Therefore, there are people seek out mental health care for the sole purpose of receiving their "letter" and consider their therapy only as a way to be approved under the "gatekeeper" requirements, as discussed below.

Certain therapists are happy to serve wholly as the gatekeeper for an individual, seeing a client for anywhere from a few sessions to a few years for this purpose. Other therapists are only interested in working with clients who want to more deeply examine their gender and overall life journey, working with their client before, during, and after receiving medical care. Changes to hormones and bodies can have an intense effect; stirring up both new and old emotions, physical sensations or abilities, and social interactions. Ongoing care for gender-related mental health beyond transition, and inclusive of topics other than gender, is considered normal for these reasons.

The Gatekeeper System

Under the current WPATH Standards of Care (World Professional Association for Transgender Health), one letter from a licensed therapist is required for hormone replacement therapy or various upper body surgeries. Two additional letters are needed for genital surgeries[2]. Though not universally required, the WPATH standards are followed very closely by many mental and medical professionals in the United States. They are also taken under consideration by some insurance companies that cover trans medical care[3].

Because of this system, there are trans people who consider therapists to be the gatekeepers of the care they need. There are many trans people for whom this system is appropriate, to make sure that they have experienced consistent and persistent gender experiences, and fully consent to the real effects of HRT and various surgeries before undertaking them. Others experience this as a simple requirement for their care. Both are challenging for those who have limited resources, with some considering it a form of systematic oppression[4].

The other gatekeeper is the insurance system. Many providers require proof of coverage and approval before doing expensive surgical procedures, along with attachment of formal diagnosis to a patient's electronic medical record. These systems can also require proving their trans reality to those in administrative roles who may or may not have training in transgender medical experience.

For those who do not have insurance coverage, the cost for every appointment needs to be taken into consideration when budgeting for care. It is not just the cost of hormones and surgeries that need to be kept in mind, but therapists, injection needles, beauty products, hair removal, and days off work. The costs alone have the potential to cause stress and anxiety for trans people, in turn affecting their mental health.

For those that fall outside the FtM or MtF binaries, there are not set standards for mental health care or access to medical care at this time. This especially comes into play for those who do not experience gender dysphoria – where this pathologized requirement for a gatekeeper isn't always met within their expected definitions. A person may not be deemed "trans enough" for a variety of reasons, which is why it is important to seek out mental health professionals who have experience, or empathy, for people outside of the binary. Being up front with a provider, and asking about their stance on non-binary gender during a first visit, also tests the waters.

Having a therapist that is a match is important, whether they are for ongoing or short duration care. There are mental health providers who do not believe that transgender experience exists at all, considering it a form of illness and delusion. Others believe that only people who are transitioning to a binary heterosexual experience fit their definition of transgender, and people outside those experiences will likely not be a good fit for their care. Trusting a mental health professional with personal truths, only to have them purposefully use the wrong pronouns, let alone vilify their gender journey, has the potential to be harmful to a person's long-term mental health.

Standards of Care

Within mental health care, there are a web of concepts that sometimes get confusing. In the 5th edition of the Diagnostic and Statistical Manual of Mental Disorders Manual (DSM-V)[5], "gender dysphoria" is considered a medical condition, as compared to the diagnosis of "gender identity disorder" that was considered a mental health condition in the DSM-IV[6]. This is an empowering step for transgender people because it took away the assumption that just because one is transgender, you were automatically struggling with a mental instability, or could be "cured."

Needing to be "cured" is what led to the notion of conversion, or reparative, therapy. These various systems attempted to "help" trans people overcome their trans desires or identities. These methods have never proven effective, and are discouraged by the American Psychology Association, American Academy of Pediatrics, and the American Psychiatric Association. Transgender conversion therapy programs are closing, including disavowal from some of the top former-advocates of such work[7].

Part of the desire by parents to have a child not be trans is based off wanting their child to have a happier life, where they do not face oppression by their peers or society. Other parents believe that they caused their child to be trans, and want to correct what happened. These can manifest in questions like "what did I do wrong," or "how do we fix this problem."

This attempt to help a child comes from a place of good intentions. Their desire for a child's success in life, as well as what it means about them as parents, are based in fear and love alike. That unfortunately does not help the people in their life who are looking for love and support, in a way that actually shows love and support to them as they are. It can seem like their loved one's journey is a "problem." Instead of the notions of repair or conversion, being trans should be approached as a normal part of the diversity of human existence. A trans person is beautiful and wonderful as they are, and should be supported, no matter their path.

The idea that being "normal" equating to being happy was the logic previously used to pathologize homosexuality until 1973. Though there are homosexual people who have mental health needs of all sorts, and there are people who do find distress in the fact that they are homosexual based on their history and environment; being homosexual does not mean that a person is mentally ill. So it is with the transgender experience. Just as the old world view said that only heterosexual people could be happy, which is not true, there is a shift away from the perspective that only cisgender people can be happy. When given the opportunity to build socially, medically, and mentally healthy lives, all people have the capacity to achieve happiness.

The primary system currently used by health care providers, called the Standards of Care (SOC), were constructed to help transgender people make sure that transition is truly the path they wish to take. This is important because there is a distinct difference between the fantasy of gender transition and the actuality of it. Living as a woman or man full-time is not the erotic or idyllic experience some people believe those genders will be. Clinicians encourage people to look at any underlying issues that could spur a desire to change gender – such as vilifying their body because of a history of abuse – to make sure that those issues are not unduly influencing their decision. Following the SOC is believed to allow medical professionals to help a person assess how transition will affect their life, by seeing if they are making choices from a place of unachievable self-destructive fantasy, or from a place of building stability for their complete health as an individual.

Within the Western medical model there are current Standards of Care (SOC) that have been put in place by the World Professional Association for Transgender Health[8]. These SOC are used by most mental and medical health professionals to establish the diagnostic label of gender dysphoria, which is the feeling that one's emotional and psychological identity is in opposition to their biological sex. It is often necessary to obtain a diagnosis of gender dysphoria for health insurance coverage of sex reassignment therapy. The challenge with this model is that gender dysphoria, as a diagnosis, uses distress as a diagnostic tool. An individual who is not actively in a place of distress concerning their transgender experience might not be considered to have gender dysphoria, and might therefore be unable to transition medically or surgically through health insurance coverage due to the SOC.

The Standards of Care are challenging in another way as they are also used to standardize trans individuals along more binary transitions in general. A person who has no interest in a binary gender transition might not as easily be diagnosed with gender dysphoria. Luckily, the newest SOC are beginning to encompass a broader diversity of non-binary gender, empowering those who do not identify as women or men to qualify for gender-affirming care and medical transitions[9].

The Standards of Care have historically operated from a triadic approach under version 6[10]:

- Real-life Experience
- Hormones
- Surgical Procedures

The 7th version of the SOC no longer uses the language of "real-life experience." This is a very important, and positive, move. Transgender is now seen as being about diversity, not pathology. Under the previous model, a trans person was required to dress and live in the gender of their identity. By living full-time within their gender expression, the trans person was believed to come to understand the experience of what their new life will be, which is very useful and empowering for many trans people.

This concept of dress was both disempowering and dangerous for certain trans populations. It infers a story of what a specific gender is expected to look like. For example, a trans woman may be expected to wear dresses, skirts and makeup, which excludes the diversity of ways women express themselves worldwide. It requires a vision of what a "real man/woman" is, which is invalidating to all men and women, and is about gendered behaviors in society rather than gender identity.

Living as the gender of personal identity is also physically dangerous for some trans people. In various areas of the United States, people who appear to be outside of gender norms are at a higher risk of experiencing verbal, sexual, and physical violence. This is especially true for people who were designated male at birth. Though these changes have been made under the newest Standards of Care, there are many medical professionals and insurance companies who have not taken on the newest model. It is important for any trans person to keep the concept of diversity in mind – just as it should be remembered by their mental and medical care team when setting them up for best success in their journey.

Gender Dysphoria

Gender dysphoria (GD) takes place in individuals from diverse age, assigned gender, race and class backgrounds. Adults with GD are at increased risk for stress, isolation, anxiety, depression, poor self-esteem and suicide. Symptoms of GD in children include disgust at their own genitalia, social isolation from their peers, anxiety, loneliness and depression. For people experiencing gender dysphoria, seeing their own body, or having their body seen by others, can be traumatic. This may also include having intense emotional responses to people using the incorrect pronoun, or pointing out the gender they were assigned at birth.

These individuals are experiencing intense stress and suffering. Trivializing that pain has the potential to make it feel even worse[11]. Asking a person with GD what support they would like is almost always more helpful than assuming that you know what will help them. If unsure where to start, or are concerned that in the asking it will cause further stress, many of the general tools for being an ally as discussed in chapter 10 are a great place to begin.

People that are trans beyond the binary experience GD as well. For a person who is androgynous, having a body with dramatic secondary sex traits, can be equally stressful. Agender people have a complex relationship with GD, because there is an assumption by many people and therapists that if one feels like they shouldn't be male, that they should be female. The answer of "none of

the above" is outside the understanding or scope of some therapists, who are unaware that GD may still be an applicable diagnosis when it is disruptive to a person's daily life.

Not all trans people experience gender dysphoria, even if they seek medical transitions. They are able to operate within their current body expression, and simply have an awareness that they would feel better if it were otherwise. These trans and gender nonconforming individuals sometimes choose to modify their body, but do not do so from a place of dysphoria. This approach to body transformation is similar to someone who goes in for liposuction as a way to present in a different way, without having a deep incongruence with their current form.

Trans experience doesn't have to involve changing one's body. Instead, someone can be happy to live in their current bodily expression, changing their name, pronoun, or fashion from what their designation at birth assumed. There are also those who have no interest in "changing" anything, choosing to embrace many pieces of identity to create their gender. Within the trans and gender nonconforming communities, there are also those who argue that the "born in the wrong body" model infers a victim mentality.

For those that have a drive to realign their gender and bodily expression with identity, underlying issues will not automatically be resolved by those actions. One example is that 9% of Americans from all walks of life struggle with some form of depression[12]. It is not exclusive to trans folks. Whether a person experiences GD or not it is important to ascertain over the course of care whether a person's stress, isolation, anxiety, depression, poor self-esteem, or suicidal tendencies are related to their discordant gender experience, or to other root causes. This allows comprehensive care to be provided for all parts of a person's mental health.

Gender dysphoria is occasionally conflated with body dysmorphia, where a person has an obsessive preoccupation upon perceived flaws with their body[13]. Body dysmorphia is a mental health condition that causes intense duress – affecting a person's interpersonal relationships and quality of life at large. Though there are people with gender dysphoria that experience body dysmorphia, it is not universal. Even flaws that are real become obsessed over, debilitating or leading to self-harm through pursuit of correcting or "fixing" the trait. Trans people are only a small number of those with body dysmorphic disorder, with others including those who perceive themselves to be too small, too fat, have a crooked nose they obsess over, or diverse other experiences. Do not assume that everyone with gender dysphoria has body dysmorphia.

Suicidal Ideation and Actions

Emotional pain for trans people has been known to include suicidal thoughts, as well as carrying out the desire to end their suffering through death. One study of 6,450 transgender people in the United States found 41% had attempted suicide, compared to a national average of 1.6%. That study also found that suicide attempts were less common among transgender people whose family ties had remained strong after they came out. Even transgender people who are at comparatively low risk amongst their trans peers were still much more likely to have attempted suicide than the general population[14]. These numbers only include those who survived, and do not take into account those who "successfully" commit suicide each year[15].

This does not mean that people who transition become more suicidal than they once were. It means that suicidal ideation is sometimes part of the human experience when doubt, pain, or societal anguish experienced by a person. People who are disenfranchised, bullied, hurt, or are rejected experience further suffering, which puts trans people at increased risk[16].

Those who have been provided love, support, help, or have found appropriate care, have much lower risks. Trans people who find or have social health are more supported in their mental health. The *It Gets Better* campaign[17] argues that making it through the hard years is worth it for gay teens, and the same is often argued for trans people. The pain is understandable, and should not be vilified. Instead, providing social and medical health for trans people can help people have the breathing room to work through the rest of their complex mental health challenges.

Individuals struggling with suicidal thoughts or intense emotional distress are encouraged to look at the top of the resources section for a list of help-lines available to transgender and gender nonconforming individuals.

Non-Medical Mental Health Systems

Therapy is a form of paid, trained, perspective, as well as an opportunity for reflection. It is not the only option for supporting and expanding a person's mental health. Many therapists encourage people to have multiple forms of care, including having a trans or gender variant person consciously develop their social health systems. This means questioning and assessing which people in their social network are supportive – or harmful – to that health.

Peer support networks are another option available. These groups gather at various LGBT centers, universities, churches, mental health facilities, and more. Online groups are also fairly common, and they offer both support and anonymity for people along binary transitions, as well as transitions to other genders identities. Other people find that it is important to connect with groups that share their ethnic, regional, disability, educational, or career backgrounds, many of which can be found in person, online, or started by the person seeking them out.

Another approach to mental health is through spiritual or faith-based counseling. Different belief systems may or may not support trans journeys, and that is important to consider when looking at available options for mental health support and personal exploration[18]. Just as with therapists, testing the water with basic questions, even in the third person ("I have a friend who told me they were trans"), gleans a lot of information about whether they are a good fit. For people with a strong spiritual background, having this affirming and supportive counsel is a boon.

Beyond formal groups and care, developing and maintaining personal tools for internal wellbeing and balance is important. This involves finding peace with a gender journey as well as systems for self-love and life success as a whole. If this degree of work feels intimidating, the tool of H.A.L.T.[19] can go a long way. Making decisions from any one of these four places will not likely support quality mental health, or overall health:

- Hungry
- Angry
- Lonely
- Tired

If someone fits any of these points, taking the time to address them before acting upon major decisions, sets them up for better likelihood of long-term, and even short-term, success.

There are also diverse ways people find a sense of balance and harmony before, during, and after transition. Some will be a result of new disciplines, and others will be tried and true enjoyments or hobbies you have enjoyed your whole life. These range from going on a walk, helping others, dancing, meditation, reading a book, writing in a journal, playing video games, and so many more. Taking the time to consider the best tools to calm a person will help when social support systems or key people are not available. Making sure to take the time to do those things. Even if it is taking a long shower rather than engaging in an angry thread of dialogue on the internet, or listening to music during a commute, acting on behaviors you have set out for yourself as positive and empowering helps encourage overall health and wellbeing.

Examining the options available around social health in chapter 10 gives additional ideas on supporting a trans person's mental health throughout the transition process.

Gender Loss and Grief

Mixed in with all of this transformation and relief, is the concept of grief and processing the potential loss from earlier aspects of a person's life. Someone who is trans or gender nonconforming may be shifting away from specific ways of life, activities, or spaces that were related to the gender they were previously seen as. These expressions of loss and grief manifest as everything from anger to depression.

This sense of loss can come from losing access to sexuality or gender-based community spaces. For those who were previously involved in the LGBT communities, they won't necessarily be welcomed into those spaces in the same way. People who are FtM are sometimes asked to disengage from women's and feminist community spaces, including ones they helped form. Though there are women's spaces that continue to embrace the trans men they

know and love, others feel uncomfortable doing so, or want to show them respect by treating them as the gender they identify as.

MtF people may experience a loss of access to gay men's spaces, or no longer feel like they are a fit in with people they once did drag. This is especially true for people who now are perceived as being heterosexual as compared to being seen as homosexual. Queer communities might or might not embrace those who no longer fit the mold of what queer "should" look like, whether by personal appearance or perceived partnerships.

The same can be true for gender-specific spaces in society at large. People who had an active part in the world of sports may feel a loss at not being welcome amidst their former peers. Trans women might no longer be a part of playing baseball for example, even if their former teammates are supportive of her transition. When social time with friends is based almost entirely on the time on the field, this can lead to an additional sense of sorrow. Even if the social time is off the field, there can be an unconscious discordance with a group of guys hanging out with a woman now in their midst – even if she was once one of the guys. This experience of the discomfort of gendered spaces can also happen everywhere from book clubs to bars, addiction support groups to political action committees.

Not only people who were once gay or lesbian experience the loss of orientation-based spaces. Our culture is based on heterosexual privilege; and the world at large may not embrace established partnerships that were once deemed heterosexual, as they are now seen by outsiders to be homosexual. A heterosexual married couple, where the husband transitions to being a woman, leads to the couple now being perceived as lesbian by the outside viewer. Just because their mate transitioned does not mean that the partner sees themselves as a new orientation, adding a potential sense of loss for partners as well. These partners are not intending to judge – or be against – their lover's transition; they are just struggling with their own simultaneous journey.

Some partners have challenges reconciling their affection with a partner's new presentation, unsure how to stay connected with their loved one. For those with a specific sexual orientation, their partner may experience a grief or loss as well. Even for partners who stay with a trans person through transition, there can be a sense of loss for either party of the things that have been set aside with that previous gender – giving birth to children, images of what it would look like growing old, or attending certain events together. Sex lives are also affected, with a partner potentially experiencing sadness around not getting to have a specific type of sexual connection ever again.

These various feelings do not mean that a person does not want to transition, or that transitioning is a bad choice for their mental health. It is about grief. In much the same way that a divorce may be a healthy choice for someone, they will still grieve the loss of parts of that relationship. Loss can manifest for even the most supportive of friends and family, even as they love and embrace the new sides of the person they care for.

For all parties, feeling various emotions is part of the journey. All major life changes bring up emotions. Even expressions of pure delight require processing, whether it is about a gender journey, or otherwise.

Celebrating a New Gender

After years of struggle or debate, fully engaging with the world under their own gender can be a hugely empowering experience for a trans person.

This involve getting to embrace, and be embraced, along their new path. Anything that helps encourage the mental health of the individual through normalizing their new gender experience empowers a person's choices and identity. Having others see them with the richness in which they see themselves can feel joyful.

Gender-affirming rituals and ceremonies are one type of celebration. These can be designed with the help of therapists, with friends and family, done within support groups, or created by the trans person themselves. Or all of the above!

Examples of gender celebrations and affirmations include:

- Re-birthday parties
- Coming of age rituals
- Baptism under a new name
- Being bar/bat mitzvahed under one's true gender
- Getting a new tattoo or piercing
- Attending gender-specific events
- Going for a girls' day, or guys' day, out
- Acquiring new clothing or accessories
- Making or receiving portraits and other art
- Updating gender markers on social media

Being fully acknowledged under a new name or gender is very empowering. Having an opportunity to stop and experience these moments of joy reminds people why these journeys were taken in the first place. This is done from a place of joy, making positive memories that last for a lifetime.

Anything that helps encourage the mental health of the individual through normalizing their new gender experience also empowers a person's choices and identity. Having others see them with the richness in which they see themselves can feel delightful for some trans folks, or simply a breath of fresh air for others. Examining the options available around being an ally, in chapter 10, gives additional ideas on supporting a trans person's mental health throughout the transition process.

Chapters Eight–Ten

World at Large

No person exists in a cultural vacuum. The same is true for transgender and gender nonconforming individuals. The final three chapters of this book address the concepts of the world that surrounds, affects, and supports, trans people. This includes the laws and legislation concerning gender, transgender communities that support each other, and the ways in which allies can help make the world a better place. These are complex issues, and each of these include challenges that need to be kept in mind exploring the journeys of those who are gender diverse.

In Chapter 8 we will go through the ways that law play a part in the lives of trans people:

- changing gender on paperwork and the effects of legal gender
- discrimination in the workplace and beyond
- hate crimes and abuse of trans people
- incarceration and treatment of transgender people in the legal system

In Chapter 9 we explore the challenges and communities around trans people:

- how people make choices around transition
- the place of "passing" and gender privilege
- awareness of oppression in the context of race, disabilities and class
- support systems, communities and activism for trans people

Lastly, in Chapter 10, we consider ways that allies can be a part of this dialogue:

- ways to express love and support
- understanding and respecting boundaries and pronouns\
- tools for supporting youth
- ways to be an advocate at every level

Chapter Eight

Transgender and the Law

Individuals who are transgender or gender variant face a diverse set of legal challenges. These issues vary worldwide, and for that reason, it is important to look into your city, county, state, and national laws[1]. This chapter is intended as a starting point to share and discuss the rights of trans people, discrimination inside and outside the legal system, and the issue of hate crimes.

Through developing awareness of the legal issues currently at play, changes can be made. Working together, everyone has a chance to help improve the legal situations at play. The information in this chapter is based on the understanding of the author – who is not a legal professional – and is also a snapshot in time from when the book was published. Laws of all sorts change over time, and those governing the rights and realities of trans and gender nonconforming people are no exception.

Legal Gender

The gender markers on birth certificates, state identification, and passports – denote legal gender. It is what gender a person is considered by the government and other formal systems. Legal gender appears on airline travel documents, resumes and work history, social security paperwork and access, green cards, military identification, and census forms. When legal gender appears in health insurance files, it also determines what care is available.

Gender markers often affect life in surprising little ways. Transgender people have to decide where to fill in an "M or F" on paperwork, paperwork that is often assumed by those asking for it to match with the person's legal gender even though it is never stated as such. There can also be legal ramifications due to instances when an individual is deemed not to have "told the truth" in the eyes of specific authorities.

These mismatches become further confusing when we look at issues such as immigration and refugee status. Without matching legal identification, it can affect the right to cross borders and to vote in the country where a person lives. Denial for access to cross borders and vote are both violations of the Universal Declaration of Human Rights[2]. If it is required to have a passport or birth certificate match the gender realities currently presented, and the former country does not allow changes, or they are refugees unable to gain access to such changes, people can be denied or be put in legal limbo. When we add in

situations for other countries whose birth certificates now have a third gender option or blank gender space, it is unclear how immigration will be handled.

The steps needed for being able to change your legal gender vary from state to state, and country to country. It is not possible to change your legal gender in every state and country, or changes are limited to certain documents. This creates situations where different pieces of documentation show a variety of name and gender combinations for a single individual. Documents that might need to be changed include birth certificates, state identification, national passports, social security cards, military records, voter registration, and immigration documents. The time and cost involved with each change creates barriers for those who do not have the ability to take time off for standing in line at government offices, or the funds to pay for filing fees and certified proof of these changes.

At the national level in the United States, passport laws have simplified to require a letter from a physician stating that "the applicant has had appropriate clinical treatment for gender transition to the new gender."[3]

Previously, gender reassignment surgery was technically required, though many trans people received passports without having done so. Laws for changing birth certificates are different for each state[4], as does the paperwork needs for changing state identification[5].

Without modifications to birth certificates, there are states that do not allow changes to state identification. This becomes an issue when it appears like a state identification card is fake. This can occur for a person presenting female, who has identification marked as male, for example. State identification also affects death certificates, influencing whether a person will be buried as the gender they lived by. The issue of death rights for trans and non-binary individuals is still a major issue, from the way their deaths are reported in obituaries to what name and gender their family uses when the deceased is buried[6]. Without matching legal gender on paperwork – partners, children and other inheritors may have difficulties accessing the estates of their loved ones. This is part of what makes having appropriate estate planning documents for trans people – as well as their partners and spouses – essential.

Trans people have to share their legal gender, as well as their gender history, with a wide variety of people, businesses, and organizations. Credit card and housing applications give access to credit history, showing an individual's past names and genders. Legal employment often involves sharing social security numbers, which may not match current gender presentation. These situations, and many more, might require a trans person to disclose their gender history to a person to whom they did not expect to have to "out" themselves.

Even after obtaining the legal gender that matches their expressed gender, gender-based issues will come up that were never considered before. A trans person over 25 may find themselves explaining why they never previously registered for selective service (aka "the draft"); needing to apply with the government for a medical exception. Someone who transitioned after service will need to contact Veterans Affairs[7] to explain their life changes for continued access to their benefits. Whether you are "legally" listed in a given state as a child's mother or father may also come up. There are states that have moved over to "parent" on such documents, allowing for the person giving birth to be listed as "male,"[8] while other states are allowing multiple parents of the same gender to be listed on a birth certificate.[9][10] In short, trans people will need to be prepared for surprises in paperwork to continue coming up.

Gender Discrimination

As of early 2015, at least 225 cities and counties prohibit employment discrimination on the basis of gender identity in employment[11]. Elsewhere, employment discrimination is a real issue for transgender people. When jobs have different dress codes for male and female employees, it can make employment difficult for non-binary trans people. Meanwhile, the recent LGBT Workplace Discrimination executive order now prohibits federal contractors and subcontractors from discriminating based on orientation or gender identity, and will hopefully set a path forward for change[12].

In the case of *Obergefell v. Hodges*[13], the Supreme Court of the United States ruled that there is a right to marriage without regard to gender. Before this decision, there have been many instances where cisgender individuals have used a partner's transgender status as a reason for divorce, annulment, or receiving reparations[14]. Some have argued that being trans, in states where gay marriage was not legal, made the marriage itself illegal.

Others have argued that a trans person is unfit to raise a child due their trans status[15], even though children tend to have fewer negative reactions to a parent's gender transition than adults do[16]. To help trans parents, more resources are developing as time goes by[17], including the diverse tools listed in the resources section of this book.

When a marriage is what keeps someone in the country, deportation is a real issue for transgender people who proceeding with medical transition who are in the country on green cards[18] – even if changing gender on the documents themselves is legal[19]. Marriage has historically been uncertain access for those who have already transitioned[20]. New marriage rulings approving gay marriage will shift the dialogue. Outside of marriage and children, housing is also a regular place of discrimination where rental landlords express that they will

not make their spaces available. Though the Fair Housing Act includes transgender under its sex discrimination clause[21], various groups are still working to make these policies a reality.

The "bathroom debate" is one of the most visible examples of trans discrimination, transphobia, and trans vilification. These campaigns argue that if trans women are allowed in the women's restroom, they will cause harm. In the 2015 campaign in Dallas asking for access to bathrooms for all trans people, the media advertising went so far as to picture a man in a women's bathroom ominously walking into the stall of a small child[22]. This discriminates against trans women's rights to urinate, which is a basic human need. It also endangers trans women, who themselves have been assaulted in men's restrooms[23].

This debate has argued that the birth sex of a person should be able to be checked if they are entering a bathroom[24]. This would require folks to share their gender realities to random strangers, creating literal states of oppression where only specific people are required to prove the validity of their presence in a specific bathroom or other gendered space. This is comparable to state laws that require proof of legal immigration status at all times in places where supposedly "random" checks are only done by people of white European ethnic heritage, to people with non-white skin tone, or non-white appearing ethnic heritage[25].

Both of these types of discriminatory laws are forms of profiling based on how much a trans individual "passes;" a notion discussed in chapter 9. A counter-campaign has begun by trans folks of all genders, including trans men who have taken pictures of themselves in women's bathrooms, asking "who is more invasive here."[26] On a potentially positive note, discriminatory debates have led to further discussions and implementation of all-gender and gender neutral bathrooms in some parts of the country[27]. This is especially empowering for some trans people who do not identify with the labels male or female, now having bathroom access that includes their experience.

Outside of the bathroom debate, laws that are discriminatory against trans people are brought before city, state[28][29] and national governments. Different legislation passes[30], is overturned[31], gets denied[32], or remain standing from before trans people gained such visibility in recent times[33]. The fact that they continue to be part of the dialogue around transgender rights means that legalized discrimination by the government is fueling a toxic culture for trans and gender variant people. There is hope though, as various cities[34] and states[35][36] are passing bills against transgender discrimination, while countries like Ireland have passed national gender recognition and rights[37].

Hate Crimes

People have diverse reactions when they are told – or discover – that a person is transgender. While some are joyous, others respond with violence. The most common form of violence is verbal attacks. Ranging from slurs to threats of physical and sexual assault, they can come from strangers as well as those close to the trans person. People who verbally attack trans people may be doing so from a place of peer pressure, while others have personal beliefs that justify attacks on people whose only "crime" is their own existence.

Verbal slurs are not seen as a "big deal" by everyone, but are often terrifying. There are transgender individuals who have chosen to "reclaim" words of violence as a sort of insider language. A prime example of this is the use of the word "tranny." There are parts of the trans community that find this term deeply offensive[38], having had it be a slur used against them or those they care about. Others use it as a playful[39], reclaimed, or empowering word. There are even people who note that there is no reclaiming needed, as it was initially used as an intra-community term before it was used as a derogatory term[40]. No matter the history though, when a term is used in the context of hate, it transfers that hate.

Trans people are beaten, sexually assaulted, disfigured and killed for being transgender. Others are attacked in acts of domestic violence[41]. Every  year, the staggering numbers of death are memorialized on Trans Day of Remembrance[42], an event that began as a candlelight vigil in 1999 to "Remember Our Dead" after the murder of Rita Heister. These deaths are important to remember. Proof of this can be found through the fact that between 2008 and 2015, more than 1,700 trans people were killed worldwide[43]. This does not include those deaths that were never reported.

These numbers are disproportionately large amongst trans women of color. However, trans people across the spectrum experience verbal, sexual and physical violence. This applies whether someone is agender, genderqueer[44], or a crossdresser. In short, not conforming to gender assumptions comes with risk in a violent and toxic culture.

In some areas of the United States, police responses to trans murders and sexual assaults are not treated with the same care as crimes perpetuated against cisgender individuals. They may even be the perpetrators, with 15% of transgender people in jail reporting being sexually assaulted by police, with numbers amongst African-Americans double that figure[45]. When cases go to trial, there are lawyers that find it acceptable to use offensive arguments that state that transgender lives have less value than other lives[46]. Others use "trans panic" as an approach, defending that the surprise of finding out someone is trans makes it acceptable to kill them[47]. These defenses might almost be laughable – if they were not believed or acceptable by parts of the American population – and if real people were not dying. Luckily, some states are starting to step up and make these defenses illegal[48], and hopefully this direction will continue.

Step by step, the issue of hate crimes based on gender identity is being brought to the political forefront. In 2009, President Barak Obama passed the first federal law to recognize the existence of – and provide civil rights protections for – transgender people.[49] Numerous states have also passed transgender-inclusive hate crimes laws[50]. Passing such laws allow for the people who commit crimes to be held liable for the horrible nature of their actions; discouraging people from doing so in the future.

Treatment in Legal Systems

Within the legal system, transgender people also face challenges. Trans women have been arrested for carrying condoms, or even "loitering for the purpose of prostitution."[51] For those who go to prison, the question of which prison someone should go to comes into play. Trans individuals may be housed under their current legal gender, while others are housed based on their gender assigned at birth[52]. When this happens, trans women end up kept in men's prisons, and vice versa. This can lead to sexual assault by prisoners and guards alike, as well as other forms of abuse[53].

In Italy, they have turned to the creative solution of constructing a transgender-only prison[54]. There are attempts being made to address trans-appropriate housing, names of address, health care, and discrimination – with the evolution taking place on a case by case basis. In some cases, the attempted answer is to have trans people kept in solitary confinement for extended lengths of time as a form of "protection," an action usually reserved as a further punitive act within the legal system[55]; effectively making being trans worthy of that punishment[56]. Many trans women have chosen to take their lives over the years, rather than live under such conditions and abuse[57].

This discrimination and negative treatment of trans and gender nonconforming individuals affects not just adults who are incarcerated, but juveniles as well. Systems need developed to care for youth in detention, as  well as the youth affected by their parents being incarcerated. Many gender variant teens who become homeless chose to run away not just from bad situations with their parents, but also from foster parents[58]. Training for potential foster parents[59], as well as making sure that people taking on youth beyond a gender binary understand trans issues, is important for building a better system for the future.

There is a slowly growing movement to address these issues, but there is a very long way to go. It will take the help of people inside the governmental and legal systems, as well as people passionate enough to bring awareness to these issues, to change people's minds. There are also social media campaigns that are making a difference[60]. With all of these working together, along with the voices of those inside the legal system with a platform to be heard – there is hope.

Chapter Nine

Challenges and Communities

As transgender people are experiencing profoundly personal and individual journeys; they are also embedded in a larger world. Whether the issues are their family, faith, ethnicity, age, disabilities, or class and socioeconomic struggles – we cannot pretend that trans people are only struggling with their own dysphoria. That is painful to say, because that struggle alone is hard for so many.

In this chapter we will examine these challenges, while also looking at how the concept of "passing" and gender privilege intertwine. These meld into the support that transgender and gender nonconforming communities offer, and how all people move together to create change through trans activism, and activism that overlaps with trans and gender nonconforming concerns.

Weighing Out What Matters

When embarking on their path, people who are trans have to identify their circles of disclosure. Who will they tell first? How will they tell them? Will it be coming dressed in different garb to a gathering of open-minded friends, or a quiet side conversation with one family member at a time? There are those that test the water with questions of gender in general, or dive into the topic. Is being in person the right choice for success with a loved one, or having a phone conversation with someone that has the time to talk?

In the current dialogues around being out and proud as trans people, it is occasionally forgotten that individuals are stuck with intense choices around when, how, and if, to transition. They ask themselves what matters more. Is it safety, family, personal expression, community, culture, religion, psychological health, or individual identity? There are people for who being "out" about their gender identity does not affect these issues. Others have serious debates with themselves and the people whose opinions they care about; over what they are concerned they will "lose" by transitioning. Being "out," after all, is not a requirement for being trans – or a choice everyone decides to make.

People who have been disclosed to, sometimes share what they learn, either on purpose, or by accident. This means keeping in mind who is likely to tell others. Within certain family dynamics, it is appropriate to talk with specific siblings before talking with parents, talk with parents before talking with siblings, or sharing with a spouse before talking with your children. Each person will respond based on what they think they know about transgender people in general, as well as how they have interacted with this specific trans person before their disclosure. How they respond may or may not be reflective of how others in the same family or social networks will respond.

Circles of disclosure include the larger circles that will need to find out as well. These circles include:

- Family (spouse, children, siblings, parents)
- Extended family (grandparents, aunts, uncles, cousins, step-parents, siblings)
- Close friends and family of choice
- Extended friendship and social networks
- Lovers
- Roommates
- Employer and co-workers
- Spiritual guides and mentors
- Neighbors
- Teachers

These and others have been discussed in the context of social health in chapter 4. Who a transgender person will disclose their gender history, or gender journey, to will come up as a question throughout their life. Each time they will need to make decisions on if – and how much – of that journey to share. There are trans and gender variant people that desire to share everything with everyone they meet. This isn't comfortable for everyone they talk to. Strangers, for example, don't necessarily want to know all details. Other transgender individuals desire to keep their circles of disclosure very small, perhaps only sharing only basic information with their medical providers. These decisions are deeply personal and should be respected.

Religion and Faith-based Communities

There are people for whom there is deep meaning provided in their life by their faith, and for the communities that faith provides. Every theology, faith, practice, worship, and spirituality has a different approach or connection to gender. In turn, each congregation, temple, mosque, church, coven, gathering, and group has its own relationship and interpretation of that approach or connection to gender.

Some religious groups and congregations whose policies and behaviors are so discriminatory that a person will decide to leave by choice. Other communities may inform a person that they are no longer welcome. Both of these can be traumatic for people whose identity, community, or family are or were embedded in their spiritual spaces. They may also find themselves questioning the faith whose community no longer welcomes them.

Meanwhile, others find themselves drawn to a new faith – or community from within the same faith – during their transition, due to the love and support offered to them. Some stay deeply connected to their current community, having their roles shift, or remain unchanged. There are trans people who find faith during transition, helped by groups that are specifically supportive of trans issues from varying traditions[1]. There are also traditions that have specifically accepted trans congregants, or have done deep reformation work to become actively inclusive of all genders. There are also a variety of religions and cultures that feature trans and gender nonconforming deities that become inspirations for their journey[2].

Certain faiths are based off of a gender binary, and have spaces that are only allowed to people of those genders. This includes Orthodox Judaism and certain Muslim, Hindu, Christian, Catholic, and Pagan spaces. Other religious-based cultures have requirements for wardrobe at religious gatherings – or in life at large. Transgender individuals face specific challenges and opportunities in these communities, and often seek out the council and different opinions from their religious leaders for guidance.

Family members and trans people alike, who believe in specific faith practices, struggle during times of transition. There are those who believe that transition is going against the will of divinity, or that force made an error. Others believe in the infallibility of divinity, and that those transitioning hold a specific precious and sacred role based on their specific journey. These beliefs are deeply personal, and may or may not be in accordance with the beliefs of others.

Other trans people traverse their faith spaces through not transitioning publicly. They operate in their personal gender of identity elsewhere, or not transition at all, to be able to maintain those connections or their

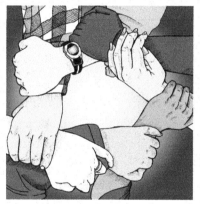

faith. Some come back to their faith after transition, not disclosing their gender history to their community.

Mixed in with the potential losses, are the hopeful gains from coming out and undertaking transition. Family members may surprise them with love, affection, and deeper connection to their true self. Their friends can embrace them with a new level of respect and compassion. They might not face as many internal struggles with suicide or depression, while getting to truly express who they are. New communities open up – or the communities they are part of embrace them even deeper. Their culture and faith may have a place for them that did not previously exist, and in finding such a space, they take on places of leadership or love. There are also trans and gender nonconforming individuals sometimes choose to leave their arms open for when people who disagreed with their transition want to connect with them later in life.

All trans people weigh out what matters to them – even if weighing it out hurts, or heals. In the end, this choice is theirs to make, and should not be made for them by anyone else.

"Passing" and Gender Privilege

Referring to the ability of a person to be regarded as a member a different social group than their own, "passing" is often done for the purposes of social acceptance, safety, or having the privileges of that social group. Originally referring to African-Americans who could "pass" as white, this term has been adopted in many parts of the trans community[3]. The idea of passing infers that a trans person who passes as cisgender is more "successful" at being seen as their gender, than those who do not.

There may seem like there is an inference, by using the word passing, that a trans person is fake, posing as something they are not. This is not true. If you are a woman, you are not lying when you say you are a woman, whether you are transgender or cisgender. If you are a man, you are not lying when you say you are a man, whether you are transgender or cisgender. This sort of language can be hugely self-stigmatizing by painting a picture around one's authenticity and realness.

Whether a person passes is based on expectations of beauty and aesthetics in culture. There is a story of what a woman should look like, and if a trans woman can't meet those expectations, then they "clearly aren't women." This same system is used to oppress ciswomen who do not match society's expectations of beauty as well.

For those that pass, and choose not share their transgender history, one of the terms used to describe the behavior or experience is to be "stealth." Safety, being seen in their gender, legal realities, partnerships, and it being no one else's business, are all common reasons for choosing to be stealth. People occasionally move to locations far away from where they grew up, or transitioned, for this purpose. Their partners may not even be aware of their history. The term stealth is confusing for people who experience their body changes were based entirely on medical abnormalities rather than a gender journey. To them, there is nothing to be stealth about; just as someone who has had their appendix removed would be confused about the notion that thy are being stealth about their condition. The choice to be stealth is their right, since people choose to maintain privacy concerning their medical history.

The capacity to pass is the counterbalance to how people "read" a transgender, or cisgender, person. What people perceive another individual's gender is. This is tied into the question of "are they a boy or a girl." This question and concept causes challenges for people who transition in non-binary ways because people do not know how to read them. Being read as one's own gender identity is a form of privilege because that individual experiences advantages in the world due to that congruence. People whose body realities or journey do not pass are sometimes oppressed or vilified for that incongruence. For genderqueer people, being read as genderqueer or androgynous can still be confusing for the viewer.

Even for people who pass, refusing to dress "correctly" also leads to stigmatization. This happens to cisgender people as well, where men who wear makeup are ridiculed or abused, and women who do not present in a culturally feminine manner are issued slurs based on their appearance, or perceived orientation based on that appearance. There are also people who specifically do not want to pass. They consider being forced to pass is a form of oppression caused in a world where being cisgender is considered the only form of "normal," or simply have no interest in doing so[4]. They demand to be seen as a person of value, no matter how they express themselves.

For people who pass, or are stealth, being outed by others can be damaging. Whether accidental or purposeful; it still causes harm. A person risks the loss of jobs, family, friends, or even legal issues. In some regions, it also affects safety. Even for those who pass, or gain advantages based on their gender, there is a chance that if some learns their history, they will lose these privileges. Permission should always be gained in advance before sharing anyone else's history, whether they pass in your eyes or otherwise. Just because you read someone as being transgender, or cisgender, does not mean that anyone else has the same perspective on that person. There are cisgender people who are read as transgender, and transgender people who are read as cisgender – all the time.

This issue is interwoven with that of gender privilege. These are the advantages that someone experiences because of their gender. Examples includes the idea that men tend to receive higher pay, or that women are given permission to express emotion. Gender privilege does not automatically transfer to trans people upon transition. When a trans woman loses male privilege, she does not gain female advantages unless she passes and lives life stealth. She risks the chance loosing that privilege if her gender history is shared with others.

Gender privilege does not make it a privilege to be that gender. It refers to the fact that specific genders come with specific advantages, as does being cisgender. Upon transition, a trans man may find that he no longer is able to hug his female friends as often as he used to, as that was part of how women interact with other women. He may also experience women crossing the street to get away from him at night – as that is part of how women interact with fear towards men in some cultural contexts. Trans women have been known to experience different degrees of objectification, get paid less money, or treated as less intelligent that she once was.

A concept that is brought up in some feminist[5] and conservative circles argues that the different genders have intrinsic – or essential – differences. Essentialism states that only women have the ability to understand or experience women's privilege, because of this intrinsic state of womanhood. Binary belief enforces a notion of "not enough of a wo/man" to ever gain those advantages or intrinsic gender qualities[6].

There are individuals for whom their trans experience becomes part of their new gender. This can be expressed in those who embrace transwoman as their gender; as compared to trans man, or man who has a trans history. The flip side of gender essentialism applies that by their very journey, trans people experience a trans essential experience. Having lived in multiple genders, they experience an advantage, and according to certain perspectives, a supremacy. From this theory, it states that trans people have an advantage based of having a more diverse perspective on the world.

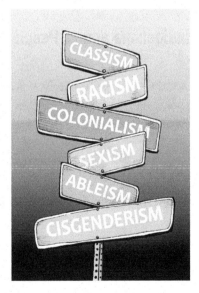

Oppression Awareness: Race, Disabilities, and Class

Just as there is gender privilege, there are also racial, ableist, class, and socioeconomic privilege. This means that a trans or gender nonconforming person still has other forms of privilege; things in life that set them up at an advantage compared to others. This is true even while a person faces oppression concerning their gender. There is not always a clear line between oppressor and ally, especially with these layers at play. Having an awareness of various layers of oppression various trans person may face, brings empathy to diverse life experiences.

These concepts tie into what is called systematic oppression[7]; also known as institutional oppression[8], it is the culture-wide, and sometimes unconscious, mistreatment of people from a segment of the population based on a trait that population shares. It is considered systematic because it is often integrated into laws and customs, and is so pervasive that it is rarely noticed by those who are not affected by it. In the case of each type of oppression, remember that these various forms of systematic oppression may be overt or subtle, conscious or unconscious – and negatively affect not just the oppressed parties – but everyone in the long run. The following perspectives are focused within the context of the United States, with each of these issues appearing in different ways worldwide.

Indigenous and/or People of Color

As mentioned in chapter 2, there are diverse gender journeys expressed worldwide. Unfortunately, colonialism has erased many indigenous histories, or re-written them from a western viewpoint. Simplified terminology can leave out swaths of population from the conversation around issues facing trans people

today. This is especially true when those populations may not identify as transgender, or feel like they are being assimilated under a transgender umbrella.

The transgender stories that have been in the West do not often include the experiences of people of color. This happens in modern a context as well – when expectations of how cisgender men and women of various ethnic backgrounds express different perspectives on what it "means to be a man or woman." When manhood and womanhood as a whole are seen in a different light, and responses from family and peers are different around transition, the choices concerning whether to transition or not will be different. Even though people of color have been the people on the front lines of the battle for transgender rights, they are often not the stories who make it to the front pages – though recent appearances of trans women of color in the media provides hope for a shift.

Racial inequality especially affects trans women of color. Black and Latina trans women are at higher risk of STDs, homelessness and violence than white trans women in the United States[9]. This inequality includes lack of access to healthcare, drug use, and financial duress leading to sex work[10]. More trans women of color are killed than any other trans population in the United States[11]. With memorials held many places during Trans Day of Remembrance to honor those that have been killed in the past year, the readings of names at the memorials remind us of these numbers. This is emblematic of culture at large as well, with African-Americans twice as likely as whites to be killed by police[12]. In a world where trans women are further marginalized, being both black and trans feminine is dangerous.

This is not to say that all indigenous individual or people of color are more disadvantaged, as advantage and privilege is not a contest that should be weighed out. Instead, there should be awareness and support built for those who are in need, not just those who have constant visibility. Allowing transgender people of every experience to share their stories helps all of use become better allies, whether we are transgender or cisgender. Supporting the work of groups such as the *National Black Justice Coalition*[13] and the *Trans People of Color Coalition*[14] helps work to effect such change, along with the various projects currently undertaken to support trans immigration[15] and two-spirit visibility[16].

Persons with Disabilities

Differently abled individuals are unconsciously, or consciously, considered outside the range of "normal" by society. Just as passing takes energy and work for many trans folk, it is similar for individuals with disabilities who work to pass as able-bodied[17]. This is true even within trans communities. This includes people in wheelchairs who are pressured to march in pride parades, individuals who are deaf that want to attend events that don't provide translators, and people with agoraphobia pushed to tell their stories at Trans Day of Remembrance.

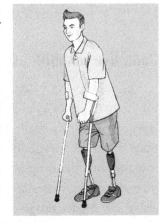

Physical Disabilities

For those with physical disabilities, some are visible, while others are invisible. Visible disability includes being in a wheelchair, while epilepsy is an invisible physical disability. Inaccessible spaces keep disabled trans and gender variant people from attending events – or being able to fully participate – such as venues without ramps or elevator access. Transitioning can also affect access to disability communities. Just as bigoted leaders cause challenges for trans people to be involved in certain workplaces or social networks – it is the same – only that losing peership for people with disabilities can also include potential loss of services.

A trans person may also not be seen as their new gender by their providers and care givers, who continue to use the wrong pronoun, or refuse to call their patient by their preferred name. Hormones and various procedures may not be an option for those who require complex medical care. Their condition, such as certain auto immune disorders, can restrict access to surgery. Even when medical options can technically be undertaken, there are surgeons and doctors that choose not to perform them for people with disabilities

Deaf and Hard of Hearing

People who are deaf or hard of hearing (HoH) are not be disabled, but their shared differences affects their trans journey. American sign language (ASL) is a more direct, or blunt, language than spoken English – making the signs around gender journeys to be less delicate. The terminology concerning trans issues in ASL is shifting as trans awareness is developed in culture at large. Deaf and HoH people will also need additional layers of support[18] when traversing the medical system and finding mental health providers.

Cognitive Disabilities

Though all individuals with disabilities risk the chance of being infantilized for their differences; people with mental or cognitive differences face additional layers around this challenge. The ability to decide for themselves if they are trans might be questioned by caretakers, family, and friends. This is especially true for family and caregivers who do not understand the individual's desires, or transgender issues as a whole. A person with cognitive disabilities may also have challenges giving full consent for receiving care when they do not understand all of the complexities involved, from how medical transitions affect the body to the details of legal and social transition.

There are also individuals who have cognitive differences who see and experience gender differently. For example, one study has shown that individuals with autism spectrum disorders are dramatically more likely to experience gender identity disorder than the population at large[19]. Those that do may also experience what markers show them as expressing their gender differently than how others do, such as experiencing clothing and gendered behaviors to have more value in gender expression than passing does[20].

Mental Health

Much activism has gone into removing GID from the *DSM*; stating that trans people are not mentally ill. For those that do have mental health challenges, the trans community occasionally responds in a stigmatizing manner, because the trans community has fought so hard to not have gender journeys and mental health challenges conflated. They may be ostracized from communities, or have providers doubt their trans journey due to other diagnoses. For those that end up in mental health facilities, they may get denied their ongoing trans care – or housed on different floors than their identity. This further exacerbates issues for those whose crisis are based on gender dysphoria or body dysmorphia. Even though these facilities focus on mental health; they may have little to no training in gender diversity or trans concerns.

Class and Socioeconomic Issues

People with fewer finances do not have access to the same degree of medical care, mental health care, or social networks available to others. Those without medical care may end up using street hormones without regular testing, or have to re-use needles out of necessity. When various procedures cost hundreds or thousands of dollars, they are not viable for people who cannot afford to pay their rent.

That assumes that a person is able to pay the rent, as one in five trans people have reported having been homeless in their lifetime[21]. For those needing access to homeless shelters, they are not always kind to trans women or genderqueer individuals[22]. There is important work happening at a national level beginning to address these safety concerns[23], with much more left to do[24].

Class and socioeconomic realities affect access to clothes, food, and shelter, as well as access to information. People without internet at home will often not be able to tap into the vast materials about transgender rights and realities that are being shared online. Announcing support groups and clinic information online is not enough, because many of the people that need to be reached don't know the events are happening. Unless fliers are posted in local libraries, shelters, soup kitchens, unemployment offices, or peers from different communities are able to get the word out – people who need the assistance won't even know it is available.

Trans Communities

Based out of both necessity and peership, communities of trans people have gathered together over the years. Some of these are sponsored by therapists or LGBT groups, while others are formed through word of mouth and local circumstance. Trans-specific communities often help provide resources. These resources include:

- Emotional support from others on gender journeys
- Techniques for presentation and passing
- Acquiring clothes, binders, and other material goods
- Help traversing legal gender challenges
- Safe spaces for gathering and housing
- Information on local groups, gatherings, and care
- Remind each other of the positive aspects of being trans[25]

No two trans groups are identical. Some are created to support people of specific gender experience, ethnicity, geographic region, sexual orientation, or economic challenges. Others are more general support for all trans and gender nonconforming people. Groups also focus around a shared struggle, such as maintaining sobriety[26]. They vary in size from a group of a few peers who get together for safety and information, to thousands gathering together for trans pride parades and political action.

Trans communities often help trans people feel empowered because there are others who understand their joys and struggles. Even finding one other person online helps people feel connected, protected, and more informed about their own journey. There are groups that set up mentorship connections[27] between experienced trans people and those who are new to the journey; assuring that people have a person to turn to, so that they don't feel alone. These connections come as intergenerational support, as well as between peers.

An example of intergenerational support appears in Ball culture, or ballroom community. Developed by African American drag queens in the late 1960s, this movement created a safe space for predominantly latin@ and

African American gender nonconforming individuals to be themselves and partake in performance-based events[28]. Part of this support is based on the notion of "houses," where people form intimate bonds; helping each other not only with learning skills, but having someone who transitioned previously who would help their house "children" during hard times. This is an especially important concept for people  who lack parental support in their life. The Kiki scene[29], a spinoff for youth, has been known to provide support between peers as well who have been disenfranchised by the world around them.

With such a broad collection of individuals worldwide, trans communities are not perfect. This can lead to stress and struggles when views do not match. However, trans communities that are able to pull together with shared strength, are able to make making change, as well as providing each other with resources where everyone benefits.

Community Symbols

There are pride symbols that help transgender individuals be able to identify peers and allies. They are flown at pride parades, worn as lapel pins, printed on clothing, posted outside of buildings, and appear anywhere else a flag or symbol is displayed.

The most common of these is transgender pride flag. It shows five horizontal stripes: two blue, two pink, and one white.

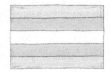

In Israel, a neon green flag is used that has a black graphic on it. The symbol is a blending between the male, female, and the combined Greek symbols.

A third flag also features five stripes, that begin with pink at the top and blue at the bottom, and shows transitioning colors between the two.

The gender fluid community has its own flag with five stripes: pink, white, purple, black and blue.

Genderqueer pride communities have a three stripe flag that does not show a pink or blue at all, instead showing purple, white and green.

The agender community expresses its own pride through a seven stripe flag: two black, two grey, two white, and one pale green.

Beyond the various flags, there are also two other symbols that have been used over the years – a butterfly expressing the notion of gender change, and a yin yang made from the colors pink and blue.

Activism for Transgender Rights

In the face of challenges, supported by communities and allies alike, there are opportunities to improve the rights and realities of transgender people. One is through remembrance. On November 20th each year, people gather together in candlelight vigils and social gatherings to remember those that have been killed for being transgender[30]. Through reading the names of the dead, they become more than statistics[31] – they become people who died[32] because of intolerance and hate. Whether we are transgender or otherwise, putting newspaper articles out and sharing stories about the past can help fight transphobia.

The anger and sorrow raised through remembering those murdered can be channeled into the work done on the Trans Day of Action on June 26th. Founded by *TransJustice* of the Audre Lorde Project, a Lesbian, Gay, Bisexual, Two-Spirit, Trans and Gender Non-Conforming People of Color Center for Community Organizing[33], this push for social and economic justice is about working for the rights of trans and gender nonconforming people in need. By creating points of unity, the day works to end profiling, harassment, and brutality at the hands of the police, create access to respectful and safe housing, and support full legalization of all immigrants. In addition, it pushes for access to health care, safe public transit systems, and equal access to education – reminding us that every human deserves these rights.

Working towards these points of action happens even on the smallest of levels, from helping do trainings for police and health care providers, to writing letters to the editor advocating for those who cannot advocate for themselves. Privilege comes with opportunity to speak up for oppressed or underrepresented populations, while simultaneously handing them the microphone to speak for themselves. Working beyond a framework of LGBT, or even LGBTQQIAA; a movement towards overall GSRM (Gender, Sexual, and Romantic Minorities) is also creating a further opportunity for dialogue and activism.

Activism also comes in the form of visibility. Having transgender individuals, their partners, friends, family, and allies share their truths on Trans Day of Visibility, March 31st, lets people in the world at large see the diversity of trans and gender nonconforming journeys. This day is an opportunity to celebrate gender diversity through marches, parties, and other special events. There are small, local gatherings, as well as large, organized occasions.

Some people take this as an opportunity to learn about the amazing array of trans and gender diverse people that have lived in the United States and around the world. Oftentimes, only tales of celebrities from within specific populations are shared. This day of visibility gives an opportunity to bring other stories out for the world to learn from. These include the stories of trans people living today, asking people in local communities to share their images of love and life alike. Those who are out give support to those who are not; showing the world that trans people are not alone.

During the summertime, other pride events also take place. These are sometimes done in conjunction with various LGBT pride events, helping remind people that the "T" needs to be part of the conversation. This is especially important when, in the quest for gay rights, there are sometimes attempt to quiet gender diverse populations on issues such as immigration[34][35], or the rights of transgender people to marry[36].

Street activism also takes place in the form of protests, picketing businesses that have anti-trans policies, or bringing awareness to unjust laws. After all, the 1969 Stonewall Riots – pivotal to LGBT activism – were led by trans women of color[37]. Even before that, the 1966 Compton Riots, were started by a small group of trans women and drag queens, and is considered by some to be the birth of the gay-rights movement[38]. Today, trans and gender nonconforming individuals are not only fighting on the front lines for trans rights, but working in collaboration with other rights groups[39][40]; knowing that helping other oppressed populations helps change the world at large.

First-hand political activism is also important, with trans people and those who fight for them having face-to-face conversations with politicians. Having a succinct and personal story that shares a human side to an issue shifts hearts and minds alike. It is important to have people be present at government hearings on trans issues, and rally people to vote on every gender and sexuality issues on ballots. Having transgender and trans-friendly politicians run for government offices of all sorts affects change through having trans people not just be political issues – but be people who change politics from the inside.

It is also worth remembering that in their darkest of times, trans people need help remembering that they are not alone. Groups like *Trans Lifeline*[41] are there for people of all ages, and the *Trevor Project*[42] for teens to call when in places of crisis – or when they just need someone to listen. Volunteering for these groups, as well as other support groups and resource centers, is a great way to help others.

Chapter Ten

Being a Trans Ally

An ally is an individual who supports and advocates for members of a community other than their own. By working beyond any differences they have; mutual goals are met, creating change for people worldwide. Allies of transgender people might be cisgender, might be somewhere on a gender journey themselves, or both!

The fact that you are already looking into these issues and expanding your knowledge is a great start. There are lots of other tools out there as well, and easy actions that can be taken. These actions can help smooth transitions, create safety for trans people, and make the laws affecting these issues align with the needs of gender diverse people. These may be things you are already doing, while others are steps you can take from here forward.

Express Love and Support

One of the fears trans people experience is that of abandonment. How will people react? Will people still like them if they follow their path? This applies for people who get outed as well; they often wonder if people they care about will feel the same way about them if they know the truth.

Having ongoing connections and support from friends, family, and social networks, shows them that they are still wanted. Remind people that they are still appreciated and cherished – no matter their gender. Though there are people that need time to adjust, learning about their trans or gender nonconforming love one or ally's journey, make sure not to alienate the trans person in the process. Let them know you care about them – rather than pushing them away after they had the courage to share something so intimate.

A person's gender, and their path, are about their own experience, health, happiness, and wellbeing. Guilt or self-blame on the part of significant others, family, friends and allies (SOFFA) can get in the way of actually offering support or building connection between people. These feelings are valid, but can cause blockages to actually helping a trans a friend, colleague, neighbor, or loved one. This is especially true if their transition is somehow declared by the ally to be *about* the ally. Moving beyond guilt and self-blame allows for the opportunity to see the person who is in need, and help them forward.

Not every piece of information about transitioning or gender will apply to every trans person. Not every trans woman will want skills on how to present as high femme, walk in heels, or need makeup advice. Not every trans man is interested in learning about sports, hunting, or being macho. There is no right way to transition, after all. There are more common – and less common – paths of transitioning. There are not correct – or incorrect – ways to transition.

This is especially important for trans people who are offering support to someone else transitioning. Their transition is unique to them, and will not look identical to the path that any other trans person has taken. Hold patience for a trans person as they find their way, and ask what ways you can support them in the path they are on.

Every person has an emotional response when they find out a person in their life is transitioning. They may fear for their loved one's safety, be upset about potential condemnation from a community, have grief around a perceived loss, or worry about what else they don't know about. It is not wrong for an ally to feel loss, even as they are celebrating the joys of the person they care for, but a trans person may not have the ability to hold their hand through that perceived loss.

No matter the emotions you experience, you get to choose how you respond, and how you behave. Take a deep breath. Having an ally taking a moment to assess themselves before moving forward with whatever they were going to say next does a lot of good, rather than regretting words said out of fear, upset, grief, or worry imprint upon future relations with the trans person they care about. A person's responses to their gender disclosure will inform a trans person about whether you are appropriate for them to have you around them right now.

For each person on a gender journey, there are a wide number of people around that person who are affected. The transition isn't *about* the ally, but it involves them. It touches their life and impacts how they move in the world. Each of these people will also need love and support. The trans person who came out may not be able

Find a PFLAG Chapter Near You

to provide all of the care and assistance that their significant other, friend, family, or ally needs or wants. There are chapters of PFLAG[1] in every state, various online groups, and other diverse resources available for significant others, family, friends, and allies of trans and gender variant people. After all, no one person needs to feel alone.

Providing support includes providing and encouraging safe spaces[2] for trans people. Respond to online bullies so that trans people are not alone against the hate. Help find physical venues for support groups and special events. Get the word out about groups, events, and resources online, through social media, printed advertising, and word of mouth. Stand up to legal bodies and politicians making individual spaces – as well as entire countries – dangerous for trans people to live in.

Think through compliments before giving them, such as "I would never have known you were a guy," or "you are handsome for a trans man." They are usually well-intended. Unfortunately, these types of statements point out that the person is perceived differently than others. "You are lovely" and "you are handsome" do the same job, without using caveats. This allows for the opportunity to share your true feeling (that they were lovely; or handsome), rather than what may be seen as a veiled attack (that you think of them as a guy, not a woman; or that they would be more handsome if they were a real man.) After all, the compliment was likely meant to be just that, a compliment.

Check with a trans person before offering unsolicited advice or resources.

It seems helpful to give knowledge, ideas, tips or tricks concerning their gender journey. This is not the case though. If they are not interested, or are

too busy, it is far from helpful. They may be too overwhelmed to take in more information. Perhaps they need to hear ideas at another time, or in a different place. Do not take it personally if a trans person, or group, does not want the help that you offer. Most of the time it isn't about the person offering. You never know, perhaps they will come back later, open to receive the offer you gave before.

Names and Pronouns

Many people go by names or nicknames other than what they were named at birth, or even what their government identification shows. Calling any person by their preferred name is a simple form of respect, and applies to trans people as well. There are those who argue that if they used to know someone under the name Jenny, then they should not have to ever call them Robert. After all, they knew them as Jenny. There are cisgender people who were named Jenny that now go by Jennifer, and hate their childhood nickname. It is appropriate to change to the name person now prefers, no matter who they are.

When not using someone's name, it is common to fill in a reference to that person with a pronoun. There are numerous gender-neutral pronouns that be easily used in group situations[3]:

- Good morning folks.
- Hi, everyone.
- Can I get you all something?

It is also simple to use language that is inclusive of all genders when discussing or talking to a single person:

- What is their name?
- Can you ask them about it?
- And for you?

Gender-specific terms can be used once a person has shared their preferred pronouns. "What is your preferred pronoun," is a direct and simple question that can be asked to anyone. If the person being asked is confused by the question, it becomes a chance to educate about the fact that different people prefer different pronouns. It also normalizes the question, rather than only asking it of people who are perceived as trans or gender nonconforming. If a preferred pronoun has not been ascertained, it is common to use gender-neutral ones until they have seen others use a specific one for a person. They then model the behavior accordingly, though it is possible that others have been incorrect in their pronoun use as well.

Subject	Object	Possessive	Possessive Pronoun	Reflexive
E	Em	Eir	Eirs	Eirself
She	Her	Her	Hers	Herself
He	Him	His	His	Himself
They	Them	Their	Theirs	Themself
Ze	Zim/Zem	Zir	Zirs	Zirself
Ne	Nem	Ner	Ners	Nerself

The same question could read as:

- Have you seen em?

- Have you seen her?

- Have you seen him?

- Have you seen them?

- Have you seen zim?

- Have you seen nem?

It is also easy to fill in any of these with a person's preferred name. In the case of Robert, this question would then be:

- Have you seen Robert?

If an error is made regarding someone's gender or use of their former name, it is best to quietly apologize and move forward, rather than constantly apologizing and drawing further attention to the issue. The goal is to use the name and labels a person wants used for themselves, just as we want someone to call us by the name and labels we prefer.

As a culture we do this all of the time when we meet a small child, or a pet. If the parent or pet-owner corrects us about the name or gender, we move forward with the new information. The same is true when we find out someone goes by Miss rather than Mrs. as an honorific. We do not dwell on it. When being informed that a different name or gender is preferred, making a brief apology and using the correct one moving forward – is appropriate.

This is different than defending or making excuses. "The pronoun 'they' is so hard to use in the singular," or, "it's not my fault because I've known my friend for so long," feel like true statements. This is different than telling someone you're honestly trying, and that you care about them. Focusing on it and arguing the validity of a name or pronoun puts focus on your discomfort, rather than allowing a conversation to continue forward. It may even have the trans person feel like they have to defend themselves, and have them withdraw emotionally. Slip-ups happen. By practicing and continuing to use the correct pronoun, whether they are around or not, will help embed their new terminology into the mind, and help others do the same.

It's tempting to say that pronouns and labels don't matter. For a trans or gender nonconforming person, they matter quite a lot. Saying that they do not can invalidate their struggle. Other people's genders or lack thereof are about their gender is not meant to cause affront. They are choosing "ze" as their pronoun not because they are mean, or like giving people a challenge, but because "ze" feels true and authentic to them. They may prefer the honorific Miss, Mrs., Mr., Mx., Mre., or dislike honorifics altogether. Willingness to use people's preferred name, pronoun, and honorific – whether they are trans or otherwise – helps make for deeper connection and trust.

Respecting Boundaries and Autonomy

Another action that allies can take is to learn and model respecting the boundaries of trans people. When wanting to ask questions about someone's gender, social, and medical realities, it is important to consider whether a given moment is an appropriate time or space to ask the question. It is also key to consider whether a question is even necessary to ask. It's tempting to say that you "need to know" about their gender, social, and medical realities. The reality is that only that person's partners and medical practitioners "need to know."

One example is surgical procedures. If it is inappropriate to ask another stranger about their health realities, it is also inappropriate to ask a trans person. If you do ask, do so from a clear place of whether you want to know about trans bodies in general, or their body specifically. Ask yourself why you want to know. This includes in the case of former names. If there is not an explicit situation where the information is pertinent, curiosity is not enough of a reason to dig into someone's past unless they have shared that they are open to any, or all, questions.

No matter the topic, there are people who are private. That does not mean they are carrying secrets or are hiding anything. Being private is okay, and should be respected. Part of allowing people their privacy includes not disclosing whether they are transgender – or cisgender – without their permission. Just because you know doesn't mean others do. Asking the individual privately if the rest of the folks here know – if you want to bring their history up – is an option.

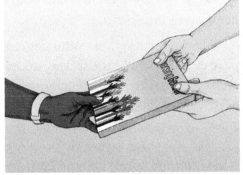

This includes when telling stories about a person's past, or accidentally using their former name. It is inappropriate to use a person's name or history in certain settings due to potentially outing them. Take a moment to ask yourself how the story can be translated to their current information, including changing names, pronouns, and omitting or neutralizing gender-specific elements. If the story is explicitly gendered, consider whether the story is necessary. Asking the trans person how they want to have past stories that are explicitly gendered be shared, whether referring to past names, genders, relationships, or groups they were part of, allows the trans person the chance to help their social circle traverse the topic. There are also trans people who are proactive, letting their social circles know how to handle these things before they come up.

Helping other people respect a trans person's history is often appreciated. If other people say they "need to know" about someone's past, making a comment like "I don't think their history is anyone's business other than their own" goes a long way. Hold their friends and family to respecting the trans person as well. It is sometimes the people closest to a trans or gender nonconforming person that are the most reluctant to use preferred names and pronouns, let alone acknowledge other parts of their life. Lovingly encouraging them to acknowledge their loved ones' autonomy and truth go a long way, by giving them the opportunity to hear it from someone else.

Speaking out about trans issues and why they should be respected helps those who are struggling with "trans fatigue." Modeled after the notion of racial fatigue[4], where a person of color is tired of talking about issues of race, trans fatigue is where a trans person is tired of talking about issues about gender. So many trans people find themselves having to teach trans 101 on an ongoing basis, just because of who they are. Having allies step up and do the work provides a momentary respite. There are 101 books[5], pamphlets[6], PDFs[7], television episodes[8], videos[9], and websites[10] available to share with people to help answer their basic questions.

Allies can struggle with this concept of fatigue as well. Remember that it okay to let those who are seeking information turn elsewhere. There are other resources out there, including those at the back of this book. Offering people a few website links, a book to read, or support groups for friends and allies to attend, goes a long way. Trans and gender nonconforming people also turn to allies who have extensive knowledge. Offering support on their path is wonderful, and deeply helpful. Each ally needs to know their own boundaries and capacity though, rather than risking resentment or burnout while helping those they care for.

Moving Beyond Assumptions

In 2015, between 16 [11]and 22%[12] of people said they personally knew a trans person. For all others, transgender people are only a theory, a person they have perhaps heard of on television, or a type of person they've heard remarks about. There are remarks and media that hold trans people in a positive light. Others do not.

Whether someone knows a trans person directly or not, they may be basing their assumptions and information only on what they see from the outside. It is important to move beyond theory, and to learn more about a person than their wrapping. Be curious, not demanding. Listen to transgender people when they share their stories. Let their stories inform you of the world from a different viewpoint and history. Learn their language and what they mean by it. When a person shares a term of any sort, ask them what they mean by that term. Labels make for great conversation-starters, but too easily become conversation-enders. Assumptions about a label can overshadow what folks were really trying to share. Let us grow through dialogue and discovery as we build awareness.

In being an ally, shifts in general outlook also effects change. Allow people of all genders to choose whether they share emotions or not; offering them compassion in general. Support everyone in their desires to pursue their own careers, no matter their sex or gender. When out in public and are uncertain of a person's gender… stop worrying about it. It doesn't matter. They are a person.

Remember, each person who is transgender is more than just transgender. Every person who is cisgender is more than just cisgender. That is one point of who they happen to be. Get to know them as a person. Move beyond the assumptions of someone's story based solely on their exterior. Each person is more than their gender experience.

Helping the Next Generation

In supporting all people to express themselves and be themselves – no matter their gender – we begin to make a better world for the next generation. We can help kids by letting them live their childhood, and life – rather a gender story.

This starts at home. Parents need to know that kids are allowed to be attracted to the toys and clothes that draw them, and that those interests are not necessarily about being trans. A toy does not have an innate gender after all, and saying boys shouldn't play with dolls sets up another generation of men with a bundle of debunked gender-biased myths. This is supported by changes at the corporate level to remove gender labels from the toy aisle and at the customer service level by training workers to enable people to shop in any clothing department without ridicule.

Online allies can defend parents whose children do not "match" other people's biases. Teachers have the ability to encourage students to pursue classes they are passionate about; rather than assuming which classes should be appropriate based on a history of gender norms. Librarians and people on school boards can purchase books with trans and gender diverse characters in them. School administrators and counselors working towards bully-free spaces for all students that allow kids to live without fear and suffering. We do so by making bathrooms accessible, and gyms safe for trans kids, while fighting against laws that impede that access[13].

Peer youth allies can work towards enabling normalcy for trans kids in their school. If a classmate is being teased, stand up for them. Talk to them and learn their story. Let them know they are not strange, weird, or unwelcome just because they are on their own unique journey. Make space for kids at school to move at their own rate, and be themselves, no matter who they are.

Not every child has been supported or shown compassion. There are folks who have been kicked out of their home, bullied, assaulted, or suffered other harm. Financial support and volunteering for programs that help trans kids who have been kicked out or are homeless is important. Safe foster homes for trans and gender adventurous kids are rare, and people with the capacity to offer those spaces are needed. Given that homelessness and suicide rates for trans kids are lower when they were shown compassion and support at home; assistance is also needed for the parents of trans kids. Let them know that they are not alone, and that allies are available to turn to when needing help and resources themselves.

The same is true for kids whose parents are transitioning. Legal activists are needed to protect kids from being taken away from loving parents whose only "issue" is that they are not cisgender. Children also need to know that they are still loved and cared for. During shifts in a household, this is especially important. There are youth camps for trans kids[14] as well as the kids of LGBTQ parents[15]. Letting them know that they are not the only youth whose parents are not the same as they once were – can let them know they are not alone.

So will having an ally support and show acceptance of a parent's transition in front of their children, modeling love, compassion, and a healthy journey forward.

Advocacy at Every Level

We do advocacy at the individual, community, school, media, corporate and political level. Every one of us have the ability to do something.

On the individual level, it starts with not tolerating disrespectful jokes at the office, comments at family gatherings, slanderous newspaper articles, and negative posts on social media. It may not change the mind of the person who made the comment – but if even one individual who overheard the discussion decides not to pass on a tasteless joke – the world is that much better.

This is about making the world safer for everyone, not just about an ally feeling better about themselves for every act they take. Trans and gender nonconforming individuals cannot be responsible for thanking and congratulating every action an ally does. Know instead that these sorts of actions are appreciated, and do make a difference. Every time a friend, family member, neighbor, coworker, or random stranger on the internet is able to navigate the world with more grace and ease – the thanks are silently being given for the work that everyone together has done.

Guiding conversations about transgender issues, and confronting anti-transgender statements, are a form of direct action. Indirect action includes making proposals at the office such as making the only bathroom in your area gender-neutral, or adding "preferred name" to intake paperwork. These are not trans-explicit, but effect change for trans people. When asked why these changes should happen, offering reasons that help everyone (such as outlined in chapter 5) – along with the fact that it also helps trans people – is a way to slip in the idea of trans rights into the minds of others. Trans-explicit activism involves doing work that is specifically for trans and gender nonconforming people – such as offering a variety of boxes or fill-in options for both assigned sex and gender on paperwork.

Sharing useful and accurate information also effects change. At the same time, it is a chance to stop the spread of misinformation and disinformation. False statements and rumors about trans people, such as the idea that "trans women are really just men in dresses" – cause real harm. We need activism in every form, from picketing, protests, and media action to quiet conversations with people who are curious and confused – to help people become more aware.

Running trans-awareness trainings[16] at the workplace, organizational, or community level helps people learn in a more systematic manner. There are people who learn better in a formal setting about social issues, while others do better with personal stories or meeting trans people who have struggled and have learned how to share those struggles. Having allies set up all of these opportunities for learning; creating entire groups who are now working together to change the culture in their workplace, organization, or community.

When sharing stories, it is important not only to share those of celebrities. Tell the tales of people across the spectrum of race, ethnicity, history, and journey. People with celebrity are given a platform to do activism on a broad level, and we can help them succeed by enabling them to plant quality information in the minds of others. Get to know diverse trans and gender variant stories. Look up the names mentioned in chapter 2, and in doing so, learn about people from every walk of life. Attending, and helping with, Trans Day of Remembrance also gives a chance to remember the names of those whose stories that are not known, and work with the media to not let those names be forgotten.

Make sure when sharing stories to make space for trans and gender nonconforming people to share their own stories. This is referred to as "step up, step back." It is important for allies to speak up for trans people, but it is also important not to keep those same individuals from speaking themselves. Take a moment to ask yourself whether a person directly affected by these issues can be given a platform to have their voice heard directly. Direct stories have great power, as does empowering people on gender journeys to be in the spotlight – in contrast to only having allies center-stage.

When working with the media, remember that people will ask potentially inappropriate questions. Try to practice your answers in advance, coming back with quality information. Know that your statements will be cut down into single sentences, and that speaking in sound bites is important. Complex concepts can sometimes be confusing when taken out of context. Know your talking points, diving in with clarity and passion alike, changes people's hearts, minds, and behavior.

Supporting political acts and legislation also effects real change. Become part of advocacy on National Gender Lobby Day[17]. Read up on your local laws, go to your city council, and push for equal gender rights. Show up to state legislative meetings, meet your representatives, present quality talking points, and run for government positions. It has been shown that when government officials and representatives meet the people who their laws will affect, especially brave teens who can share their stories from the heart[18], that they are less likely to pass harmful legislation.

Vote. Help others register. Even if it seems like "only one vote," each of those votes add up. By voting, we speak up for those who currently don't have the right to vote. With so many people who don't vote, an active minority has a chance when they turn up in numbers.

Each person can change the world, one conversation or law at a time.

The Journey Ahead

Take a moment and breathe. This has been a wild ride across a vast topic.

As we traverse gender, it is a journey for all of us. Gender affects every one of us, whether or not we notice gender on a day to day basis. The expectations of our family and friends. How we operate in culture. It is embedded in our society, and each of us lives with it all around us.

Our language around gender, and transgender issues specifically, is constantly evolving. This is because as more people speak about their own journeys, language will shift to meet the needs of the people involved. The theories, concepts and information presented in this book are a snapshot. Our hope is that it provides a basic map as you continue forward.

As the dialogue continues to shift, the concerns and fear around these topics will also shift. Through knowledge and awareness, we each have a chance to learn and grow. With each new story learned, and each new personal reflection, consciousness expands. Through inclusiveness and world improvement for everyone, we make space for us all to be ourselves. What helps trans and gender nonconforming populations – helps *everyone*.

Though this has been a road map to diverse gender journeys, the map is not the journey itself. Navigating these issues first-hand will reveal new truths and personal awareness. The hope is that by each of us learning about these issues through hearing the stories of others, having conversations, and reading books like this one – we will all grow together.

Help spread the word. Together we help make the world a better place, one life at a time. We have quite the journey ahead, but we can do it.

None of us are alone.

Citations

Introduction

1. Gary J. Gates. "*How many people are lesbian, gay, bisexual, and transgender?*" University of California Williams Institute, 2016. Retrieved March 2016, http://williamsinstitute.law.ucla.edu/wp-content/uploads/Gates-How-Many-People-LGBT-Apr-2011.pdf

2. Stacy S. Meier and Christine Labuski. "The demographics of the transgender population." In Amanda K. Baumle (Ed.), *The International Handbook of the Demography of Sexuality* (pp. 289-327). Springer Press, 2013.

3. "Born this way: Stories of young transgender children." *CBS News*, 8 June 2014. Retrieved March 2016, http://www.cbsnews.com/news/born-this-way-stories-of-young-transgender-children/

4. Laura Erickson-Schroth, ed. *Trans Bodies, Trans Selves: A Resource Guide for the Transgender Community*. Oxford University Press, 2014.

Chapter 1: Sex, Gender, and Orientation

1. "How common is intersex?" *Intersex Society of North America*. Retrieved March 2016, http://www.isna.org/faq/frequency

2. Dr. Dennis O'Neil. "HUMAN CHROMOSOMAL ABNORMALITIES: An Introduction to Common Gross Defects of Human Chromosomes." *Behavioral Sciences Department, Palomar College.* Retrieved March 2016, http://anthro.palomar.edu/abnormal/

3. Claire Ainsworth. "Sex Redefined: The idea of two sexes is simplistic. Biologists now think there is a wider spectrum than that." *Nature International Weekly Journal of Science*, 18 Feb 2015. Retrieved March 2016, http://www.nature.com/news/sex-redefined-1.16943

4. Erika Moen and Matthew Nolan. "Homologous Genitals." *Oh Joy Sex Toy*, 17 Nov 2015. Retrieved March 2016, http://www.ohjoysextoy.com/genitals/

5. "LGBT Rights: Frequently Asked Questions" *Office of the UN High Commissioner for Human Rights*. Retrieved March 2016, https://www.unfe.org/en/fact-sheets

6. "Is a person who is intersex a hermaphrodite?" *Intersex Society of North America*. Retrieved March 2016, http://www.isna.org/faq/hermaphrodite

7. "Hermaphroditos." *Theoi Greek Mythology*. Retrieved March 2016, http://www.theoi.com/Ouranios/ErosHermaphroditos.html

8. Alice Domurat Drege. "Ambiguous Sex"--or Ambivalent Medicine?" *The Hastings Center Report* May/Jun 1998, Volume 28, Issue 3 Pages 24-35. Retrieved March 2016, http://www.isna.org/articles/ambivalent_medicine

9. Alice Domurat Dreger. "Ambiguous Sex"--or Ambivalent Medicine?" *The Hastings Center Report* May/Jun 1998, Volume 28, Issue 3 Pages 24-35. Retrieved March 2016, http://www.isna.org/articles/ambivalent_medicine

10. Intersexion: Gender Ambiguity Unveiled. Dir. Grant Lahood. *XiveTV*, 2012.

11. Paisley Currah, Richard Juang, and Shannon Price Minter, eds. *Transgender Rights*. Minneapolis, MN: University of Minnesota Press. 2006.

12. John Colapinto. *As Nature Made Him: The Boy Who Was Raised as a Girl.* 2nd Edition. Harper Perennial, 2006.

13. Lydia Parafianowicz. "Swedish parents keep 2-year-old's gender secret." *The Local*, 23 Jun 2009. Retrieved March 2016, http://www.thelocal.se/20090623/20232

14. Thomas Beatie. *Labor of Love: The Story of One Man's Extraordinary Pregnancy*. Seal Press, 2008.

15. Emanuella Grinberg. "Target to move away from gender-based signs." *CNN News*, 8 Aug 2015. Retrieved March 2016, http://www.cnn.com/2015/08/08/living/gender-based-signs-target-feat/index.html

16. Patrick Kingsley. "Egyptian woman who has lived as man for 40 years voted 'best mum.'" *The Guardian*, 22 March 2015. Retrieved March 2016, http://www.theguardian.com/world/2015/mar/22/egyptian-woman-award-lived-as-man

17. Lisa Bloom. "How to Talk to Little Girls." *Huffington Post*, 26 Sept 2011. Retrieved March 2016, http://www.huffingtonpost.com/lisa-bloom/how-to-talk-to-little-gir_b_882510.html

18. Lynette Rice. "Trans stories find a home on reality TV following Orange is the New Black, Transparent success." *Entertainment Weekly*, 30 Mar 2015. Retrieved March 2016, http://www.ew.com/article/2015/03/30/trans-stories-find-home-reality-tv-following-orange-new-black-transparent-success

19. "Top 10 inspiring transgender movies." *Sundance TV*, 28 Aug 2014. Retrieved March 2016, http://www.sundance.tv/blog/2014/08/transgender-films

20. "Transgender identity in the news." *CNN News*, 16 Dec 2015. Retrieved March 2016, http://www.cnn.com/2015/04/22/living/gallery/transgender-identity/index.html

21. *"Transgender Experience Led Stanford Scientist to Critique Gender Difference." Stanford University Medical Center. 14 July 2006.* Retrieved March 2016. http://www.sciencedaily.com/releases/2006/07/060714174545.htm

22. "Gender Identity Map." *IMPACT: The LGBT Health and Development Program at Northwestern University.* Retrieved March 2016, http://www.impactprogram.org/interactive-media/gendermap/

23. Margaret Nydell. *Understanding Arabs: A Guide To Modern Times.* Boston, MA: Intercultural Pres. 2005.

24. Trans Theology. Retrieved March 2016, http://www.transtheology.org/

25. Trans Respect Versus Transphobia Worldwide. Retrieved March 2016, http://transrespect.org/en/

26. "Lawrence v. Texas 539 U.S. 558 (2003)." *US Supreme Court*, 2003. Retrieved March 2016, https://supreme.justia.com/cases/federal/us/539/558/

27. Julia O'Donoghue. "Louisiana House votes 27-67 to keep unconstitutional anti-sodomy law on the books." *NOLA.com*, 15 Apr 2014. Retrieved March 2016, http://www.nola.com/politics/index.ssf/2014/04/post_558.html

28. *Be Like Others (a.k.a. Transsexual in Iran)*. Dir. Tanaz Eshaghian. Wolfe Video, 2008.

29. Aengus Carroll and Lucas Paoli Itaborahy. "State Sponsored Homophobia: A World Survey of Laws: criminalization, protection and recognition of same-sex love." May 2015, 10th Edition. Retrieved March 2016, http://old.ilga.org/Statehomophobia/ILGA_State_Sponsored_Homophobia_2015.pdf

30. Miriam Elder. "Russia passes law banning gay 'propaganda.'" *The Guardian*, 11 June 2013. Retrieved March 2016, http://www.theguardian.com/world/2013/jun/11/russia-law-banning-gay-propaganda

31. "LGBT rights by country." *Wikipedia*. Retrieved March 2016, https://en.wikipedia.org/wiki/LGBT_rights_by_country_or_territory

32. Aengus Carroll and Lucas Paoli Itaborahy. "State Sponsored Homophobia: A World Survey of Laws: criminalization, protection and recognition of same-sex love." May 2015, 10th Edition. Retrieved March 2016, http://old.ilga.org/Statehomophobia/ILGA_State_Sponsored_Homophobia_2015.pdf

Chapter 2: Diversity of Transgender Journeys

1. Sam Dylan Finch. "Trauma and Transness: Why I Didn't 'Always Know' I Was Transgender." *Let's Queer Things Up!*, 16 Jan 2016. Retrieved March 2016, http://letsqueerthingsup.com/2016/01/16/trauma-and-transness-why-i-didnt-always-know-i-was-transgender/

2. Sunnivie Brydum. "The True Meaning of 'Cisgender.'" *The Advocate*, 31 July 2015. Retrieved March 2016, http://www.advocate.com/transgender/2015/07/31/true-meaning-word-cisgender

3. David Oliver Cauldwell. "Psychopathia Transexualis." *Sexology: Sex Science Magazine* 16, 1949.

4. Susan Stryker. *Transgender History*. Seal Press, 2008

5. Dr. Magnus Hirschfeld. "Die intersexuelle Konstitution" in *Jarhbuch fuer sexuelle Zwischenstufen*, 1923

6. Harry Benjamin. *The transsexual phenomenon, page 23*. Julian Press, 1966.

7. Harry Benjamin. *The transsexual phenomenon, page 23*. Julian Press, 1966.

8. Andrea James. "Standards of Care for women in transition." From *Trans Road Map*, retrieved March 2016, http://www.tsroadmap.com/reality/wpath-standards.html

9. World Professional Association for Transgender Health. Retrieved March 2016, http://www.wpath.org

10. ICATH (Informed Consent for Access to Trans Health). Retrieved March 2016, http://www.icath.org/

11. *Joanne Meyerowitz. How Sex Changed: A History of Transsexuality in the United States. Harvard University Press, 2002.*

12. Buzz Bissinger. "Caitlyn Jenner: The Full Story." *Vanity Fair*, 30 June 2015. Retrieved March 2016, http://www.vanityfair.com/hollywood/2015/06/caitlyn-jenner-bruce-cover-annie-leibovitz

13. Nevo Zisin. "'I was not born a girl': Why we need to change transgender language." *SBS*, 8 March 2016. Retrieved March 2016, http://www.sbs.com.au/news/insight/article/2016/03/07/i-was-not-born-girl-why-we-need-change-transgender-language

14. Naim Rasul. "Race, Ethniticity, and Culture." From Laura Erickson-Schroth, ed. *Trans Bodies, Trans Selves: A Resource Guide for the Transgender Community*. Oxford University Press, 2014.

15. "Transgender Man Leads 'Men's Health' Cover Model Contest." *National Public Radio*, 19 Apr 2015. Retrieved March 2016, http://www.npr.org/2015/04/19/400826487/transgender-man-leads-mens-health-cover-model-contest

16. "In interview with Oprah, pregnant man says baby will be a miracle." *NY Daily News*, 3 Apr 2008. Retrieved March 2016, http://www.huffingtonpost.com/2012/11/28/thomas-beatie-the-pregnant-man-oprah_n_2199936.html

17. The Brown Bois Project. Retrieved March 2016, http://www.brownboiproject.org/

18. Naim Rasul. "Race, Ethniticity, and Culture." From Laura Erickson-Schroth, ed. *Trans Bodies, Trans Selves: A Resource Guide for the Transgender Community*. Oxford University Press, 2014.

19. "Boi (slang)." *Wikipedia*. Retrieved March 2016, https://en.wikipedia.org/wiki/Boi_%28slang%29

20. Sue-Ellen Jacobs, Wesley Thomas and Sabine Lang, eds. *Two-Spirit People: Native American Gender Identity, Sexuality and Spirituality*. University of Illinois Press, 1997

21. Chadwick Moore. "Joining the annual gathering of the Two Spirit Society in Montana." *OUT*, 22 Sept 2015. Retrieved March 2016, http://www.out.com/news-opinion/2015/9/22/joining-annual-gathering-two-spirit-society-montana

22. Cody Gohl. "The World's Only Two-Spirit Powwow Comes to San Francisco." *New Now Next*, 16 Feb 2016. Retrieved March 2016, http://www.newnownext.com/the-worlds-only-two-spirit-powwow/02/2016/

23. Federal and State Recognized Tribes. *National Conference of State Legislatures*. Retrieved March 2016, http://www.ncsl.org/research/state-tribal-institute/list-of-federal-and-state-recognized-tribes.aspx

24. D. Roy Mitchell IV. "Transgender Alaska Natives in the 18th and 19th centuries." Lecture at the *University of Alaska Anchorage*. Nov 2014.

25. Sue-Ellen Jacobs and Wesley Thomas, eds. *Two Spirit People: Native American Gender Identity, Sexuality, and Spiritual*. University of Illinois Press, 1997.

26. Will Roscoe. *Changing Ones: Third and Fourth Genders in Native North America*. Palgrave Macmillan, 2000.

27. Will Roscoe, ed. *Living the Spirit: A Gay American Indian Anthology*. St. Martin's Griffin. 1988.

28. "Meet the "Muxes", an integral part of Zapotec culture." *The Yucatan Times*, 13 Mar 2014. Retrieved March 2016, http://www.theyucatantimes.com/2014/03/meet-the-muxes-an-integral-part-of-zapotec-culture

29. Jason Burke. "Pakistan's once-ridiculed transgender community fight elections for first time." *The Guardian*, 9 May 2013. Retrieved March 2016, http://www.theguardian.com/world/2013/may/09/pakistan-transgender-elections-campaign-trail

30. Rabbi Elliot Kulka. "Terms for Gender Diversity in Classical Jewish Texts." *Trans Torah*, 2006. Retrieved March 2016, http://www.transtorah. org/PDFs/Classical_Jewish_Terms_for_Gender_Diversity.pdf

31. "3rd International Intersex Forum Concluded." *European Region of the International Lesbian, Gay, Bisexual, Trans and Intersex Association.* Retrieved March 2016, http://www.ilga-europe.org/resources/news/latest-news/3rd-international-intersex-forum-concluded

32. "New Australian passports allow third gender option." *BBC News*, 15 Sept 2011. Retrieved March 2016, http://www.bbc.co.uk/news/world-asia-pacific-14926598

33. James Michael Nichols. "Germany to Allow Parents to Choose No Gender for Babies on Birth Certificates." *Huffington Post*, 31 Oct 2013. Retrieved March 2016, http://www.huffingtonpost.com/2013/10/31/germany-intersex_n_4181449.html

34. Terrence McCoy. *"India now recognizes transgender citizens as 'third gender.'"* Washington Post, 15 Apr 2014. Retrieved March 2016, http://www.washingtonpost.com/news/morning-mix/wp/2014/04/15/india-now-recognizes-transgender-citizens-as-third-gender

35. "Nepal pioneers a third gender on official documents, but concerns persist." *Four Two Nine Magazine*, 6 Mar 2013. Retrieved March 2016, http://dot429.com/articles/1599-nepal-pioneers-a-third-gender-on-official-documents-but-concerns-persist

36. Simon Collins. "X marks the spot on passport for transgender travelers." *New Zealand Herald*, 5 Dec 2012. Retrieved March 2016, http://www.nzherald.co.nz/nz/news/article.cfm?c_id=1&objectid=10852012

37. Deron Dalton. "The 22 trans women murdered in 2015." *The Daily Dot.* Retrieved March 2016, http://www.dailydot.com/politics/trans-women-of-color-murdered

38. Timothy White. *Rock Lives: Profiles and Interviews.* Holt Paperbacks, 1991.

39. "Hollywood Stars: Steven Tyler says he's both a man and a woman?" *Examiner*, 17 May 2011. Retrieved March 2016, http://www.examiner.com/article/hollywood-stars-steven-tyler-says-he-s-both-man-and-woman

40. Faux Queens. Retrieved March 2016, http://www.fauxqueens.com

41. Decca Aitenhead. "Eddie Izzard on going into politics: 'Why shouldn't I be mayor of London?'" *The Guardian*, 13 Dec 2013. Retrieved March 2016, http://www.theguardian.com/culture/2013/dec/13/eddie-izzard-going-into-politics

42. Intersex Awareness Day. Retrieved March 2016, http://intersexday.org

Chapter 3: Time Periods of Transition

1. "Transgender kids show consistent gender identity across measures." *Medical Xpress*, 29 Jan 2015. Retrieved March 2016, http://medicalxpress.com/news/2015-01-transgender-kids-gender-identity.html

2. Ellen C. Perrin, Edgardo J. Menvielle, and Catherine Tuerk. "To the Beat of a Different Drummer: The Gender Variant Child." *ntemporary Pediatrics*, 2007. Retrieved March 2016, http://imatyfa.org/permanent_files/to-the-beat-of-a-different-drummer-6-2007.pdf

3. "Transgender and Gender Variant Children and Youth: Resources for Parents/Guardians, Family Members, Educators and Allies." *Safe Schools Coalition*. Retrieved March 2016, http://www.safeschoolscoalition.org/RG-gender_nonconforming_trans_youth.html

4. "A school's gender neutral uniform policy." *BBC World Update*, 21 Jan 2016. Retrieved March 2016, http://www.bbc.co.uk/programmes/p03g4sbn

5. Charlize Veritas. "Becoming the Parent of a Transgender Child." *The Huffington Post*, 27 Jan 2016. Retrieved March 2016, http://www.huffingtonpost.com/charlize-veritas/becoming-a-transgender-pa_b_9082832.html

6. Jaime M. Grant, Lisa A. Mottet, and Justin Tannis, with Jack Harrison, Jody Herman and Mara Keisling. "Executive Summary: Injustice at every turn: A report of the national transgender discrimination survey." *National Center for Transgender Equality and National Gay and Lesbian Task Force*, 2011. Retrieved March 2016, http://www.thetaskforce.org/static_html/downloads/reports/reports/ntds_summary.pdf

7. Lisa Aliferis. "Transgender Children Living Openly Are Doing Well, Study Says." *KQED News*, 25 Feb 2016. Retrieved March 2016, http://ww2.kqed.org/stateofhealth/2016/02/25/transgender-children-living-openly-are-doing-well-study-shows

8. Stephanie Brill and Rachel Pepper. *The Transgender Child: A handbook for Families and Professionals*. Cleis Press, 2008.

9. "Parenting Trans Youth." *Southern Arizona Gender Alliance*. Retrieved March 2016, http://sagatucson.org/wp/parenting-trans-youth

10. "Camps for LGBT Youth." *Trans Student Educational Resources*. Retrieved March 2016, http://www.transstudent.org/camps

11. "Gender Spectrum Youth Program." *Gender Spectrum*. Retrieved March 2016, https://www.genderspectrum.org/quick-links/events/youth-program

12. Gender Odyssey Family. Retrieved March 2016, http://www.genderodysseyfamily.org

13. TransYouth Family Allies. Retrieved March 2016, http://www.imatyfa.org

14. "Looking at Gender Identity with Children's Books." *Welcoming Schools: A Project of the Human Rights Campaign Foundation*. Retrieved March 2016, http://www.welcomingschools.org/pages/looking-at-gender-identity-with-childrens-books

15. Florence Dillon. "Why Don't You Tell Them I'm a Boy? Raising a Gender-Nonconforming Child." *Safe Schools Coalition*, 1999. Retrieved March 2016, http://www.safeschoolscoalition.org/whydontyoutellthem.pdf

16. PFLAG: Parents, Families, Friends, and Allies United with LGBTQ People. Retrieved March 2016, http://community.pflag.org

17. "Find a PFLAG Chapter." *PFLAG: Parents, Families, Friends, and Allies United with LGBTQ People*. Retrieved March 2016, http://www.pflag.org/find

18. "The 2011 National School Climate Survey: The Experiences of Lesbian, Gay, Bisexual and Transgender Youth in Our Nation's Schools." *Gay, Lesbian & Straight Education Network (GLSEN)*. Retrieved March 2016, http://www.glsen.org/sites/default/files/2011%20National%20School%20Climate%20Survey%20Full%20Report.pdf

19. "Strengths and Silences: The Experiences of Lesbian, Gay, Bisexual and Transgender Students in Rural and Small Town Schools." *Gay, Lesbian & Straight Education Network (GLSEN)*. Retrieved March 2016, http://www.glsen.org/sites/default/files/Strengths%20%26%20Silences.pdf

20. Associated Press. "Bullied transgender teen commits suicide. *New York Post*, 10 Apr 2015. Retrieved March 2016, http://nypost.com/2015/04/10/bullied-transgender-teen-commits-suicide/

21. GSA Network. Retrieved March 2016, https://gsanetwork.org/

22. "Toolbox: Activist Resources." *Amplify: A Project of Advocates of Youth*. Retrieved March 2016, http://amplifyyourvoice.org/toolbox

23. "Beyond the Binary Campaign." *GSA Network*. Retrieved March 2016, https://gsanetwork.org/get-involved/change-your-school/campaigns/beyond-binary

24. "Bending the Mold: An Action Kit for Transgender Students." *Lambda Legal*. Retrieved March 2016, http://www.lambdalegal.org/publications/bending-the-mold

25. *Kicked Out*, edited by Sassafras Lowrey and Jennifer Clare Burke. Homofactus Press, 2010.

26. "Homeless Youth." *National Coalition for the Homeless*, June 2008. Retrieved March 2016, http://www.nationalhomeless.org/factsheets/youth.html

27. "Incidence and Vulnerability of LGBTQ Homeless Youth." *National Alliance to End Homelessness* Solution Brief, 8 Dec 2008. Retrieved March 2016, http://www.endhomelessness.org/content/article/detail/2141/

28. Nicholas Ray. "Lesbian, Gay, Bisexual and Transgender Youth: An Epidemic of Homelessness." *National LGBTQ Task Force*, 2006. Retrieved March 2016, http://www.thetaskforce.org/lgbt-youth-an-epidemic-of-homelessness/

29. Nico Sifra Quintana, Josh Rosenthal, and Jeff Krehely. "On the Streets: The Federal Response to Gay and Transgender Homeless Youth." *Center for American Progress*, 21 June 2010. Retrieved March 2016, https://www.americanprogress.org/issues/lgbt/report/2010/06/21/7983/on-the-streets/

30. True Colors Fund. Retrieved March 2016, https://truecolorsfund.org/

31. "Health Outcomes Subcommittee: Puberty Blocking & Hormone Therapy for Transgender Adolescents." *Trans Active*, 2014. Retrieved March 2016, http://gendercreativekids.ca/wp-content/uploads/2014/01/TransActive-OHSC-Testimony.pdf

32. Margaret Talbot. "About A Boy: Transgender surgery at sixteen." *The New Yorker*, 18 Mar 2013. Retrieved March 2016, http://www.newyorker.com/magazine/2013/03/18/about-a-boy-2

33. "National Collegiate Athletics Association (NCAA) Inclusion of Transgender Student Athletes" *NCAA*, August 2011. Retrieved March 2016, http://www.ncaa.org/sites/default/files/Transgender_Handbook_2011_Final.pdf

34. Transgender On-Campus Non-Discrimination Information (TONI Project). Retrieved March 2016, http://transstudents.org/

35. Alex Morris. "My Husband Is Now My Wife: The spouses of transgender people face their own dramatic transformations – only no one celebrates them." *The Cut*, 22 Sept 2015. Retrieved March 2016, http://nymag.com/thecut/2015/09/trans-wives-transitioning.html

36. Helen Boyd. *She's Not the Man I Married: My Life with a Transgender Husband*. Seal Press, 2014.

37. "Workplace Gender Transition Guidelines." *Human Rights Campaign*. Retrieved March 2016, http://www.hrc.org/resources/workplace-gender-transition-guidelines

38. "A Broken Bargain for Transgender Workers. *LGBT MAP*, September 2013. Retrieved March 2016, http://www.lgbtmap.org/file/a-broken-bargain-for-transgender-workers.pdf

39. "FAQ: Answers to Common Questions About Transgender Workplace Rights." *Lambda Legal*. Retrieved March 2016, http://www.lambdalegal.org/know-your-rights/transgender/trans-workplace-faq

40. Julia Baird. "The Courage of Transgender Soldiers." *The New York Times*, 21 Feb 2014. Retrieved March 2016, http://www.nytimes.com/2014/02/22/opinion/sunday/baird-the-courage-of-trans-soldiers.html]

41. Harper Jean Tobin; Raffi Freedman-Gurspan and Lisa Mottet. "Chapter 14: Open Military Service." from *A Blueprint for Equality: Federal Agenda for Transgender People*. National Center for Transgender Equality, June 2015. Retrieved March 2016, http://www.transequality.org/sites/default/files/docs/resources/NCTE_Blueprint_June2015_0.pdf

42. Amanda Terkel. "Pentagon Set to End Ban On Transgender Service Members in May." *The Huffington Post*, 26 Aug 2015. Retrieved March 2016, http://www.huffingtonpost.com/entry/pentagon-transgender-ban_55ddec92e4b0a40aa3ad0ae7

43. Transgender American Veterans Association. Retrieved March 2016, http://tavausa.org/

44. Jacob Bernstein. "For Some in Transgender Community, It's Never Too Late to Make a Change." *NY Times*, 6 Mar 2015. Retrieved March 2016, http://www.nytimes.com/2015/03/08/fashion/for-some-in-transgender-community-its-never-too-late-to-make-a-change.html

45. "Improving the lives of transgender older adults: Recommendations for policy and practice." *SAGE (Services and Advocacy for GLBT Elders) and the National Center for Transgender Equality (NCTE)*, 2012. Retrieved March 2016, http://www.lgbtagingcenter.org/resources/pdfs/TransAgingPolicyReportFull.pdf

46. "Transgender Aging." *National Resource Center on LGBT Aging*. Retrieved March 2016, http://www.lgbtagingcenter.org

47. "Aging Fiercely While Trans with Kate Bornstein, Sheila Cunningham, Miss Major, and Jay Toole." *Visual Aids and the NYC Oral History Project*, 11 July 2015. Retrieved March 2016, https://www.visualaids.org/events/detail/aging-fiercely

48. National Resource Center on LGBT Aging. Retrieved March 2016, https://www.lgbtagingcenter.org

49. Mo Perry. "The Challenge of Being Transgender in a Nursing Home." *The Atlantic*, 12 Aug 2015. Retrieved March 2016, http://www.theatlantic.com/health/archive/2015/08/transgender-nursing-home-aging/400580/

50. Joe Ippolito and Tarynn M. Witten. "Aging." From Laura Erickson-Schroth, ed. *Trans Bodies, Trans Selves: A Resource Guide for the Transgender Community*. Oxford University Press, 2014.

51. Liana Aghajanian. "Aging Trans People Are Systematically Locked Out of the Health Care System." *Newsweek*, 4 Nov 2015. Retrieved March 2016, http://www.newsweek.com/2015/11/13/trans-people-cant-get-health-care-390375.html

52. Karen I. Fredricksen-Golden, PhD; Hyun-Jun Kim, PhD; Charles A. Emlet, PhD; Anna Muraco, PhD; Elena A. Erosheva, PhD; Charles P. Hoy-Ellis, MSW; Kayn Goldsen, BS; and Heidi Petry, PhD. "The Aging and Health Report: Disparities and Resilience among Lesbian, Gay, Bisexual, and Transgender Older Adults." *Caring and Aging*, 16 Nov 2011. Retrieved March 2016, http://caringandaging.org/wordpress/wp-content/uploads/2011/05/Full-Report-FINAL-11-16-11.pdf

53. "Transgender Aging: Aging poses unique challenges for transgender older adults." *SAGE: Services & Advocacy for Gay, Lesbian, Bisexual & Transgender Elders.* Retrieved March 2016, http://www.sageusa.org/issues/transgender.cfm

Chapters 4-7 – Health

1. John W. Santrock. *A Topical Approach to Human Life-span Development* (3rd ed.). McGraw-Hill, 2007

Chapter 4: Social Health

1. Philadelphia Trans Health Conference. Retrieved March 2016, https://www.mazzonicenter.org/trans-health

2. The Trans Advocate. Retrieved March 2016, http://www.transadvocate.com

3. Wipe Out Transphobia. Retrieved March 2016, http://www.wipeouttransphobia.com

4. LYRIC Center for LGBTQQ Youth. Retrieved March 2016, http://lyric.org

5. "Trans Aging." FORGE. Retrieved March 2016, https://forge-forward.org/aging/

6. We Happy Trans. Retrieved March 2016, http://wehappytrans.com

7. Norah Vincent. *Self-Made Man: One Woman's Year Disguised as a Man.* Penguin Books, 2006.

8. "Tonight Show Makes Tired Transgender Jokes." *GLAAD*, 17 Aug 2009. Retrieved March 2016, http://www.glaad.org/2009/08/17/tonight-show-makes-tired-transgender-jokes/

9. Jaime M. Grant, Lisa A. Mottet, and Justin Tannis, with Jack Harrison, Jody Herman and Mara Keisling. "Injustice at every turn: A report of the national transgender discrimination survey." *Washington, DC: National Center for Transgender Equality and National Gay and Lesbian Task Force.* 2011. Retrieved March 2016, http://www.thetaskforce.org/static_html/ downloads/reports/reports/ntds_full.pdf

10. "Discrimination Against Transgender Workers." *Human Rights Campaign.* Retrieved March 2016, http://www.hrc.org/resources/discrimination-against-transgender-workers

11. "Bullied Transgender Teen Commits Suicide." *NY Post Times,* 10 Apr 2015. Retrieved March 2015, http://nypost.com/2015/04/10/bullied-transgender-teen-commits-suicide/

12. Dr. Jillian T. Weiss. "Transphobia In the Gay Community." *The Bilerco Project,* 11 Dec 2009. Retrieved March 2016, http://www.bilerico. com/2009/12/transphobia_in_the_gay_community.php

Chapter 5: Medical Health

1. "U.S. Breast Cancer Statistics." *BreastCancer.org,* 23 Oct 2015. Retrieved March 2016, http://www.breastcancer.org/symptoms/understand_bc/ statistics

2. "Primary Care Protocol for Transgender Patient Care." *Center of Excellence for Transgender Health,* Apr 2011. Retrieved March 2016, http://www. transhealth.ucsf.edu/trans?page=protocol-00-00

3. "TRANSLINE: Transgender Medical Consultation Service." *Project Health.* Retrieved December 2015, http://project-health.org/transline/

4. "Transgender Health Information Program: Medical." *Vancouver Coastal Health,* May 2014. Retrieved March 2016, http://transhealth.vch.ca/ medical-options

5. "Finding Insurance for Transgender-Related Healthcare." *Human Rights Campaign,* 8 Jan 2015. Retrieved March 2016, http://www.hrc.org/ resources/finding-insurance-for-transgender-related-healthcare

6. "Transition and insurance." *Trans Road Map.* Retrieved March 2016, http://www.tsroadmap.com/reality/insurance.html

7. Susan Rinkunas. "Insurance Companies Can't Afford Not to Cover Transgender Patients. *NY Mag*, 1 Dec 2015. Retrieved March 2016, http://nymag.com/thecut/2015/12/transgender-health-insurance-coverage-costs.html

8. "Know Your Rights: Medicare." *National Center for Transgender Equality.* Retrieved March 2016, http://www.transequality.org/know-your-rights/medicare

9. TransGenderCare. Retrieved March 2016, http://www.transgendercare.com

10. "Transgender Health." *American Medical Student Association.* Retrieved March 2016, http://www.amsa.org/advocacy/action-committees/gender-sexuality/transgender-health/

11. "Primary Care Protocol for Transgender Patient Care." *Center of Excellence for Transgender Health*, Apr 2011. Retrieved March 2016, http://www.transhealth.ucsf.edu/trans?page=protocol-00-00

12. "TRANSLINE: Transgender Medical Consultation Service." *Project Health*. Retrieved March 2016, http://project-health.org/transline/

13. "Transgender Health Information Program: Medical." *Vancouver Coastal Health*, May 2014. Retrieved March 2016, http://transhealth.vch.ca/medical-options

14. "Gender Dysphoria." *National Health Service*, 29 Apr 2014. Retrieved March 2016, http://www.nhs.uk/conditions/gender-dysphoria/Pages/Introduction.aspx

15. "Tucking." *Susan's Place*. Retrieved March 2016, https://www.susans.org/wiki/index.php/Tucking

16. Parker Marie Molloy. "Trans Woman Releases Bathroom-Finder App Refuge Restrooms." *Advocate*, 7 Feb 2014. Retrieved March 2016, http://www.advocate.com/politics/transgender/2014/02/07/trans-woman-releases-bathroom-finder-app-refuge-restrooms

17. "Youth: Special Considerations." *Center of Excellence for Transgender Health*, Apr 2011. Retrieved March 2016, http://www.transhealth.ucsf.edu/trans?page=protocol-youth

18. "Standards of Care for the Health of Transsexual, Transgender, and Gender-Nonconforming People, Version 7." *The World Association for Transgender Health*, 2012. Retrieved March 2016, http://www.wpath.org/uploaded_files/140/files/Standards%20of%20Care,%20V7%20Full%20Book.pdf

19. "Informed Consent for Masculinizing Hormone Therapy." *Howard Brown Health Center*, 25 Sept 2013. Retrieved March 2016, http://howardbrown.org/uploadedFiles/Services_and_Programs/Transgender_Health/Informed%20Consent%20for%20Masculinizing%20Hormone%20Therapy.pdf

20. Informed Consent for Access to Trans Health. Retrieved March 2016, http://www.icath.org

21. TransLine Medical Consultation Service. Retrieved March 2016, https://transline.zendesk.com/home

22. Cheri Cheng. "One-Third of Endocrinologists Do Not Want to Treat Trans Patients, Survey Says." *HNGN*, 10 Mar 2016. Retrieved March 2016, http://www.hngn.com/articles/187428/20160310/one-third-endocrinologists-want-treat-transgender-patients-survey.htm

23. "Feminizing Hormones." *Vancouver Coastal Health: Transgender Health Information Project*. Retrieved March 2016, http://transhealth.vch.ca/medical-options/hormones/feminizing-hormones

24. Enid Vázquez. "A Transgender Therapy Primer." *The BODY: The Complete HIV/AIDS Resource*, August 2008. Retrieved March 2016, http://www.thebody.com/content/art48428.html

25. "Testosterone Side Effects." *Drugs.com*. Retrieved March 2016, http://www.drugs.com/sfx/testosterone-side-effects.html

26. "Masculinizing Hormones." *Vancouver Coastal Health: Transgender Health Information Project*. Retrieved March 2016, http://transhealth.vch.ca/medical-options/hormones/masculinizing-hormones

27. "FTM Testosterone Therapy Basics." *Hudson's FTM Resource Guide*. Retrieved March 2016, http://www.ftmguide.org/ttherapybasics.html

28. "Health Insurance Main." *United States Census Bureau*, 2014. Retrieved March 2016, http://www.census.gov/hhes/www/hlthins/

29. "Transgender Health Injection Guide." *Fenway Health*, July 2015. Retrieved March 2016, http://fenwayhealth.org/wp-content/uploads/2015/07/COM-1880-trans-health_injection-guide_small_v2.pdf

30. Jager Weatherby. "Transgender Rajee Narinesingh on the Aftermath of Illegal Injections: 'It Was So Bad, the Knife Broke During Surgery.'" *Real Self*, 16 Apr 2015. Retrieved March 2016, https://www.realself.com/blog/transgender-woman-illegal-injections-bad-the-knife-broke-surgery

31. "Silicone Injections." *Trans Road Map*, 31 May 2015. Retrieved March 2016, http://www.tsroadmap.com/physical/silicone/index.html

32. Trystan T. Cotton. *Hung Jury: Testimonies of Genital Surgery by Transsexual Men*. Transgress Press, 2012.

33. Cameron Bowman and Joshua Goldman. "Care of the Patient Undergoing Sex Reassignment Surgery (SRS)." *Vancouver Coastal Health, Transcend Transgender Support & Education Society, and the Canadian Rainbow Health Coalition*, June 2006. Retrieved December 2015, http://amsasites.wpengine.com/wp-content/uploads/2015/04/CareOfThePatientUndergoingSRS.pdf

34. Elissa Miolene. "Transgender Patients Say Georgetown Is Denying Them Care." *Washingtonian*, 9 Jul 2015. Retrieved March 2016, http://www.washingtonian.com/2015/07/09/transgender-population-still-struggling-with-access-to-health-care/

35. Susan Donaldson James. "Trans Man Denied Cancer Treatment; Now Feds Say It's Illegal." *ABC News*, 8 Aug 2012. Retrieved March 2016, http://abcnews.go.com/Health/transgender-bias-now-banned-federal-law/story?id=16949817

Chapter 6: Sexual Health

1. Stephanie A. Sanders, Brandon J. Hill, William L. Yarber, Cynthia A. Graham, Richard A. Crosby, and Robin R. Milhausen. "Misclassification bias: diversity in conceptualizations about having 'had sex.'" *Sexual Health* 7(1): 31–34, 2010. Retrieved March 2016, http://kinseyinstitute.org/publications/PDF/had%20sex%20study.pdf

2. B.J. Hill, Q. Rahman, D.A. Bright and S.A. Sanders. "The semantics of sexual behavior and their implications for HIV/AIDS research and sexual health: U.S. and U.K. gay men's definitions of having 'had sex.'" *The Kinsey Institute for Research in Sex, Gender, and Reproduction. AIDS Care*, 16: 1-7, 2010. Retrieved March 2016, http://www.ncbi.nlm.nih.gov/pubmed/20640953

3. Katia Hetter. "I Don't Own My Child's Body." *CNN*, 20 June 2012. Retrieved March 2016, http://www.cnn.com/2012/06/20/give-grandma-hug-child/index.html

4. Dr. Nerdlove. "Getting a yes (instead of avoiding a no): The standard of enthusiastic consent." Paging Dr. Nerdlove. Retrieved March 2016, http://www.Doctornerdlove.com/2013/03/enthusiastic-consent

5. Paris Lees. "Should Trans People Have to Disclose Their Birth Gender Before Sex?" *Vice*, 1 Jul 2013. Retrieved March 2016, http://www.vice.com/read/should-trans-people-have-to-disclose-their-birth-gender-before-sex

6. Nick Duffy. "Trans man convicted over 'sex deception' after using fake penis to 'dupe' girlfriend." *Pink News*, 16 Dec 2015. Retrieved March 2016, http://www.pinknews.co.uk/2015/12/16/trans-man-convicted-over-sex-by-deception-after-using-fake-penis-to-dupe-girlfriend/

7. Hilleke E. Hulshoff Pol; Peggy T. Cohen-Kettenis; Neeltje E. M. Van Haren; Jiska S. Peper; Rachel G. H. Brans; Wiepke Cahn; Hugo G Schnack, Louis J G Gooren; and René S. Kahn. "Changing your sex changes your brain: influences of testosterone and estrogen on adult human brain structure." *European Journal of Endocrinology*, 2006. Retrieved December 2015, http://www.eje-online.org/content/155/suppl_1/S107.full.pdf

8. "Sex, Alcohol, and Drugs." *Planned Parenthood*, 2014. Retrieved March 2016, https://www.plannedparenthood.org/teens/sex/sex-alcohol-and-other-drugs

9. Dean G. Kilpatrick, Heidi S. Resnick, Kenneth J. Ruggiero, Lauren M. Conoscenti, and Jenna McCauley "Drug-facilitated, Incapacitated, and Forcible Rape: A National Study." *U.S. Department of Justice*. Retrieved March 2016, https://www.ncjrs.gov/pdffiles1/nij/grants/219181.pdf

10. Jaime M. Grant, Lisa A. Mottet, and Justin Tannis, with Jack Harrison, Jody Herman and Mara Keisling. "Injustice at every turn: A report of the national transgender discrimination survey." *National Center for Transgender Equality and National Gay and Lesbian*

11. "Being Safe, Being Me: Results of the Canadian Trans Youth Health Survey." *Stigma and Resilience Among Vulnerable Youth Center*, 2015. Retrieved March 2016, http://delongis.psych.ubc.ca/wp-content/uploads/2014/02/Being-safe-being-me-Results-of-the-Canadian-Trans-Youth-Health-Survey-.pdf

12. "Responding to Transgender Victims of Sexual Assault." *Office for Victims of Crime*, June 2014. Retrieved December 2015, http://www.ovc.gov/pubs/forge/sexual_numbers.html

13. Sunnivie Brydum and Mitch Kellaway. "This Black Trans Man Is in Prison For Killing His Rapist." *The Advocate*, 8 Apr 2015. Retrieved March 2016, http://www.advocate.com/politics/transgender/2015/04/08/black-trans-man-prison-killing-his-rapist

14. Angelo Louw. "Men Are Also 'Corrective Rape' Victims." *Mail & Guardian*, 11 Apr 2014 Retrieved March 2016, http://mg.co.za/article/2014-04-11-men-are-also-corrective-rape-victims

15. Survivor Project. Retrieved March 2016, http://survivorproject.org

16. Kathryn Stamoulis. "Teaching Our Sons Not to Rape." Psychology Today, 21 Jan 2015. Retrieved March 2016, https://www.psychologytoday.com/blog/the-new-teen-age/201501/teaching-our-sons-not-rape

17. Finn Wightman. "A Letter To My Son About Consent." *The Good Men Project*, 25 Mar 2015. Retrieved March 2016, http://goodmenproject.com/ethics-values/a-letter-to-my-son-about-consent/

18. "Responding to Transgender Victims of Sexual Assault." *Office for Victims of Crime*, June 2014. Retrieved March 2016, http://www.ovc.gov/pubs/forge/sexual_numbers.html

19. Denise Grady. "Uterus Transplants May Soon Help Some Infertile Women in the U.S. Become Pregnant." *The New York Times*, 12 Nov 2015. Retrieved March 2016, http://www.nytimes.com/2015/11/13/health/uterus-transplants-may-soon-help-some-infertile-women-in-the-us-become-pregnant.html

20. Oliver Wheaton. "Revolutionary New Surgery Could Allow Trans Women to Carry Children." *Metro UK*, 22 Nov 15. Retrieved March 2016, http://metro.co.uk/2015/11/22/revolutionary-new-surgery-could-allow-trans-women-to-carry-children-5519000/

21. Gabrielle Birkner. "Jewish Transgender Man Gives Birth and Embraces Life as a Single 'Abba'." *The Jewish World*, 25 Jan 2016. Retrieved March 2016, http://jewishworldnews.org/jewish-transgender-man-gives-birth-and-embraces-life-as-a-single-abba/

22. "Q: Safe sex for transgender men?" *The Condom Depot Learning Center*, 21 Mar 2014. Retrieved March 2016, http://learn.condomdepot. com/2014/03/21/q-safe-sex-for-transgender-men/

23. Elizabeth Boskey, PhD. "How to Make a Dental Dam from a Latex Glove." *About Health*, 3 Feb 2014. Retrieved March 2016, http://std. about.com/od/oralsextips/ss/How-To-Make-A-Dental-Dam-From-A-Latex-Glove.htm

24. Sam Dylan Finch. "5 Ways to Support a Trans Person Experiencing Body Dysphoria." *Everyday Feminism*, 23 March 2015. Retrieved March 2016, everydayfeminism.com/2015/03/supporting-trans-person-with-dysphoria/

25. Spicy-Gear. "Safer Sex for *Trans People." *BlogHer*, 9 April 2014. Retrieved March 2016, http://www.blogher.com/safer-sex-trans-people

26. "Q: Safe sex for transgender women?" *The Condom Depot Learning Center*, 28 Mar 2014. Retrieved March 2016, http://learn.condomdepot. com/2014/03/28/q-safer-sex-for-transgender-women/

27. "Public Health Crisis: The Impact of Using Condoms as Evidence of Prostitution in New York City." *The Pros Network, Sex Workers Project*, 2012. Retrieved March 2016, http://sexworkersproject.org/ downloads/2012/20120417-public-health-crisis.pdf

28. Tooru Nemoto, PhD, Don Operario, PhD, JoAnne Keatley, MSW, Lei Han, PhD, and Toho Soma, MPH. "HIV Risk Behaviors Among Male-to-Female Transgender Persons of Color in San Francisco." *American Journal of Public Health*, 2004. Retrieved March 2016, http://www.cdc.gov/ hiv/group/gender/transgender/index.html

29. Jaime M. Grant, Lisa A. Mottet, and Justin Tannis, with Jack Harrison, Jody Herman and Mara Keisling. "Executive Summary: Injustice at every turn: A report of the national transgender discrimination survey." Washington, DC: *National Center for Transgender Equality and National Gay and Lesbian Task Force*. 2011. Retrieved March 2016, http://www.thetaskforce.org/static_ html/downloads/reports/reports/ntds_summary.pdf

30. Spicy-Gear. "Safer Sex for Trans* People." *Blog Her*, 9 Apr 2014. Retrieved March 2016, http://www.blogher.com/safer-sex-trans-people

31. Dr. Alex Müller. "Sexual Health for Transgender and Gender Non-Conforming People." *Gender Dynamix*. Retrieved March 2016, http://www.academia.edu/3541149/Sexual_Health_for_Transgender_and_Gender_Non-Conforming_People

Chapter 7: Mental Health

1. "Gender Dysphoria Fact Sheet." *American Psychiatric Publishing: A Division of American Psychiatric Association*, 2013. Retrieved March 2016, http://www.dsm5.org/Documents/Gender%20Dysphoria%20Fact%20 Sheet.pdf

2. "Standards of Care for the Health of Transsexual, Transgender, and Gender Nonconforming People, Version 7." *The World Professional Association for Transgender Health*. Retrieved March 2016, http://www. wpath.org/uploaded_files/140/files/Standards%20of%20Care,%20 V7%20Full%20Book.pdf

3. "Gender Reassignment Surgery." *Aetna Insurance*. Retrieved March 2016, http://www.aetna.com/cpb/medical/data/600_699/0615.html

4. B. Binaohan. *DeColonizing Trans/Gender 101*. Biyuti Publishing, 2014.

5. "Gender Dysphoria Fact Sheet." *American Psychiatric Publishing: A Division of American Psychiatric Association*, 2013. Retrieved March 2016, http://www.dsm5.org/Documents/Gender%20Dysphoria%20Fact%20 Sheet.pdf

6. "Gender Identity Disorder from DSM IV." *American Psychiatric Association*, 1994. Retrieved March 2016, http://www.geekbabe.com/ annie/feature/dsmiv.html

7. Zack Ford. "Infamous Reparative Therapy Clinic For Transgender Youth Set To Close." *Think Progress*, 16 Dec 2015. Retrieved March 2016, http:// thinkprogress.org/lgbt/2015/12/16/3732840/ex-trans-reparative-therapy-clinic-closing/

8. "Standards of Care for the Health of Transsexual, Transgender, and Gender Nonconforming People, Version 7." *The World Professional Association for Transgender Health.* Retrieved March 2016, http://www. wpath.org/uploaded_files/140/files/Standards%20of%20Care,%20 V7%20Full%20Book.pdf

9. "Standards of Care for the Health of Transsexual, Transgender, and Gender Nonconforming People, Version 7." *The World Professional Association for Transgender Health.* Retrieved March 2016, http://www. wpath.org/uploaded_files/140/files/Standards%20of%20Care,%20 V7%20Full%20Book.pdf

10. "Standards of Care for Women in Transition." *Trans Road Map*, 31 May 2015. Retrieved March 2016, http://www.tsroadmap.com/reality/wpath-standards.html

11. Sam Dylan Finch. "5 Ways to Support a Trans Person Experiencing Body Dysphoria." *Everyday Feminism*, 23 Mar 2015. Retrieved March 2016, http://everydayfeminism.com/2015/03/supporting-trans-person-with-dysphoria/

12. Chris Iliades, MD. "Stats and Facts About Depression in America." *Everyday Health*, 23 Jan 2013. Retrieved March 2016, http://www. everydayhealth.com/hs/major-depression/depression-statistics/

13. "Body Dysmorphic Disorder – Definition." *The Mayo Clinic.* Retrieved March 2016, http://www.mayoclinic.org/diseases-conditions/body-dysmorphic-disorder/basics/definition/CON-20029953

14. Jaime, M. Grant; Lisa Mottet, Justin Tanis; Jack Harrison; Jody Herman; and Mara Keisling. "Injustice at Every Turn: A Report of the National Transgender Discrimination Survey." *National Center for Transgender Equality and National Gay and Lesbian Task Force*, 2011. Retrieved March 2016, http://www.thetaskforce.org/static_html/downloads/reports/reports/ntds_full.pdf

15. Nillin Dennison. "TDoR 2015: Memorial List of 27 Reported Deaths by Suicide." *Planet Transgender*, 16 Nov 2015. Retrieved March 2016, http://planettransgender.com/tdor-2015-memorial-list-27-reported-deaths-suicide/

16. "8 Things the Statistics Actually Say About Trans Suicide." *What's Gender Got To Do With It? (A Trans Psychology Blog)*, 28 Oct 2015. Retrieved March 2016, http://blog.sebastianmitchellbarr.com/post/132094750755/8-things-the-statistics-actually-say-about-trans

17. It Gets Better Project. Retrieved December 2015, http://www.itgetsbetter.org

18. Delfin Bautista and Quince Mountain, with Health Mackenzie Reynolds. "Religion and Spirituality." From Laura, Erickson-Schroth, ed. *Trans Bodies, Trans Selves: A Resource Guide for the Transgender Community*. Oxford University Press, 2014.

19. "Hungry, Angry, Lonely, Tired = H.A.L.T." *Need Encouragement*, 23 July 2014. Retrieved March 2016, https://needencouragement.com/hungry-angry-lonely-tired/

Chapter 8: Transgender and the Law

1. "Legal Aspects of Transgenderism." *Wikipedia*. Retrieved March 2016, https://en.wikipedia.org/wiki/Legal_aspects_of_transgenderism

2. "Universal Declaration of Human Rights." *United Nations Human Rights: Office of the High Commissioner*. 10 Dec 1948. Retrieved March 2016, http://www.ohchr.org/EN/UDHR/Documents/UDHR_Translations/eng.pdf

3. "7 Fam 1310 Appendix M Summary" *U.S. Department of State*, 13 Nov 2014. Retrieved March 2016, https://fam.state.gov/FAM/07FAM/07FAM1300apM.html

4. Becky Allison, M.D. "U.S. States and Canadian Provinces: Instructions for Changing Name and Sex on Birth Certificate." Retrieved March 2016, http://www.drbecky.com/birthcert.html

5. "ID Documents Center." *National Center for Transgender Equality*. Retrieved March 2016, http://www.transequality.org/documents

6. Nicole Hensley. "Transgender woman buried by family as a man in Idaho funeral." *NY Daily Times*, 24 Nov 2014. Retrieved March 2016, http://www.nydailynews.com/news/national/transgender-woman-buried-family-man-idaho-funeral-article-1.2020992

7. "Know Your Rights." *Transgender American Veterans Association*. Retrieved March 2016, http://transveteran.org/for-veterans/know-your-rights/

8. Leonard Greene. "Birth certificates ask parents if 'woman giving birth' is female." *New York Post*, 30 Jan 2015. Retrieved March 2016, http://nypost.com/2015/01/30/birth-certificates-ask-parents-if-woman-giving-birth-is-female

9. Julia Glum. "Texas to List Same-Sex Parents On Birth Certificates After Court Order; Software Update." *International Business Times*, 14 Aug 2015. Retrieved March 2016, http://www.ibtimes.com/texas-list-same-sex-parents-birth-certificates-after-court-order-software-update-2054467

10. Lindsay Whitehurst. "Judge Rules Utah Must Recognize Same Sex Parents on Child's Birth Certificate." *The Huffington Post*, 15 July 2015. Retrieved March 2016, http://www.huffingtonpost.com/entry/judge-rules-utah-must-recognize-same-sex-parents-on-childs-birth-certificate_55a6fcabe4b0896514d054f7

11. "Cities and Countries with Non-Discrimination Ordinances that Include Gender Identity." *Human Rights Campaign*. Retrieved March 2016, http://www.hrc.org/resources/entry/cities-and-counties-with-non-discrimination-ordinances-that-include-gender

12. "Remarks by the President at Signing of Executive Order on LGBT Workplace Discrimination." *The White House*. 21 July, 2015. Retrieved March 2016, https://www.whitehouse.gov/the-press-office/2014/07/21/remarks-president-signing-executive-order-lgbt-workplace-discrimination

13. *Oberfell v. Hodges*, 14-566. U.S. Supreme Court, 26 June 2015. Retrieved March 2016, http://www.supremecourt.gov/opinions/14pdf/14-556_3204.pdf

14. Kristina-Maia DeMott. "Transition and Divorce." *Trans Road Map*. Retrieved March 2016, http://www.tsroadmap.com/family/divorce.html

15. Christine Salek. "Transgender Rights: What Happens to Custody When Mommy Becomes Daddy?" *Mic*, 6 Apr 2013. Retrieved March 2016, http://mic.com/articles/33137/transgender-rights-what-happens-to-custody-when-mommy-becomes-daddy

16. "FAQ About Transgender Parenting." *Lambda Legal*. Retrieved March 2016, http://www.lambdalegal.org/know-your-rights/transgender/trans-parenting-faq

17. "Resources for Transgender Parents." *Lambda Legal.* Retrieved March 2016, http://www.lambdalegal.org/know-your-rights/transgender/trans-parents-resources

18. Fong & Aquino. "Marriage-based Green Cards and Transgender Persons." *Immigration Visa Attorney Blog,* 1 Jun 2015. Retrieved March 2016, http://www.immigrationvisaattorneyblog.com/2015/06/marriage-based-green-cards-and.html

19. "Victory for Transgender Immigrants." *Transgender Law Center.* Retrieved March 2016, http://transgenderlawcenter.org/archives/882

20. Kate Kuorbatova and Elana Redfield. "Immigration." From Laura, Erickson-Schroth, ed. *Trans Bodies, Trans Selves: A Resource Guide for the Transgender Community.* Oxford University Press, 2014.

21. "Know Your Rights: Housing and Homeless Shelters." *National Center for Transgender Equality.* Retrieved March 2016, http://www.transequality.org/know-your-rights/housing-and-homeless-shelters

22. Russell Berman. "How Bathroom Fears Conquered Transgender Rights in Houston." *The Atlantic,* 3 Nov 2015. Retrieved March 2016, http://www.theatlantic.com/politics/archive/2015/11/how-bathroom-fears-conquered-transgender-rights-in-houston/414016/

23. Casey Jaywork. "Why Everyone Should Care About the Legislature's Attack on Trans Rights." *Seattle Weekly News,* 26 Jan 2016. Retrieved March 2016, http://www.seattleweekly.com/home/962787-129/why-everyone-should-care-about-the

24. Ryan Broderick. "Everything You Need to Know About Arizona's Transgender 'Bathroom Bill'." *BuzzFeed,* 28 Mar 2013. Retrieved March 2016, http://www.buzzfeed.com/ryanhatesthis/everything-you-need-to-know-about-arizonas-transgender-bathr

25. Arian Campo-Flores. "Arizona's Immigration Law and Racial Profiling." *Newsweek,* 26 Apr 2010. Retrieved March 2016, http://www.newsweek.com/arizonas-immigration-law-and-racial-profiling-70683

26. Claire-Renee Kohner. "Trans Man Behind #WeJustNeedtoPee Isn't Selfie-Centered." *Advocate,* 17 Mar 2015. Retrieved March 2016, http://www.advocate.com/politics/transgender/2015/03/17/trans-man-behind-wejustneedtopee-isnt-selfie-centered

27. Aimee Lee Ball. "In All-Gender Restrooms, the Signs Reflect the Times." *The New York Times*, 5 Nov 2015. Retrieved March 2016, http://www. nytimes.com/2015/11/08/style/transgender-restroom-all-gender.html

28. Maggie Shepard. "Bill would let businesses shun gays, transgenders." *Albuquerque Journal*, 21 Dec 2015. Retrieved March 2016, http://www. abqjournal.com/694736/abqnewsseeker/bill-would-let-businesses-shun-gays-transgenders.html

29. Wilson Dizard. "Florida bill seeks to ban transgender people from choosing their bathrooms." *Al Jazeera America*, 6 Feb 2015. Retrieved March 2016, http://america.aljazeera.com/articles/2015/2/6/florida-bill-seeks-to-set-bathroom-rules-for-trans-people.html

30. "Arizona Bathroom Bill Flushed Away – For Now." *Transgender Law Center*, 6 June 2013. Retrieved March 2016, http://transgenderlawcenter. org/archives/8128

31. Fiona Ortiz. "Feds Order High School To Let Transgender Students Use Girls' Locker Room" *The Huffington Post*, 11 Mar 2015. Retrieved March 2016, http://www.huffingtonpost.com/entry/transgender-high-school-locker-room_56387949e4b00a4d2e0bb825

32. Curtis Wong. "Trans Texans Share Emotional Responses On Rejection of LGBT Discrimination Measure." *The Huffington Post*, 11 Nov 2015. Retrieved March 2016, http://www.huffingtonpost.com/entry/houston-transgender-hero-response_56437f7ee4b045bf3ded55ba

33. Alissa Scheller and Cameron Love. "Transgender People Are More Visible Than Ever, But It's Still Legal to Discriminate Against Them in Most States." *The Huffington Post*, 3 June 2015. Retrieved March 2016, http://www.huffingtonpost.com/2015/06/03/transgender-discrimination-laws_n_7502266.html

34. Ellen Wulfhorst. "New York City Lays Out Transgender Protection On Dress Codes, Bathroom Use." *The Huffington Post*, 22 Dec 2015. Retrieved March 2016, http://www.huffingtonpost.com/2015/12/22/new-york-transgender-protections_n_8862628.html

35. Emma Margolin. "Maryland legislature passes transgender equality bill." *MSNBC*, 27 Mar 2014. Retrieved March 2016, http://www.msnbc.com/msnbc/maryland-passes-transgender-equality-bill

36. Cleis Abeni. "New Protections Make New York Among Nations Most Trans-Affirmative." *The Advocate*, 21 Dec 2015. Retrieved March 2016, http://www.advocate.com/transgender/2015/12/21/new-protections-make-new-york-among-nations-most-trans-affirmative

37. Kyle Knight. "Dispatches: Ireland Steps Out as Global Transgender Leader." *Human Rights Watch*, 16 July 2015. Retrieved March 2016, https://www.hrw.org/news/2015/07/16/dispatches-ireland-steps-out-global-transgender-leader

38. "'Tranny' Is a Form of Hate Speech." *The Gender Blender Blog*, 1 Apr 2009. Retrieved March 2016, https://thegenderblenderblog.wordpress.com/2009/04/01/tranny-is-a-form-of-hate-speech/

39. James Nichols. "RuPaul Responds to Controversy Over the Word Tranny." *The Huffington Post*, 22 May 2014. Retrieved March 2016, http://www.huffingtonpost.com/2014/05/22/rupaul-responds-tranny_n_5374897.html

40. Kate Bornstein. "Tranny, Revisited by Auntie Kate." *Queer and Pleasant Danger Blog*, 25 May 2014. Retrieved March 2016, http://katebornstein.typepad.com/kate_bornsteins_blog/2014/05/tranny-revisited-by-auntie-kate.html

41. Amy Sun. "Let's Talk About Domestic Violence in the Trans* Community." *Everyday Feminism*, 25 Mar 2014. Retrieved March 2016, http://everydayfeminism.com/2014/03/domestic-violence-trans-community

42. *International Trans Day of Remembrance*. Retrieved March 2016, http://tdor.info

43. "Alarming Figures: Over 1,700 Trans People Killed in the Last 7 Years." *Trans Respect Versus Transphobia Worldwide*, 8 May 2015. Retrieved March 2016, http://www.transrespect-transphobia.org/en_US/tvt-project/tmm-results/idahot-2015.htm

44. Jenna Garrett. "Agender: Portraits of young people who identify as neither male or female." *Feature Shoot*, 19 Mar 2014. Retrieved March 2016, http://www.featureshoot.com/2014/05/chloe-aftel

45. "Hate Violence against Lesbian, Gay, Bisexual, and Transgender People in the United States." *National Coalition of Anti-Violence Programs*, 2008. Retrieved March 2016, http://www.ncavp.org/common/document_files/Reports/2008%20HV%20Report%20smaller%20file.pdf

46. Dan Arel. "Attorney: Transgender murder victim's life worth less than 'high class' victim." *Pantheos*, 22 Oct 2015. Retrieved March 2016, http://www.patheos.com/blogs/danthropology/2015/10/attorney-argues-that-a-transgender-murder-victims-life-is-worth-less-than-a-higher-class-victim/

47. Meredith Talusan. "The Failed Logic of "Trans Panic" Criminal Defenses." *BuzzFeed*, 25 Aug 2015, Retrieved March 2016, www.buzzfeed.com/meredithtalusan/trans-panic-criminal-defense

48. Parker Marie Molloy. "California Becomes First State to Bag Gay, Trans 'Panic' Defenses." *Advocate*, 29 Sept 2015. Retrieved March 2016, www.advocate.com/crime/2014/09/29/california-becomes-first-state-ban-gay-trans-panic-defenses

49. "Obama Signs Trans-Inclusive Hate Crimes Law." *Massachusetts Transgender Political Coalition*, 28 Oct 2009. Retrieved March 2016, http://www.masstpc.org/massachusetts-transgender-political-coalition-praises-federal-hate-crimes-law-signing/

50. "Hate Crime Laws." *Transgender Law & Policy Institute*. Retrieved March 2016, http://www.transgenderlaw.org/hatecrimelaws/index.htm

51. Emily Gogolak. "Profiled by NYPD, Transgender People in New York Fear Carrying Condoms." *The Village Voice*, 7 Mar 2013. Retrieved March 2016, http://www.villagevoice.com/news/profiled-by-nypd-transgendered-people-in-new-york-fear-carrying-condoms-6663034

52. Ani Uncar. "In the Gay Wing of L.A. Men's Central Jail, It's Not Shanks and Muggings but Hand-Sewn Gowns and Tears." *LA Weekly*, 18 Nov 2014. Retrieved March 2016, http://www.laweekly.com/news/in-the-gay-wing-of-la-mens-central-jail-its-not-shanks-and-muggings-but-hand-sewn-gowns-and-tears-5218552

53. Kylar W. Broadus and Shannon Price Minter. "Chapter 10: Legal Issues." From Laura Erickson-Schroth, ed. *Trans Bodies, Trans Selves: A Resource Guide for the Transgender Community*. Oxford, England: Oxford University Press, 2014.

54. "Italy's Transgender Prison: Safety or Segregation." *Gender Across Borders*, 19 Jan 2010. Retrieved March 2016, http://www.genderacrossborders.com/2010/01/19/italys-transgender-prison-safety-or-segregation

55. Aviva Stahl. "The Horrors Endured by Transgender Women in Prison." *Alternet*, 7 Aug 2014. Retrieved March 2016, http://www.alternet.org/horrors-endured-transgender-women-prison

56. Andrew Harmon. "Eight months in solidarity: Is a government turf war over immigration putting transgender lives at risk." *The Advocate*, 7 May 2012. Retrieved March 2016, from http://www.advocate.com/news/news-features/2012/05/07/transgender-detainees-face-challenges-broken-immigration-system

57. Johanna-Alice Cooke. "Second Transwoman Dies in Male Prison." *KaleidoScot*, 2 Dec 2015. Retrieved March 2016, http://www.kaleidoscot.com/second-transwoman-dies-male-prison-5888

58. "Homeless Youth." *National Coalition for the Homeless*, June 2008. Retrieved March 2016, http://www.nationalhomeless.org/factsheets/youth.html

59. "Supporting Your LGBTQ Youth: A Guide for Foster Parents." *Child Welfare Information Gateway*. Retrieved March 2016, https://www.childwelfare.gov/pubPDFs/LGBTQyouth.pdf

60. Leela Ginelle. "In the World's Most Lethal Country for Trans People, a Brutal Beating Sparks Protest." *Bitch Media*, 30 Apr 2015. Retrieved March 2016, https://bitchmedia.org/post/in-the-worlds-most-dangerous-country-for-trans-people-a-brutal-beating-sparks-protest

Chapter 9: Challenges and Communities

1. Delfin Bautista and Quince Mountain with Health Mackenzie Reynolds. "Religion and Spirituality." From Laura Erickson-Schroth, ed. *Trans Bodies, Trans Selves: A Resource Guide for the Transgender Community*. Oxford University Press, 2014.

2. Raven Kaldera. *Hermaphrodieties: The Transgender Spirituality Workbook*. Asphodel Press, 2010.

3. Koa Beck. "The Trouble With 'Passing' for Another Race/Sexuality/Religion ..." *The Guardian*, 2 Jan 2014. Retrieved March 2016, http://www.theguardian.com/commentisfree/2014/jan/02/trouble-with-passing-race-sexuality-religion

4. Abe Forman-Greenwald. "'I'm a Guy.'" *BuzzFeed*, 22 Sept 2014. Retrieved March 2016, www.buzzfeed.com/abefg/what-its-like-to-be-transgender-without-transitioning

5. "Trans-exclusionary Radical Feminism." *RationalWiki*. Retrieved March 2016, http://rationalwiki.org/wiki/Trans-exclusionary_radical_feminism

6. "Germaine Greer: Transgender women are 'not women.'" *BBC News*, 24 Oct 2015. Retrieved March 2016, http://www.bbc.com/news/uk-34625512

7. Niveen Nabulsi, Brittney Mikrut and Alondra Ibarra. "Systematic Oppression." *Prezi*, 5 Dec 2012. Retrieved March 2016, https://prezi.com/fjdvhirx6e4s/systematic-oppression/

8. Carol Cheney, Jeannie LaFrance and Terrie Quinteros. "Institutionalized Oppression Definitions." From *Tools for Diversity*, Tri-County Domestic & Sexual Violence Intervention Network Anti-Oppression Training for Trainers, 2006. Retrieved March 2016, http://www.pcc.edu/resources/illumination/documents/institutionalized-oppression-definitions.pdf

9. Jaime M. Grant, Lisa A. Mottet, and Justin Tannis, with Jack Harrison, Jody Herman and Mara Keisling. "Injustice at every turn: A report of the national transgender discrimination survey." *National Center for Transgender Equality and National Gay and Lesbian Task Force*, 2011. Retrieved March 2016, http://www.thetaskforce.org/static_html/downloads/reports/reports/ntds_full.pdf

10. "HIV Among Transgender People." *Centers for Disease Control and Prevention*. Retrieved March 2016, http://www.cdc.gov/hiv/group/gender/transgender/index.html

11. *International Trans Day of Remembrance*. Retrieved March 2016, http://tdor.info

12. Jon Swaine. "Black Americans killed by police twice as likely to be unarmed as white people." *The Guardian*, 1 Jun 2015. Retrieved March 2016, http://www.theguardian.com/us-news/2015/jun/01/black-americans-killed-by-police-analysis

13. National Black Justice Coalition. Retrieved March 2016, http://nbjc.org

14. Trans People of Color Coalition. Retrieved March 2016, http://www.transpoc.org

15. "Resources and Support for Transgender Immigrants." *Lambda Legal.* Retrieved March 2016, http://www.lambdalegal.org/know-your-rights/ transgender/resources-trans-immigrants

16. "Two Spirit Resource Center." *Native OUT.* Retrieved March 2016, http://nativeout.com/twospirit-rc/

17. Ashley Mog and Amanda Lock Swarr. "Threads of Commonality in Transgender and Disability Studies." *Disability Studies Quarterly*, Fall 2008. Retrieved March 2016, http://dsq-sds.org/article/view/152/152

18. Planet DeafQueer. Retrieved March 2016, http://planet.deafqueer.com

19. Laura A. Jacobs, Katherine Rachin, Laura Erickson-Schroth, and Aron Janssen. "Gender Dysphoria and Co-Occurring Autism Spectrum Disorders: Review, Case Examples, and Treatment Considerations." *LGBT Health*, 2014. Retrieved March 2016, http://www.academia.edu/8037960/ Gender_Dysphoria_and_Co-Occurring_Autism_Spectrum_Disorders_ Review_Case_Examples_and_Treatment_Considerations

20. Sola Agustsson. "What My Female-Born Transgender Autistic Brother Can Teach You About How We Construct Our Identities." *Alternet*, 24 Apr 2015. Retrieved March 2016, http://www.alternet.org/personal-health/what-my- female-born-transgender-autistic-brother-can-teach-you-about-how-we

21. Jaime M. Grant, Lisa A. Mottet, and Justin Tannis, with Jack Harrison, Jody Herman and Mara Keisling. "Injustice at every turn: A report of the national transgender discrimination survey." *National Center for Transgender Equality and National Gay and Lesbian Task Force.* 2011. Retrieved March 2016, http://www.thetaskforce.org/static_html/ downloads/reports/reports/ntds_full.pdf

22. Zack Ford. "Salvation Army Refuses Housing Shelter to Transgender Woman." *Think Progress*, 4 May 2014. Retrieved March 2016, http:// thinkprogress.org/lgbt/2014/05/04/3433957/salvation-army-transgender- shelter/

23. Lisa Mottet and John M. Ohle. "Transitioning Our Shelters: A Guide to Making Homeless Shelters Safe for Transgender People." *National Gay and Lesbian Task Force Policy Institute: National Coalition for the Homeless*, 2003. Retrieved March 2016, http://srlp.org/wp-content/ uploads/2012/08/TransitioningOurShelters.pdf

24. "Shelter for All Genders: Best Practices for Homeless Shelters, Services, and Programs in Massachusetts in Serving Transgender Adults and Gender Non-Conforming Guests." *Massachusetts Transgender Political Coalition Policy Committee*, Dec 2013. Retrieved March 2016, http://www. masstpc.org/wp-content/uploads/2012/10/Shelter-for-all-Genders.pdf

25. We Happy Trans. Retrieved March 2016, http://wehappytrans.com

26. Transobriety Yahoo Group. Retrieved March 2016, https://groups.yahoo. com/neo/groups/transobriety/info

27. TransMentors International. Retrieved March 2016, http://transmentors.org

28. Guy Trebay. "Legends of the Ball." *The Village Voice*, 11 Jan 2000. Retrieved March 2016, http://www.villagevoice.com/news/legends-of-the-ball-6395676

29. Rebecca Smyene. "Welcome to the Kiki Ball: The Next Gen Ballroom Scene." *Fader*, 13 Nov 2014. Retrieved March 2016, http://www.thefader. com/2014/11/13/kiki-ball-photo-essay

30. *International Trans Day of Remembrance*. Retrieved March 2016, http://tdor.info

31. "Trans Murder Monitoring." *Trans Respect Versus Transphobia Worldwide*. Retrieved March 2016, http://transrespect.org/en/research/trans-murder-monitoring/

32. Nillin Dennison. "TDoR 2015: Memorial List of 27 Reported Deaths by Suicide." *Planet Transgender*, 16 Nov 2015. Retrieved March 2016, http:// planettransgender.com/tdor-2015-memorial-list-27-reported-deaths-suicide/

33. "Trans Day of Action for Social and Economic Justice – Points of Unity." *The Audre Lorde Project*. Retrieved March 2016, http://alp.org/tdoa_pou

34. Paul Bedard. "Massive LGBT 'civil disobedience' immigration protest for D.C., border detention centers." *Washington Examiner*, 9 Sept 2014. Retrieved March 2016, http://www.washingtonexaminer.com/massive-lgbt-civil-disobedience-immigration-protest-for-d.c.-border-detention-centers/article/2553073

35. "Our Moment for Reform: Immigration and Transgender People." *National Center for Transgender Equality*, 4 Oct 2013. Retrieved March 2016, http://www.transequality.org/issues/resources/our-moment-reform-immigration-and-transgender-people

36. "Why Marriage Matters to Transgender Persons." *Freedom to Marry*. Retrieved March 2016, http://www.freedomtomarry.org/communities/ entry/c/transgender

37. Jamilah King. "Meet the Trans Women of Color Who Helped Put Stonewall on the Map." *Mic*, 25 Jun 2015. http://mic.com/ articles/121256/meet-marsha-p-johnson-and-sylvia-rivera-transgender-stonewall-veterans

38. Amanda Michaels. "The Compton Riots." *TGLife*, 20 Sept 2011. Retrieved March 2016, http://tgreporter.com/index.php/history/ item/132-compton-riots

39. Deron Dalton. "How 4 Black Lives Matter Activists Handle Queerness and Trans Issues." *The Daily Dot*, 11 Oct 2015. Retrieved March 2016, http://www.dailydot.com/politics/black-lives-matter-queer-trans-issues/

40. David Badash. "Occupy Wall Street: NYPD Chains Transgender Man to Jail Restroom For 8 Hours." *The New Civil Rights Movement*, 4 Oct 2011. Retrieved March 2016, http://www.thenewcivilrightsmovement.com/ occupy-wall-street-nypd-chains-transgender-man-to-jail-restroom-for-8-hours/discrimination/2011/10/04/27860

41. Trans Lifeline. Retrieved March 2016, http://www.translifeline.org

42. The Trevor Project. Retrieved March 2016, http://www.thetrevorproject.org

Chapter 10: Being a Trans Ally

1. Parents, Families, Friends, and Allies United with LGBTQ People (PFLAG). Retrieved March, 2016, http://community.pflag.org

2. "Glossary." *Advocates for Youth*. Retrieved March 2016, http://www. advocatesforyouth.org/index.php?option=com_content&task=view&id= 607&Itemid=177

3. "Gender Pronouns." *Lesbian, Gay, Bisexual, Transgender Resource Center of the University of Milwaukee*. Retrieved March 2016, http://uwm.edu/ lgbtrc/support/gender-pronouns/

4. Akilah Huges. "Racial Discussion Fatigue Syndrome #RDFS" *YouTube*, 17 July 2015. Retrieved March 2016, https://m.youtube.com/ watch?v=j6Kcsm5wp-4

5. Mel Reiff Hill, Jay Mays and Robin Mack. *The Gender Book, 2013*. Marshall House Press. Retrieved March 2016, http://www. TheGenderbook.com

6. Skype Brown. "Trans* 101 For Significant Others, Partners, Friends, Family, and Allies (SOFFAs) of Trans* People." Retrieved March 2016, http://www.kinseyinstitute.org/resources/pdf/Trans101forSOFFAs_v4.pdf

7. "Our Trans Loved Ones: Questions and Answers for Parents, Families, and Friends of People Who Are Transgender and Gender Expansive." *PFLAG*. Retrieved March 2016, http://community.pflag.org/document. doc?id=921

8. John Oliver. "Transgender Rights." *Last Week Tonight with John Oliver*, 28 Jun 2015. Retrieved March 2016, https://www.youtube.com/ watch?v=hmoAX9f6MOc

9. Crystal Waterton. "Trans Being Human (Mature)." Retrieved March 2016, https://vimeo.com/149715056

10. "Transgender FAQ." *GLADD*. Retrieved March 2016, http://www.glaad. org/transgender/transfaq

11. Seth Adams and Matt Goodman. "Number of Americans who report knowing a transgender person doubles in seven years according to new GLAAD survey." *GLAAD*, 17 Sept 2015. Retrieved March 2016, http://www.glaad.org/releases/number-americans-who-report-knowing-transgender-person-doubles-seven-years-according-new]

12. Liz Halloran. "Survey Shows Striking Increase in Americans Who Know and Support Transgender People." *Human Rights Campaign*, 24 April 2015. Retrieved March 2016, http://www.hrc.org/blog/survey-shows-striking-increase-in-americans-who-know-and-support-transgende

13. Dominic Holden. "South Dakota Becomes First State To Pass Anti-Transgender Student Restroom Bill." BuzzFeed News, 16 Feb 2016. Retrieved March 2016, http://www.buzzfeed.com/en/south-dakota-becomes-first-state-to-pass-anti-transgender-st

14. Camp Aranu'tiq. Retrieved March 2016, http://www.camparanutiq.org

15. Camp Ten Trees. Retrieved March 2016, http://camptentrees.org

16. Eli R. Green, PhD. "6 Questions For Allies to Consider When Facilitating Transgender Training." *The Teaching Transgender Toolkit*, 3 Oct 2015. Retrieved March 2016, http://www.teachingtransgender.org/facilitating-transgender-trainings-as-a-cisgender-ally/

17. "Trans Lobby Day Debrief." *National Center for Transgender Equality*. Retrieved March 2016, https://transgenderequality.wordpress.com/2013/06/27/trans-lobby-day-debrief/

18. Jos Truitt. "Tennessee Anti-Transgender Bill Defeated By Voices of Young Trans People." *Feministing*, 22 March 2016. Retrieved March 2016, http://feministing.com/2016/03/22/tennessee-anti-transgender-bill-defeated-by-the-voices-of-young-trans-people/

Acknowledgements

Twenty-two years ago, a young man went to his first therapist's appointment, encouraged to do so by his mother. She said that if he needed to explore the topic of gender transition, she'd do everything she could to support him. This was the book that I wish that the two of them had at their disposal. This book has brewed in the back of my mind for some time, because it is the book I wish my mother and I had available to us; a book I could have handed to my doctor (who was unsure how to proceed), my therapist (who was unkind on a number of levels), my father (who didn't cope well), and my teachers (who just assumed it was part of my artistic streak).

I was lucky. My gender journey has taken me on a wild ride; baby designated female at birth to androgynous youth; gender curious trans teen boy to high femme adventurer; polygender being to transman; and now thriving as a metrosexual man... this is a book I wish I'd had along the way. At times the journey felt so alone.

My hope is this book can help someone – even one person – not feel so alone.

With my laptop, and too many hours in my office or coffee shops, this project began to form thanks to Butterfly, Coral Mallow, David Wraith, and others who actively encouraged me to make it happen. And then? Thanks to Andy Izenson, I read *decolonizing trans/gender 101* by b. binaohan. The author kicked my ass. The fault in my work had been that, like other authors who have been publishing on this topic, I came from a Caucasian, American, English-speaking perspective, and has access to health care. That does not make me a bad person, but it made me really examine how to make voices beyond mine heard, and acknowledge the privilege I carry. It took a lot of sweat, and tears, to make this book happen. I also know that no single book can, or will, speak to (and for) everyone. My hope is that this will help some of these dialogues forward, or at least not make them worse.

This project could not have happened alone. My partner, Butterfly, gave me the space to write, edit, write again, edit again, complain on occasion, and share my delight when little joys came along. She even gave me support when I cried. Through her urging me along, it made me stick to my guns… and also convinced me not to have it be a 400-page project, so that folks could actually read the whole thing.

Since my legal and medical transition a decade ago, I've also been blessed by having hundreds of people share their stories with me in person, plus thousands through their writing, and lots of online conversations. I want to thank all of you for your intimacy, vulnerability, ideas, and feedback along the way. Partners, friends, and allies of trans and gender nonconforming individuals, also spoke up – much needed perspectives indeed.

During the process, Dr. Martha Tara Lee gave me a platform to explore the topic of trans issues on her podcast, *Eros Evolution*, which offered great clarity. Teaching on the topic at the University of Anchorage in Alaska and at the *Sex Down South Conference* also let me test-run Chapter 1, with *Sex Down South* also giving me insights into gender and cultural experiences I would have never had otherwise. Thank you all.

My readers were also invaluable. Deborah Addington, Spencer Bergstedt, Michael Eric Brown; Butterfly, Roan Coughtry, Dossie Easton, Alexa Kelley, Xander McDonald, Dani Meir, Dylan Richards, and Elena Rose, gave diverse perspectives which I was able to incorporate, which I am grateful for. Coral Mallow, however, made me go back and reconsider and reorganize large swaths of the book, for which I (and all of you, most likely), find to have been a great gift.

Once you have a book in hand, it needs a lot of massage. Rounds of massage… also known as editing. The book that went to readers was cleared up by the wonderful Jess Menton, and the final work received the delightful and caring eye of Lisa Fox. Thank you both for being both kind and vigilant. Rob River, on the other hand, manifested the book's layout, inside and out. He continues to amaze me, many projects later, in his quality of work, and his compassion.

In an email from an autistic reader, I was asked why I didn't include artwork in the book I sent them. Night one I fretted and vented that I couldn't do it. Night two I put out the call. Through a Facebook surprise, I connected with the talented Andi Fogt, who not only took my notes and brought them to life, but took feedback when needed, and made magic happen. You are a blessing and delight.

This book could only happen with courage of trans and gender nonconforming people who have shared their stories with me and with the world; the transmen and genderpunks I connected with back in the 90s; those who have shared their journeys with the whole world; people who post their anonymous vulnerability on the internet; and every day activists who share their beauty by simply being themselves. It was also made possibly through Bear, whom I do all of my work for, and the watchful eye of Djehuty, who kept me in line. And of course, my mother, Bonnie Kay Jauregui, who gave me space to be myself.

Let us remember those who died to young. Let us build up the next generation to have it better than we did. Let us support one another.

Let us remember that none of us are alone.

With much love,

Lee Harrington
Anchorage, Alaska
March 2016

Glossary

This glossary is intended to support your exploration of the world of transgender issues and various gender journeys. Remember that terminology frequently morphs within gender and sexuality communities, and a word that means one thing in amongst one group of individuals, may mean something else amongst another group.

For items with multiple definitions, any or all may apply to different individuals, circumstances, or situations. Related terms have also been listed, some of which are synonyms, while others are related concepts. Terms that are defined elsewhere in the glossary appear in italics.

Agender – A *gender identity* that includes a genderless state, or no personal experience of *gender*. (Related terms: Genderless; *Gender Neutral*; *Neutrois*; Non-Gender; None of the Above; Null-Gender)

Aggressive – A *gender identity* for an individual *designated female at birth*, that is *female* identified, and purposefully presents as *masculine*. Used most commonly in communities of color. (Related terms: Ag; *Butch*; Stud)

Ally – An individual who supports, and advocates for, individuals and/or communities other than their own.

Alphabet Soup – A synonym for *LGBTQQIAA*, *QUILTBAG*, and other gender and sexuality acronyms.

Androgynous – [1] A *gender identity* blending *male* and *female*, *masculine* and *feminine*, or devoid of specifically gendered traits. [2] Visually appearing to blend *masculine* and *feminine* traits, or be devoid of specifically gendered traits.

Asexual – [1] An *orientation* in which an individual does not experience any *sexual orientation* or attraction. (Related term: ACE) [2] A time period in an individual's life during which they do not experience any sexual attraction, or interest in *sex*.

Assigned Gender – The *gender* given at birth, most often based on the visible expression of *primary sex traits*.

Ballroom – An *LGBTQQIAA* subculture where people compete in dance and *gender performance* at balls, known for their diverse *gender expression*. (Related terms: Ball Scene; *Drag*; KiKi; Vogue)

Bigender – A *gender identity* that includes, or alternates between, two *genders*. Most commonly, someone who identifies as being both *male* and *female*. (Related terms: Dual Gender; Mixed Gender; Multi Gender; *Omnigender*; *Pangender*; Polygender)

Binding – The act of using compression garments or materials to minimize the visibility of mammary tissue.

Birth Sex – The *sex* assigned by medical providers at birth, most often based on the visible expression of *primary sex traits*, or chromosomes. (Related terms: *Assigned Gender*; *Natal Sex*)

Bisexual – A *sexual orientation* to both *genders*. (Related terms: Bi; *Pansexual*)

Body Dysmorphia – A psychological disorder characterized by body-based dissonance, and obsession, with an incongruent form, or part, of their body; causing regular, and ongoing, emotional and psychological distress.

Boi – A *gender identity*, or personal identity, used by a variety of individuals, including *trans men*, *masculine of center* individuals, *gay* men, and *lesbians*. (Related terms: *Aggressive*; *Butch*; Stud)

Bottom Surgery – Slang for lower body surgeries available *trans* and *gender nonconforming* individuals. (Related terms: Gender Confirmation Surgery (GCS); *Gender Reaffirmation Surgery*; *Gender Reassignment Surgery (GRS)*; Sex Confirmation Surgery (SCS); *Sex Change Operation*; *Sexual Reassignment Surgery* (SRS))

Butch – [1] A *gender identity* for an individual *designated female at birth*, that is *female* identified, and purposefully presents as *masculine*. [2] A gender identity for any individual that purposefully presents as distinctly masculine. Both are used most commonly in *lesbian*, *gay*, *homosexual*, and *queer* communities. (Related terms: *Aggressive*; Stud)

CD – An acronym for *crossdresser*.

Chest Surgery – Upper body surgeries available to *trans men* and *gender nonconforming* individuals *designated female at birth*. (Related terms: *Double Mastectomy*; Keyhole Surgery; Reconstructive Chest Surgery; *Top Surgery*; Torso Reconstruction Surgery)

Chican@ – A *gender identity*, or umbrella term, for *transgender* and *gender nonconforming* individuals of Mexican descent. (Related term: Chicana/o)

Cisgender – An individual whose *assigned gender* aligns with their *gender identity*. (Related terms: Cis; Cissexual; Non-transsexual)

Cisgender Privilege – The advantages given to an individual by culture, because they are *cisgender*, or perceived to be *cisgender*.

Cisgenderism – A form of bigotry, or marginalization, against *trans* people, based on an assumption that *cisgender* people are superior to *transgender* people. (Related terms: Transprejudice; Transphobia)

Cisnormative – The cultural assumption that being *cisgender* is the norm, or the appropriate way to exist.

Conversion Therapy – Systems that, in the guise of mental health, attempt to have *trans* and *gender nonconforming* individuals overcome their *gender identity* or desire to transition. These systems have never proven effective, and are considered harmful to *trans* and *gender nonconforming* individuals. (Related term: Reparative Therapy)

Conscious Gender Exploration – Engaging in, and bringing personal awareness to, various forms of *gender expression*, *gender performance*, and *gender identity*.

Crossdresser – An individual who engages in *crossdressing* on a regular or ongoing basis. (Related terms: *CD*; *Transvestite*)

Crossdressing – The act of wearing clothes classically designated, by the culture you are part of, as being for the opposite *sex*.

Designated Female at Birth – An individual whose *assigned gender* was *female*. (Related terms: Assigned Female at Birth (AFAB); *DFAB*; Female Assigned at Birth (FAAB))

Designated Male at Birth – An individual whose *assigned gender* was *male*. (Related terms: Assigned Male at Birth (AMAB); *DMAB*; Male Assigned at Birth (MAAB))

Demigender – A *gender identity* that is a specific *gender*, except in certain insistences.

DFAB – An acronym for *designated female at birth*.

Disclose – [1] To share personal information. [2] To share one's *transgender* status or history with another individual or group of people.

DMAB – An acronym for *designated male at birth*.

Drag – [1] The act of *crossdressing*, and adopting exaggerated *gendered behaviors*, to transform into a personal identity, persona or character. [2] A community of individuals and performers that adopt exaggerated *gendered behaviors*, to transform into various personal identities, personas, or characters. (Related terms: Ball Scene; *Ballroom*; *Drag King*; *Drag Queen*; Diva; *Female Impersonator*; *Male Impersonator*)

Drag King – An individual who does *drag*, taking on a *male* persona or *masculine* traits, whose *gender identity* is usually *female*. (Related terms: *Faux King*; *Male Impersonator*)

Drag Queen – An individual who does *drag*, taking on a *female* persona or *feminine* traits, whose *gender identity* is usually *male*. (Related terms: *Faux Queen*; *Female Impersonator*)

DSM – An acronym for the *Diagnostic and Statistical Manual of Mental Health Disorders*, published by the American Psychiatric Association, used by mental health providers, researchers, insurance companies, and the legal system.

Double Mastectomy – The medical term for the surgical removal of both breasts, partially or completely. (Related terms: *Chest Surgery*; Keyhole Surgery; Reconstructive Chest Surgery; *Top Surgery;* Torso Reconstructive Surgery)

Dysphoria – See *Gender Dysphoria*.

F2M – An acronym for *female-to-male*. (Related terms: *Female-to-Male*; *FtM*; FTM; *Man*; *Transgender*; *Trans Man*; *Transman*; *Transsexual*)

Faux King – A *drag king* whose *gender identity*, when not in *drag*, is *male*. (Related term: Bio King)

Faux Queen – A *drag queen* whose *gender identity* when not in *drag* is *female*. (Related term: Bio Queen)

Female – [1] The *sex* assigned by medical providers at birth, most often based on the presence of a vagina, or in the case of genetic testing, XX chromosomes. [2] An *assigned gender*, usually determined based on the presence of a vagina. [3] A multi-factorial social construct based on *assigned gender*, *gender presentation*, *perceived gender*, and/or *gender identity*.

Female Impersonator – [1] A *drag queen* taking on an exaggerated mimicking of a specific *woman*, usually one of fame or notoriety, as a form of performance. [2] A simplistic, or offensive, term for *drag queens*.

Female-to-Male – An individual that was *designated female at birth*, whose *gender identity* is *male*. (Related terms: *F2M*; *FtM*; FTM; *Man*; Trans Boy; *Transgender*, *Trans Man*; *Transman*; *Transsexual*)

Feminine – The archetypal activities, behaviors, dress, mannerisms, presentation, traits, style, and other *gendered behaviors* associated with women in a culture, or considered socially appropriate in that culture. (Related term: *Femininity*)

Feminine of Center – An individual whose *gender identity*, or *gender performance*, is closer to *female* than *male* along the *gender spectrum*. (Related term: Female of Center)

Femininity – Performance of *feminine* traits or behaviors.

FtM – An acronym for a *female-to-male transgender* or *transsexual* person. (Related terms: *Female-to-Male*; *F2M*; FTM; *Man*; *Transgender*; *Trans Man*; *Transman*; *Transsexual*)

Femme – [1] A *gender identity* for an individual *designated female at birth*, that is *female* identified, and purposefully presents as distinctly *feminine*. [2] A *gender identity* for any individual that purposefully presents as distinctly *feminine*. Both are used most commonly in *lesbian*, *gay*, *homosexual*, and *queer* communities.

Filipin@ – A *gender identity*, or umbrella term, for *transgender* and *gender nonconforming* individuals of Filipino descent. (Related term: Filipina/o)

Gay – [1] A *sexual orientation* towards men, used by men. [2] A romantic *orientation* towards men, used by men. [3] A *sexual orientation* used by *homosexual* individuals of all *genders*. [4] A community, cultural, or social identity denoted by specific speech patterns, mannerisms, tastes in media, and iconography. [5] A synonym for happy or joyous. (Related terms: *Homosexual*; *Lesbian*; *Queer*)

Gatekeeper – Slang for a mental health provider, medical provider, or insurance company, whose approval is needed to approve *hormone replacement therapy*, or various surgeries.

GD – An acronym for *Gender Dysphoria*.

Gender – A multi-factorial social construct that ascribes individuals as being *feminine, masculine, androgynous*, etc.

Gender Archetypes – Stereotypical *gender roles*, personalities, and personas, within a culture.

Gender Bending – [1] Combining *masculine, feminine*, and *androgynous* traits, to create a *gender presentation* beyond *female* or *male*, often through makeup, hair styling, or wardrobe. [2] Shifting between forms of *gender expression, gender performance*, or *gender identity*.

Gender Binary – The concept that there are only two *genders* – *male* and *female*.

Gender Conformity – To have an individual's *gender expression* align with a culture's *gender norms*.

Gender Diverse – A synonym for *gender variant*.

Gender Dysphoria – [1] A medical disorder from the *Diagnostic and Statistical Manual of Mental Health Disorders* (*DSM*). [2] Experiencing *birth sex* to not being in alignment with *gender identity*, causing emotional and psychological distress. (Related term: *Body Dysmorphia; GD*)

Gender Expression – [1] The *gender identity*, or *perceived gender*, that an individual communicates through their *gender performance*. [2] The signifiers a person uses to determine another person's *gender*. (Related terms: *Gender Performance*; *Gender Presentation*)

Gender Expansive – A synonym for *gender variant* or *gender nonconforming*.

Gender Fluid – [1] A *gender identity* marked by having no single fixed point. [2] A *gender identity* that is outside of the *gender binary*. (Related terms: *Gender Bending*; Gender Flexible; Gender Non-binary; *Genderqueer*)

Gender History – An individual's pre-transition *gender*. (Related term: *Transgender Experience*)

Gender Identity – An individual's internal, or psychological, experience of their own *gender*.

Gender Identity Disorder – A psychiatric disorder from a former publication of the *Diagnostic and Statistical Manual of Mental Health Disorders* (*DSM*-4), used to describe a person with significant *gender dysphoria*. (Related terms: *Gender Dysphoria*; *GD*; *GID*)

Gender Neutral – [1] Spaces that are inclusive of all individuals, such as *gender* neutral bathrooms. [2] Terminology used to refer to individuals and relationships that is inclusive of all individuals, such as "they" or "partner." [3] A *gender identity* that includes a genderless state, or no personal experience of *gender*. (Related terms: *Agender*; Genderless; *Neutrois*; Non-Gender; None of the Above; Mx.) [4] A style of *gender presentation* that does not express any specific *gender*.

Gender Neutral Pronouns – *Pronouns* used to reference an individual, other than their name, other than he/him/his or she/her/hers.

Gender Nonconforming – [1] A *gender identity* for individuals whose *gender expression* or experience is beyond the *gender binary*, or cultural *gender norms*. [2] An umbrella term *genders* or identities beyond the *gender binary*. (Related terms: *Gender Diverse*; *Gender Expansive*; *Gender Variant*; *Genderqueer*; *Trans*; *Trans**)

Gender Norms – Cultural expectations that an individual's *gender expression* and behaviors will be in alignment with their *assigned gender* and/or *perceived gender*.

Gender Performance – The wardrobe, styling, mannerisms, movement, name, activities, and actions an individual uses, or engages in, that express their *gender identity* or *perceived gender*. (Related terms: *Gender Expression*; *Gender Presentation*)

Gender Presentation – A synonym for *gender expression.*

Gender Privilege – The advantages given to an individual by culture, because of their *gender,* or *perceived gender.*

Gender, Sexual, and Romantic Minorities – A descriptor inclusive of LGBTQQIAA populations, alternative sexual practices, and relationship structures beyond monogamy. (Related terms: *Alphabet Soup*; *LGBT*; LGBTIQ; LGBTQQAAI; *LGBTQQIAA*; GLBT; *GSRM*; *QUILTBAG*; Sexual and Gender Diversity)

Gendered Behaviors – Activities and styles of expression, that a culture has determined by a culture to be appropriate for specific *genders.* (Related term: *Gender Roles*)

Genderqueer – [1] A *gender identity* for individuals outside of the culturally expected, or assumed, *gender binary.* [2] A combination of two or more *genders identities.* [3] An individual who falls between *cisgender* and *transgender.* [4] *Gender expression* or performance outside of culturally expected *gender norms.* (Related terms: *Gender Diverse*; *Gender Expansive*; Gender Fabulous; *Gender Nonconforming*; *Gender Variant*; *Trans*; *Trans**)

Gender Reaffirming Surgery – Surgical procedures performed to gonad or genital structure to create an aesthetic, or function, closer in alignment to a person's *gender identity.* (Related terms: *Bottom Surgery*; Gender Confirmation Surgery (GCS); *Gender Reassignment Surgery*; GRS; Sex Confirmation Surgery (SCS); *Sex Change Operation*; Sexual Reassignment Surgery (SRS))

Gender Reassignment Surgery – A synonym for *gender reaffirming surgery.*

Gender Roles – The behaviors, dress, activities, and ways of thinking, ascribed to specific genders in a culture. (Related terms: *Gendered Behaviors*; *Gender Performance*)

Gender Spectrum – The concept that there are many *genders* ranging between *female* and *male.*

Gender Variant – A *gender identity* for those who do not conform to cultural expectations of *gender.* (Related terms: *Gender Diverse*; *Gender Expansive*; *Gender Nonconforming*; *Genderqueer*; *Trans*; *Trans**)

GID – An acronym for *Gender Identity Dysphoria.*

GRS – An acronym for *gender reaffirmation surgery,* or *gender reassignment surgery.*

GSRM – An acronym for *Gender, Sexuality, and Romantic Minorities*.

Heteroflexible – A *sexual orientation* towards those of the opposite *gender* in most, but not all, situations. (Related term: *MSM*)

Heteronormative – The cultural assumption that being *cisgender*, as well as only attracted to the opposite *sex*, is the norm, or is the appropriate way to exist.

Heterosexual – A sexual or romantic *orientation* toward those of the opposite *gender*. (Related term: Straight)

Hermaphrodite – [1] A historical term for *intersex* individuals. [2] An offensive term for *intersex* individuals. [3] A reference to the god Hermaphroditus in Greek mythology.

Homoflexible – A *sexual orientation* towards those of the same *gender* in most, but not all, situations.

Homosexual – A sexual or romantic *orientation* towards those of the same *gender*. (Related terms: *Gay*; *Lesbian*; *MSM*)

Hormone Blockers – Medications used to reduce the levels of a specific hormone in the body, sometimes in conjunction with *hormone replacement therapy*. (Related term: *Puberty Blockers*)

Hormone Replacement Therapy – Medications used to supplement a lack of specific hormones in the body, or to supplement one hormone in the body with another. (Related term: *Hormone Blockers*; *HRT*)

HRT – An acronym for *hormone replacement therapy*.

IaoPoC – An acronym for indigenous individuals and/or people of color.

Informed Consent – [1] To understand the risks and ramifications of a choice being made. [2] A model of care for *transgender*, *intersex*, and *gender nonconforming* people, that states that permission to modify a person's body should be up to that individual, and not require mental health provider approval.

Intersex – An individual born with the sexual anatomy, reproductive organs, or chromosomes that do not adhere to the medical category of *male* or *female*. (Related term: Disorders of Sex Development (DSDs))

In the Closet – Keeping one's *sexual orientation*, *gender*, or *gender history* private, or un-disclosed.

Latin@ – A *gender identity*, or umbrella term, for *transgender* and *gender nonconforming* individuals of Latin American descent. (Related terms: Latina/o; Latinx; Translatina; Translatino)

Lesbian – [1] A sexual or romantic *orientation* towards women, used by women. (Related term: *Homosexual*) [2] A community, political, or social identity denoted by a distain of *male*-centered, patriarchal culture, introduced in the 1970s as a segment of second-wave feminism. [3] A resident of the Greek island of Lesbos.

Legal Gender – The *gender* listed on government documents and databases.

Legal Transition – The process of modifying various government documents and databases, to have them be in alignment with *gender identity*. (Related terms: *Legal Gender*; *Transition*; *Transitioning*)

LGBT – An acronym for *lesbian*, *gay*, *bisexual*, and *transgender*. (Related terms: LGBTIQ; *LGBTQQAAI*; LGBTQQIAA; GLBT; *GSRM*; *QUILTBAG*)

LGBTQQIAA – An acronym for *lesbian*, *gay*, *bisexual*, *transgender*, *queer*, questioning, *intersex*, *asexual*, and *agender*. Expanded in recent years from *LGBT*, to be more inclusive of alternative *gender* and sexual experiences. (Related terms: *Alphabet Soup*; *LGBT*; LGBTIQ; LGBTQQAAI; *Gender, Romantic, and Sexual Minorities*; GLBT; *GSRM*; *QUILTBAG*; Sexual and Gender Diversity)

M2F – An acronym for *male-to-female*. (Related terms: Gurl; *Male-to-Female*; *MtF*; *MTF*; *Trans Girl*; *Trans Woman*; *Transgender*; *T-girl*; *Transsexual*; *Transwoman*; Woman)

Male – [1] The *sex* assigned by medical providers at birth, most often based on the presence of a penis, or in the case of genetic testing, XY chromosomes. [2] An *assigned gender*, usually determined based on the visual presence of a penis. [3] A multi-factorial social construct based on *assigned gender*, *gender presentation*, *perceived gender*, and/or *gender identity*.

Male-to-Female – An individual that was *designated male at birth*, whose *gender identity* is *female*. (Related terms: Gurl; *M2F*; *MtF*; *MTF*; *Trans Girl*; *Trans Woman*; *Transgender*; *T-girl*; *Transsexual*; *Transwoman*; Woman)

Man – A multi-factorial social construct based on *assigned gender*, *gender presentation*, *perceived gender*, and/or *gender identity*.

Male Impersonator – [1] A *drag king* taking on an exaggerated mimicking of a specific *man*, usually one of fame or notoriety, as a form of performance. [2] A simplistic, or offensive, term for *drag kings*.

Masculine – The archetypal activities, behaviors, dress, mannerisms, presentation, traits, style, and other *gendered behaviors* associated with men in a culture, or considered socially appropriate in that culture.

Masculinity – Performance of *masculine* traits or behaviors.

Masculine of Center – An individual whose *gender identity*, or *gender performance*, is closer to *male* than *female* along the *gender spectrum*. (Related term: Male of Center)

Medical Transition – The process of engaging in *hormone replacement therapy*, having surgery, and/or engaging in other medical procedures, to be in alignment with *gender identity*. (Related terms: *Physical Transition*; *Transition*; *Transitioning*)

Metrosexual – A man, usually *heterosexual*, that meticulously grooms and presents himself.

Misgender – [1] To purposefully refer to an individual by the *gender* or *pronouns* not in accordance with their *gender identity*. [2] To mistake an individual's *gender* for one not in accordance with their *gender identity*.

MSM – Men who engage in *sexual behavior* with other men. (Related term: *Heteroflexible*)

MtF – An acronym for *male-to-female*. (Related terms: Gurl; *M2F*; *Male-to-Female*; MTF; Trans Girl; *Trans Woman*; *Transgender*; *T-girl*; *Transsexual*; *Transwoman*; *Woman*)

Natal Sex – A synonym for *birth sex*.

Neutrois – [1] A *gender identity* that includes a genderless state, or no personal experience of *gender*. [2] *A gender identity* that is neither *male* nor *female*. (Related terms: *Agender*; Genderless, *Gender Neutral*; Non-Gender; None of the Above; Null-Gender)

Nongendered – A synonym for *agender* or *neutrois*.

Non-Op – A *transgender* person who has chosen not to have any surgical procedures as part of their *transition*. (Related term: Non-Operative)

On the Down Low – Men that are in *heterosexual* relationships engaging in *sexual behaviors* with men that are not *disclosed* to their partners or others. (Related terms: Cheating; *Heteroflexible*; *MSM*)

Omnigender – A *gender identity* that includes, or alternates between, many different *genders*. (Related terms: *Bigender*; Multi Gender; *Pangender*; Polygender; Trigender)

Orientation – An attraction towards, or interest in, individuals of specific *genders*, or other identifiers.

Out – Disclosing, being open, or sharing one's *sexual orientation*, *gender*, or *gender history*. (Related terms: *Disclosure*; Out of the Closet)

Packing – [1] The act of wearing prosthetics or material to create the aesthetic of genital mass, or some form of penile function. [2] The act of wearing prosthetics or material to create the aesthetic of one's chosen *gender* presentation, most commonly breasts, hips, and penis.

Pangender – A *gender identity* that includes, or alternates between, a number of different *genders*. (Related terms: *Bigender*; Dual Gender; Mixed Gender; Multi Gender; *Omnigender*; Polygender; Trigender)

Pansexual – A *sexual orientation* towards many, or all, *genders*. (Related terms: *Bisexual*; Omnisexual; *Queer*)

Passing – [1] A *trans* or *gender nonconforming* individual being regarded as, or are mistaken for, *cisgender*. [2] An individual being regarded as a member of a different social group than their own, often done for the purposes of social acceptance, safety, or having the privileges of that social group. [3] A person of one ethnic culture who cannot be easily distinguished from another ethnic culture, such as an African-American individual who could be regarded as or mistaken for being white.

Perceived Gender – [1] The *gender* that people perceive an individual to be. [2] The *gender* that people project on an individual.

Physical Transition – The process of modifying *gender presentation*, and/or engaging in *medical transition*, to be in alignment with *gender identity*. (Related terms: *Medical Transition*; *Transition*; *Transitioning*)

PoC – An acronym for People of Color.

Post-Op – A *transgender* person who has had surgery as part of their *medical transition*. This term often refers to *bottom surgery* for *trans women*, *top surgery* for *trans men*, or either for *gender nonconforming* individuals. (Related term: Post-Operative)

Pre-Op – A *transgender* person who intends to have surgery as part of their *medical transition*, but has not yet had it. This term often refers to *bottom surgery* for *trans women*, *top surgery* for *trans men*, or either for *gender nonconforming* individuals. (Related term: Pre-Operative)

Preferred Pronoun – The *pronoun* an individual would like to have used when talking to, or referring to them. (Related term: Preferred Gender Pronoun (PGP))

Primary Sex Traits – The anatomy of the internal genitalia, anatomy of the external genitalia, and gonads.

Pronouns – Terminology used to reference an individual, other than their name. Examples include:

- E/Em/Ers (pronounced he/her/hers, without the "h")
- Ey/Em/Ers (pronounced they/them/theirs, without the "th")
- He/him/his
- Ne/Nem/Ners (pronounced he/her/hers, with a "n" instead of an "h")
- Sie/Hir/Hirs (pronounced see/hear/hears)
- She/her/hers
- They/them/theirs
- Ze/Zim/Zir (pronounced he/her/hers, with a "z" instead of an "h")

Puberty Blockers – Hormone blockers used to delay puberty for *trans* and *gender nonconforming* youth, or youth experiencing central precocious puberty (CPP).

Queer – [1] A *sexual orientation* categorized by an interest or attraction to individuals, unfettered by *gender* identities or labels. (Related terms: Omnisexual; *Pansexual*) [2] An umbrella term for individuals operating outside of or beyond social or cultural constructs of behavior, *gender*, identity or sexuality. [3] A derogatory term used against *LGBTQQIAA* people. [4] A synonym for strange or unusual.

QUILTBAG – An acronym for *queer*, undecided, *intersex, lesbian, transgender, bisexual, asexual,* and *gay*. (Related terms: *Alphabet Soup*; *LGBT*; LGBTIQ; *LGBTQQAAI*; LGBTQQIAA; *Gender, Romantic, and Sexual Minorities*; GLBT; *GSRM*)

Read – [1] To perceive someone as a specific *gender identity*. Example: "that is how I read you." [2] To perceive a *transgender* or *gender nonconforming* individual as a *gender identity* other than their own. Example: "they read me." (Related terms: *Passing*; *Perceived Gender*)

Secondary Sex Characteristics – The body characteristics that appear at puberty, including breasts, body hair, menstrual cycles, fat distribution, and overall height.

Sex – [1] A label assigned to the human form, based on an individual's chromosomes, *primary sex traits, secondary sex traits,* and hormone levels. [2] Bodily interactions between two or more people, which may include sensual experiences, oral to genital interaction, genital touch, use of vibrators or objects in a sexual manner, or different types of genital to genital contact.

Sex Change Operation – A synonym for *gender reaffirming surgery*, considered out of date.

Sexual Behavior – Bodily experiences, which may include sensual experiences, oral to genital interaction, genital touch, use of vibrators or objects in a sexual manner, masturbation, or different types of genital to genital contact. (Related term: *Sex*)

Sexual Orientation – An erotic attraction towards specific *genders*, or other identifiers. (Related term: *Orientation*)

Sex Reassignment Surgery – A synonym for *gender reaffirming surgery*.

She-Male – [1] A *gender identity* used by individuals *designated male at birth* who have had *hormone replacement therapy* and/or breast augmentation, but are not seeking lower body surgeries. [2] An offensive term used against *male-to-female transgender* individuals. [3] A category of pornography fetishizing *male-to-female transgender* individuals, and those who identify as *she-male*.

SOC – An acronym for the *standards of care* from World Professional Association for Transgender Health (WPATH).

SOFFA – An acronym for significant others, family, friends, and allies of *transgender* and *gender nonconforming* individuals.

Social Transition – The process of disclosing *gender identity*, and/or changing *gender* presentation around various friends, family, allies, social groups, and/or workplace, to be in alignment with *gender identity*. (Related terms: *Transition*; *Transitioning*)

SRS – An acronym for *sex reassignment surgery*.

Standards of Care – The system maintained by the World Professional Association for Transgender Health (WPATH), used by mental health providers, medical health providers, insurance companies, and the legal system, regularly used to approve *medical transition* and *legal transition* for *transgender* individuals. (Related term: *SOC*)

Stealth – An individual that passes, and chooses not to be *out* about, or *disclose*, their *gender*, *gender history*, and/or medical information related to *sex* and *gender*.

Straight – A synonym for *heterosexual*.

T – Slang for the hormone testosterone.

TG – An acronym for *transgender*.

T-girl – Slang used by, or for, some *trans women* and *gender nonconforming* individuals *designated male at birth*.

TGNC – [1] An acronym for *transgender* and *gender nonconforming*. [2] An acronym for *transgender* nonconforming.

T/GV – An acronym for *transgender/gender variant*.

Third Gender – A diverse category of *gender* communities, identities, experiences, and systems worldwide beyond or between *binary genders*. (Related terms: *Third Sex*; and diverse terms listed in Chapter 2)

Third Sex – [1] A synonym for *third gender*. [2] A term used to refer to *LBGT* people in general; fell out of popularity in the 1960s. [3] A term used to refer to feminists in the late 1900s.

Top Surgery – Slang for upper body surgeries available to *trans men* and *gender nonconforming* individuals *designated female at birth*. (Related terms: *Chest Surgery*; *Double Mastectomy*; Keyhole Surgery; Reconstructive Chest Surgery; Torso Reconstructive Surgery)

Tranny – [1] A derogatory or offensive term referring to *trans* individuals. [2] Slang used by *trans* individuals referring to themselves or other *trans* individuals. [3] Slang used by individuals in the *drag* community referring to themselves or other individuals in the *drag* community. [4] Controversial slang used by individuals in the fashion, gay, and queer communities for other people exhibiting fashionable, edgy, or feminine tendencies that entered pop culture in 2007 through *Project Runway*.

Trans – [1] A synonym for *transgender*. [2] An umbrella term for all forms of *transgender*, *gender nonconforming*, and other diverse gender experiences. (Related terms: *Gender Diverse*; *Gender Expansive*; *Gender Nonconforming*; *Gender Variant*; Non-*Cisgender*; *TG*; *Transgender*; *Trans**; *Transsexual*)

Trans* – [1] A synonym for *transgender,* or *trans*. [2] A politicized umbrella term inclusive of all non-*cisgender* experiences. (Related terms: *Gender Diverse*; *Gender Expansive*; *Gender Nonconforming*; *Gender Variant*; Non-*Cisgender*; *TG*; *Trans*; *Transgender*; *Transsexual*)

Trans Man – An individual that was *designated female at birth*, whose *gender identity* is *male*. (Related terms: *F2M*; *Female-to-Male*; *FtM*; FTM; *Man*; Trans Boy; *Transgender*; Transguy; *Transman*; *Transsexual*)

Trans Woman – An individual that was *designated male at birth*, whose *gender identity* is *female*. (Related terms: Gurl; *M2F*; *Male-to-Female*; *MtF*; MTF; Trans Girl; *Transgender*; *T-girl*; *Transsexual*; *Transwoman*; *Woman*)

Transfeminine – A *gender identity* for an individual *designated male at birth*, who experiences *femininity* as a key piece of their *transgender* experience. (Related terms: *Trans Woman*; *Transwoman*)

Transgender – [1] A *gender identity* for an individual whose *assigned gender* at birth does not align with their *gender identity*, or *true gender*, in some way. [2] An umbrella term for various individuals that are not *cisgender*, are *gender nonconforming*, and/or engage in *conscious gender exploration*. (Related terms: *Gender Nonconforming*; *Gender Variant*; *TG*; *Trans*; *Trans**; *Transsexual*)

Transgender Experience – A term used to denote that their *assigned gender* does not, or did not, align with their *gender identity*, or *true gender*. Example: "man of transgender experience." (Related terms: *Gender History, Trans, Transgender*)

Transgender Umbrella – An encompassing term that is inclusive of any and all individuals that are not *cisgender*, are *gender nonconforming*, or engage in *conscious gender exploration*.

Transgendered – [1] A synonym for *transgender*. [2] A synonym for *transitioned*. [3] An out of date term for *transgender* or *transitioned*.

Transition – To change one's social situation, *legal gender*, *gender presentation*, take medications, and/or undergo medical procedures, to become in alignment with an individual's *gender identity*.

Transitioning – The process of engaging in social, legal, physical, and/or a medical *transition* to be in alignment with an individual's *gender identity*.

Transmasculine – A *gender identity* for an individual *designated female at birth*, who experiences *masculinity* as a key piece of their *transgender* experience. (Related terms: *Trans Man*; *Transman*)

Transman – [1] A synonym for *trans man*. [2] A *gender identity* for *female-to-male* transgender individuals who actively acknowledge, advertise, affirm, or embrace their *transgender* experience. (Related terms: *F2M*; *Female-to-Male*; *FtM*; FTM; *Man*; Trans Boy; *Transgender*; Transguy; *Trans Man*; *Transsexual*)

Transphobia – Hostility or fear aimed at, or concerning, *transgender* or *gender nonconforming* people. (Related terms: *Cisgenderism*; Transprejudice)

Transsexual – [1] An individual whose *assigned gender* at birth does not align with their *gender identity*, or *true gender*. [2] A *gender identity* for an individual whose *assigned gender* at birth does not align with their *gender identity*, or *true gender*. [3] An individual who has undergone *medical transition*, or surgical procedures, in conjunction with their *gender transition* to the opposite *gender*. [4] A synonym for *transgender*. [5] Medical, or out of date, terminology for *transgender* experience.

Transwoman – [1] A synonym for *trans woman*. [2] A gender identity for *male-to-female* transgender individuals who actively acknowledge, advertise, affirm, or embrace their transgender experience. (Related terms: Gurl; *M2F*; *Male-to-Female*; *MtF*; MTF; Trans Girl; *Trans Woman*; *Transgender*; *T-girl*; *Transsexual*; Woman)

Transvestism – An outdated, and sometimes offensive, synonym for *crossdressing*.

True Gender – [1] Terminology used to refer to the *gender identity* of an individual whose *assigned gender* has never been aligned with their *gender identity*. [2] An offensive, or derogatory, term used referring to a *transgender* individual's *assigned gender*.

Transvestite – [1] A synonym for *crossdresser*, sometimes considered outdated. [2] A *crossdresser* who engages in *crossdressing* as an erotic activity. (Related term: *TV*)

Two-Spirit – An umbrella term used by some Native American and Canadian First Nation indigenous populations to denote individuals that exist beyond the *heterosexual cisgender* experience.

TV – An acronym for *transvestite*.

Woman – A multi-factorial social construct based on *assigned gender*, *gender presentation*, *perceived gender*, and/or *gender identity*.

Further Resources

This is a list of resources for those curious about digging deeper into the subjects discussed in this book. This list is a far from exhaustive supply of books, websites, and other resources on various topics concerning trans and gender nonconforming issues. Please dig further. New resources are being produced all the time, while other resources transform, or become no longer available. *Any information, opinions, or safety guidelines provided by various links do not represent the knowledge or beliefs of the author, publisher, or those that that sell this book.*

These resources are broken down in order of the categories and chapters mentioned in the book. Please remember to look at the back of this section for the blogs, biographies, autobiographies, television series, documentaries, and movies as well, as many of them were not included in their associated categories. Books and websites have been alphabetized in each category, with book and movie titles italicized, and online articles in quotes, for ease of distinction. Websites are listed with a short description for clarity.

As there are so many amazing and diverse resources available, an expanded resources list is available online. If you know of other resources that should be included, feel free to let us know there, to help everyone learn about tools, information, and support available.

Visit our website at – http://www.traversinggender.com

Outreach and Helpline Resources

Trans Lifeline Suicide Prevention
US: 1-877-565-8860
Canada: 1-877-330-6366
http://www.translifeline.org/

Trevor Project for LGBT Youth
1-866-4-U-TREVOR (866-788-7386)
http://www.thetrevorproject.org/

GLBT National Help Line
1-888-843-4564
Youth Hotline: 1-800-246-7743
http://www.glbthotline.org/

National Suicide Prevention Lifeline
1-800-273-8255
www.suicidepreventionlifeline.org

The Samaritans Helpline
1-877-870-HOPE (4673)
http://samaritanshope.org/

Fenway Health Clinic LGBT Helpline (25+)
1-888-340-4528
Monday – Saturday, 6:00 pm – 11:00 pm
Peer Listening Line (25 & Under)
Toll-Free: 1-800-399-PEER (7337)
Monday – Saturday, 5:30 pm – 10:00 pm
http://fenwayhealth.org/care/wellness-resources/help-lines/

Suggested Reading

The Gender Book, by Mel Reiff Hill, Jay Mays, and Robin Mack. Marshall House Press, 2013. – A short and engaging book for understanding the basics of gender concepts through cartoons, great for all ages. This book also includes a free website that has much of the book online, plus further resources; at http://www.TheGenderbook.com

My New Gender Workbook: A Step-by-Step Guide to Achieving World Peace Through Gender Anarchy and Sex Positivity 2nd Edition, by Kate Bornstein. Routledge, 2013. – Updated from the original *My Gender Workbook,* this amazing text is an invaluable guide for individuals trying to figure out their own gender journey.

Trans Bodies, Trans Selves: A Resource Guide for the Transgender Community, edited by Laura Erickson-Schroth. Oxford University Press, 2014. – An extensive and in-depth text is a must-read for transgender and gender nonconforming individuals that dives into diverse topics, including personal identity, health choices, social systems, legal issues, and more.

General Trans Resources

The Gender Creative Child: Pathways for Nurturing and Supporting Children Who Live Outside Gender Boxes, by Diane Ehrensaft PhD. The Experiment, 2016.

Gender Identity Research and Education Society (GIRES) – http://www.gires.org.uk – Resources for education, employment, health, law, research, and support for and concerning trans and gender nonconforming individuals.

Gender Outlaws: The Next Generation, edited by Kate Bornstein and S. Bear Bergman. Seal Press, 2010.

The Trans Advocate – http://www.TransAdvocate.com/ – Investigative news and editorials from a trans advocate perspective.

Transgender 101: A Simple Guide to a Complex Issue, by Nicholas. M. Teich. Columbia University Press, 2012.

Transgender Explained for Those Who Are Not, by Joann Herman. Authorhouse, 2009.

The Transgender Guidebook: Keys to a Successful Transition, by Anne L. Boedecker PhD. CreateSpace, 2011.

True Selves: Understanding Transsexualism–For Families, Friends, Coworkers, and Helping Professionals, by Mildred L. Brown and Chloe Ann Rounsley. Jossey-Bass, 2003.

Ally Resources

"5 Ways to Support a Trans Person Experiencing Body Dysphoria," by Sam Dylan Finch, 23 March 2015 – http://everydayfeminism.com/2015/03/supporting-trans-person-with-dysphoria/

The Gender Neutral Pronoun Blog – http://genderneutralpronoun.wordpress.com – Resources concerning gender neutral language, modern usage, history, and tools for allies and gender adventurers of every stripe.

GLAAD's Transgender Media Program – http://glaad.org/transgender – Information for media professionals, tips for allies, and a transgender FAQ

"Guide to Being a Straight Ally, 3rd Edition," by *Straight for Equality, a project of PFLAG*, 2011. – http://www.straightforequality.org/document.doc?id=1023

"Our Trans Loved Ones: Questions and Answers for Parents, Families, and Friends of People Who Are Transgender and Gender Expansive," by *PFLAG* – http://community.pflag.org/document.doc?id=921

"Trans* 101 For Significant Others, Partners, Friends, Family, and Allies (SOFFAs) of Trans* People," by Skye Brown – http://www.kinseyinstitute.org/resources/pdf/Trans101forSOFFAs_v4.pdf

Trans-kin: A Guide for Family & Friends of Transgender People, edited by Dr. Elanor A. Hubbard and Cameron T. Whitley. Boulder Press, 2012.

"Trans Being Human (Mature)," by Crystal Waterton – https://vimeo.com/149715056

"Transgender Rights," from *Last Week Tonight with John Oliver*, 28 June 2015. https://www.youtube.com/watch?v=hmoAX9f6MOc

Resources for Transgender and Gender Nonconforming individuals

International Foundation for Gender Education – http://www.ifge.org/ – IFGE's website shares news, and partners with events, concerning trans and gender nonconforming individuals.

Laura's Playground – http://lauras-playground.com/ – Originally begun as a resource for transwomen, this site has expanded to include extensive resources for trans and gender nonconforming experience.

Learning Trans – http://learningtrans.org/ – Highlights trans-produced and community knowledge, this website is a living history of the transgender community.

Susan's Place – http://susans.org – A news, entertainment, politics, science, art, and resources website on all things transgender.

Transbucket – http://www.transbucket.com – Social forum for resources and dialogue between transgender and gender nonconforming individuals.

TransMentrors International – http://www.transmentors.org/ Connecting trans-identified people with one another through the TransMentors project, their website also includes applicable information and resources.

Transsexual Road Map – http://tsroadmap.com – A massive, impressive, labyrinth of information and resources for people of diverse trans experience, their diversity of essays is well worth exploring.

T-Vox – http://t-vox.org – Featuring great information and resources for trans people based in the UK, and a timeline of trans history, they have material available in 7 languages, as well as a regular podcast on various trans topics.

We Happy Trans – http://wehappytrans.com – This website is an opportunity to hear about, and share, positive trans* experiences.

MtF (and Feminine of Center) Resources

Facial Feminization Surgery: A Guide for the Transgendered Woman, by Douglas K. Ousterhout MD. Addicus Books, 2010.

Fucking Trans Women (FTW): A Zine About the Sex Lives of Trans Women, By Mira Bellwether. CreateSpace, 2013.

Girl Talk. The Transgender Guide for Voice and Feminization, by M.S. Lynette Nisbet. Robertson Publishing, 2012.

I am Transgendered – test http://www.iamtransgendered.com/ Resources and advice on connecting with others, gender presentation, and various events for both trans women and male to female crossdressers.

Letters for My Sisters: Transitional Wisdom in Retrospect, edited by Andrea James and Deanne Thornton. CreateSpace, 2015.

TG Forum – http://tgforum.com – Blogs, news, editorials, articles, resources, events, transgender issues podcast, and a discussion forum for trans women. Includes select resources for crossdressers and other trans people as well.

The Transgender Companion (Male to Female): The Complete Guide to Becoming the Woman You Want to Be, by Jennifer Seeley. CreateSpace, 2007.

Transgender Guide – http://tgguide.com – Online community, collection of resources, and articles for MtF transsexuals, trans women, crossdressers, and gender variant folk.

When The Opposite Sex Isn't: Sexual Orientation in Male-to-Female Transgender People, by Sandra L. Samons. Routledge, 2008.

FTM (and Masculine of Center) Resources

Becoming a Visible Man, by Jamison Green. Vanderbilt University Press, 2004.

FTM International – http://www.ftmi.org/ – Home of the widest-circulating newsletter on FTM issues worldwide, their collection on FTM legal, family, and healthcare resources is extensive.

FtM Magazine – http://www.ftmmagazine.com/ – In addition to the print and digital magazine, their website also features various free interviews and news articles.

FTM Surgery – http://ftmsurgery.net – Information on various FtM surgeries, including before and after photos, fundraising information, navigating insurance companies, and lists of surgeons worldwide.

Hudson's FTM Resource Guide – http://www.ftmguide.org/– Resources for FtM individuals including information on presenting as male, grooming, clothing, surgeries, books, terminology, and more.

Hung Jury: Testimonies of Genital Surgery by Transsexual Men, by Trystan T. Cotton. Transgress Press, 2012.

Letters For My Brothers: Transitional Wisdom in Retrospect, edited by Megan Rohrer and Zander Keig. Wilgefortis, 2010.

Stud Magazine – http://thestudmagazine.com/ – This online magazine featuring stud and aggressive individuals, as well as transmen of color, includes articles on health, education, employment, art, and biographies of community members.

Transmen and FTMs: Identities, Bodies, Genders, and Sexualities, by Jason Cromwell. University of Illinois Press, 1999.

The Transitional Male – http://TheTransitionalMale.com – Featuring a by-state (and international) list of medical and mental health providers, they also have a collection of information for FtM individuals, including navigating therapy, disclosure, legal issues, and supporting FtM children. They also host the Big Brother Binder Program for disabled, unemployed and disenfranchised transmen.

Two-Spirit Resources

Changing Ones: Third and Fourth Genders in Native North America, by Will Roscoe. Palgrave Macmillan, 2000.

Dancing to Eagle Spirit Society – http://www.dancingtoeaglespiritsociety.org/ In addition to running gatherings and rituals, their website offers information for two-spirit individuals about traditional practices amidst other resources.

Native OUT – http://NativeOUT.com A Two-Spirit blog that includes resources and multimedia.

The North American Aboriginal Two Spirit Information Pages – http:// people.ucalgary.ca/~ptrembla/aboriginal/two-spirited-american-indian-resources.htm – An extensive collection of links and data, their collection is impressive, even with the interspersed dead links.

Queer Indigenous Studies: Critical Interventions in Theory, Politics, and Literature, edited by Dr. Qwo-Li Driskill, Chris Finley, Brain Joseph Gilley, and Scott Lauria Morgensen. University of Arizona Press, 2011.

Safe and Caring Schools for Two Spirit Youth – http://www.nnaapc.org/ publications/TwoSpiritBook.pdf – This is a toolkit on creating safer spaces for Two Spirit youth in schools created by the Two-Spirit Circle of Edmonton

Two Spirit People: Native American Gender Identity, Sexuality, and Spirituality, edited by Sue-Ellen Jacobs, Wesley Thomas and Sabine Lang. University of Illinois Press, 1997.

"Two-Spirit Resource Directory," prepared by Harlan Pruden (Cree) on behalf of the National Confederacy of Two-Spirit Organizations and NorthEast Two-Spirit Society with the Stonewall Community Foundation, 2013 – http://uwm.edu/lgbtrc/wp-content/uploads/sites/162/2014/09/two-spirit-resource-directory-jan-2013.pdf

Two Spirit Youth Speak Out! – http://www.unya.bc.ca/downloads/glbtq-twospirit-final-report.pdf – Resource created by the Urban Native Youth Association (UNYA) in Vancouver, British Columbia with a needs assessment of Two Spirit youth throughout BC through survey results and associated projects and outreach.

We Are Part of a Tradition: A Guide on Two Spirited People for First Nations Communities, by Gilbert Deschamps. 2-Spirited People of the 1St Nations, 1998. – http://2spirits.com/PDFolder/WeArePartOfTradition.pdf

Third Gender and Worldwide Perspectives

Challenging Gender Norms: Five Genders Among Bugis in Indonesia, by Sharyn Graham Davies. Wadsworth Publishing, 2006.

Ladyboys: Inside the Secret World of Thailand's Third Sex, by Susan Aldous and Pornchai Sereemongkonpol. Maverick House Publishers, 2011.

Professing Selves: Transsexuality and Same-Sex Desire in Contemporary Iran, by Afsaneh Najmabadi. Duke University Press, 2013.

Neither Man Nor Woman: The Hijras of India, 2nd Edition, by Serena Nanda. Wadsworth Publishing, 1998.

Sex in Transition: Remaking Gender & Race in South Africa, by Amanda Lock Swarr. State University of New York Press, 2012.

Toms and Dees: Transgender Identity and Female Same-Sex Relationships in Thailand, by Megan Sinnott. University of Hawaii Press, 2004.

Travesti: Sex, Gender, and Culture among Brazilian Transgendered Prostitutes, by Don Kulick. University of Chicago Press, 1998.

Tritiya-Prakriti: People of the Third Sex: Understanding Homosexuality, Transgender Identity, And Intersex Conditions Through Hinduism, by Amara Das Wilelm. Xlibris Corp., 2010.

Women Who Become Men: Albanian Sworn Virgins, by Antonia Young. Bloomsbury Academics, 2001.

Agender, Genderqueer, and Gender Nonconforming Resources

The Asexual Visibility & Education Network – http://www.asexuality.org – The AVEN website includes a forum, FAQs for different audiences, resources, media links, and their bi-monthly newsletter/magazine for the asexual community.

Neutrois Nonsense – http://neutrois.me/ – An intimate exploration of identity and finding life beyond the gender binary

Neutrois – http://www.Neutrois.com/ – Resources about agender and neutral-gender experience, as well as resources and a community for neutrois individuals.

Genderqueer Identities – http://genderqueerid.com/ – A rich collection of articles, information, history, resources, academia and more about and for genderqueer and gender nonconforming individuals.

Androgyne Online – http://androgyne.0catch.com/ – Information and resources for and about androgynous, bigender, pangender, agender, and other gender nonconforming people. Includes a rich collection of links for diverse "gender outlaws" beyond these categories as well.

Conscious Gender Exploration

Butch is a Noun, by S. Bear Bergman. Arsenal Pulp Press, 2010.

Genderqueer: And Other Gender Identities, photography by Dave Naz. Rare Bird Books, 2014.

Genderfork – http://www.genderfork.com/ – Interviews, videos, and opportunities to ask questions for people across the gender spectrum.

GenderQueer: Voices From Beyond the Gender Binary, edited by Joan, Clare Howell and Riki Wilchins. Alyson, 2002.

Brazen Femme: Queering Femininity, edited by Chloë Brushwood Rose, Anna Camilleri. Arsenal Pulp Press, 2003.

Female Masculinity, by Judith Halberstam. Duke University Press, 1998.

Drag, and Crossdressing Resources

Butch Queens Up in Pumps: Gender, Performance, and Ballroom Culture in Detroit, by Marlon M. Bailey.

CrossDreamser – http://www.crossdreamers.com/ – Articles, reflections and resources for people interested in crossdressing, of every gender experience, and trans/queer issues.

Crossdresser Heaven – https://www.crossdresserheaven.com/ – Articles, advice, and resources for individuals who crossdress, as well as a discussion forum for crossdressers and their partners.

The Drag King Book, by Judith "Jack" Halberstam and Del LaGrace Volcano. Serpent's Tail, 1999.

Drag King Dreams, by Leslie Feinberg. Seal Press, 2006.

Faux Queens – http://www.fauxqueens.com/ – A community for individuals assigned female at birth that perform as drag queens.

The Lazy Crossdresser, by Charles Anders. Greenery Press, 2015.

Legendary: Inside the House Ballroom Scene, by Gerald H. Gaskins. Duke University Press, 2013.

Unzipping Gender: Sex, Cross-Dressing and Culture, by Charlotte Suthrell. Bloomsbury Academic, 2004.

Intersex Resources

Intersex Initiative – http://www.intersexinitiative.org/ – Activism and advocacy organization whose website includes articles, publications, and information on intersex legal issues, intersex in media, their speaker's bureau, and more.

Intersex Society of North America – http://isna.org/ – Information and advocacy for and about intersex people, including an extensive library and resources section.

InterACT – http://interactadvocates.org/ – Advocacy and resources for, and concerning, intersex youth.

Intersex Roadshow Blog – http://intersexroadshow.blogspot.com/ – Articles and information for and about transgender and other gender variant populations.

Organisation Internationale des Intersexués/Organization Intersex International – http://oiiinternational.com/ – OII is a global network of intersex organizations, with resources worldwide.

Intersex Awareness Day – http://intersexday.org/ – Information on gatherings on Intersex Awareness Day (October 26th) and Intersex Day of Solidarity (November 8th), as well as additional articles on intersex experience.

European Region of the International Lesbian, Gay, Bisexual, Trans and Intersex Association. (ILGA) – http://www.ilga-europe.org/ – ILGA is an international non-governmental umbrella organization working to protect human rights for intersex individuals, as well as all people across the LGBTI spectrum in Europe.

Intersex Playtpus – http://intersexplatypus.tumblr.com/ – News, media, and resources by or about intersex individuals.

For Providers and Others:

Critical Intersex, edited by Morgan Holmes. Ashgate Press, 2009.

Disorders of Sexual Development: Accord Alliance http://www.accordalliance.org/ – Information, guidelines, and creating partnerships between patients, families, healthcare administrators, clinicians, support groups, and researchers for those affected by disorders of sex development (DSD).

Ethics and Intersex (International Library of Ethics, Law, and the New Medicine), edited by Sharon E. Sytsma. Springer Netherlands, 2006.

Fixing Sex: Intersex, Medical Authority, and Lived Experience, by Katrina Karkazis. Duke University Press, 2008.

Intersex and Identity: The Contested Self, by Sharon Preves. Rutgers University Press, 2003.

Kid's Books

Children's books are coming out all the time. The fact that this category is growing is so wonderful. But here are a few places to start that cover a wide range of topics on gender diversity and acceptance. For other ideas, or to share your own, feel free to visit www.TraversingGender.com:

- *The Adventures of Tulip, the Birthday Wish Fairy, by S. Bear Bergman. Flamingo Rampant, 2012.*

- *But I'm Not A Boy*, by Katie Leone and Alison Pfeifer. CreateSpace, 2015.

- *I Am Jazz*, by Jessica Herthel, Jazz Jennings and Shelagh McNicholas. Dial Books, 2014.

- *Jacob's New Dress*, by Sarah Hoffman, Ian Hoffman and Chris Case. Albert Whitman & Company, 2014.

- *Little Kunoichi, The Ninja Girl*, by Sanae Ishida. Little Bigfoot, 2015.

- *My Princess Boy*, by Cheryl Kilodavis, illustrated by Suzanne DeSimone. Alladin, 2010.

- *Pink is Just a Color and So is Blue*, by Niki Bhatia. CreateSpace, 2012.

- *Red: A Crayon's Story*, by Michael Hall. Greenwillow Books, 2015.

- *Roland Humphrey is Wearing a WHAT?*, by Eileen Kiernan-Johnson and Katrina Revenaugh. Huntley Rahara Press, 2013.

- *When Kayla Was Kyle*, by Amy Fabrikant and Jennifer Levine. Avid Readers Publishing Group, 2013.

If you're looking to introduce all kids at an early age to the idea the idea that every person can be unique, check out:

- *It's Okay To Be Different,* by Todd Parr. Little, Brown Books for Young Readers, 2009.

For and About Trans Youth:

Always My Child: A Parent's Guide to Understanding Your Gay, Lesbian, Bisexual, Transgendered, or Questioning Son or Daughter, by Kevin Jennings. Touchstone Publishing, 2002.

"Bending the Mold: An Action Kit for Transgender Students." *Lambda Legal,* 2008. – http://www.lambdalegal.org/publications/bending-the-mold

Gay, Lesbian, and Straight Education Network (GLSEN) http://www.glsen.org/ – With chapters across the US, GLSEN has resources for educators, tools for Gay-Straight Alliances groups, information on making schools safer, and great information that applies to kids across the gender and sexuality spectrum.

Gay Straight Alliance (GSA) Network – https://gsanetwork.org/ – Local groups bringing together youth activists and peer to peer support, as well as events, resources, and updates on the news that affects LGBT youth.

Gender Born, Gender Made: Raising Healthy Gender Non-Conforming Children, by Diane Ehrensaft, PhD. The Experiment, 2011.

Gender Creative Kids – http://GenderCreativeKids.ca/ – Resources and support to affirm gender creative kids with their families, schools and communities in Canada.

Gender Neutral Parenting: Raising Kids With the Freedom to be Themselves, by Paige Lucas-Stannard. Verity Publishing, 2013.

LGBT Youth in America's Schools, by Jason Cianciotto and Sean Cahill. University of Michigan Press, 2012.

Parents, Families, Friends, and Allies Unites with LGBTQ People (PFLAG) – http://www.pflag.org/ – Support groups, events, resources, and answers to diverse frequently asked questions concerning LGBTQ youth and loved ones. Their booklets about supporting people who are trans and gender expansive are wonderful.

Parents of Transgender Children on FaceBook – https://www.facebook.com/groups/108151199217727 – A closed discussion group for parents with trans and gender nonconforming children, it is full of other parents who freely offer support and advice.

Safe Schools Coalition – http://www.safeschoolscoalition.org/ – This public-private partnership supporting GLBTQQ youth, they offer an impressive array of useful resources, for youth, as well as those supporting them, and is well worth exploring and supporting.

Supporting Transgender and Gender Creative Youth: Schools, Families, and Communities in Action, edited by Elizabeth Meyer and Annie Pullen Sansfaçon. Peter Lang, 2014.

Trans Kids Purple Rainbow Foundation – http://www.transkidspurplerainbow.org/ – Provides financial support to programs for transkids, homeless youth shelters, trans families in needs, and research on issues affecting trans youth. Their website includes assorted resources as well.

Trans Youth Equality Foundation – http://TransYouthEquality.org Support, education and advocacy for trans and gender non-conforming youth and their families.

The Transgender Child: A Handbook for Families and Professionals, by Stephanie A. Brill and Rachel Pepper. Cleis Press, 2008.

Trans-Parenting – http://Trans-Parenting.org/ – Support and educational resources for parents and their advocates raising trans and gender independent children.

TransYouth Family Allies (TYFA) – http://www.imatyfa.org/ – With a website full of resources for parents, educators, health care professionals, and youth, TYFA's goals also include empowering youth and their families through support, education, and outreach.

Why Don't You Tell Them I'm a Boy? Raising a Gender-Nonconforming Child, by Florence Dillon. Safe Schools Coalition, 1999. – http://www. safeschoolscoalition.org/whydontyoutellthem.pdf

For and about Trans Teens:

Trevor Project for LGBT Youth
1-866-4-U-TREVOR (866-788-7386)
http://www.thetrevorproject.org/

GLBT National Youth Hotline
1-800-246-7743
http://www.glbthotline.org/

FAQ for Transgender and Gender-Nonconforming Youth, *Lamda Legal* – http://www.lambdalegal.org/know-your-rights/transgender/trans-youth-faq

Gender Identity: The Ultimate Teen Guide, by Cynthia L. Winfield. Scarecrow Press, 2006.

The Gender Quest Workbook: A Guide for Teens and Young Adults Exploring Gender Identity, by Rylan Jay Testa, Deborah Coolhart, and Jayme Peta. Instant Help, 2015.

GLBTQ: The Survival Guide for Gay, Lesbian, Bisexual, Transgender, and Questioning Teens, by Kelly Huegel, Free Spirit Publishing, 2011.

Helping Your Transgender Teen: A Guide for Parents, by Irwin Krieger. Genderwise Press, 2011.

It Gets Better Project – http://www.itgetsbetter.org/ – Built to assist LGBT youth around the world in understanding that life gets better, while creating and inspiring the changes needed to make it better for them. Full of wonderful videos, personal stories, and journeys from across the gender spectrum.

The Letter Q: Queer Writers' Letters to Their Younger Selves, edited by Sarah Moon and James Lecesne. Arthur A. Levine Books, 2014.

Speaking Out: LGBTQ Youth Stand Up, edited by Steve Berman. Bold Strokes Books, 2011.

Trans Teen Survival Guide – http://transgenderteensurvivalguide.tumblr. com/ – A site for people of all trans and gender diverse experiences to ask questions about their gender identity, designed originally for teens, but available for people of all ages.

The Transgender Teen, by Stephanie A. Brill. Cleis Press, 2016.

Transparent: Love, Family, and Living the T with Transgender Teenagers, by Cris Beam. Mariner Books, 2008.

Transphobia: Deal With It and Be a Gender Transcender, by J. Wallace Skelton and Nick Johnson. Lorimer Books, 2015.

For young adult fiction books, here some great places to start:

- *Almost Perfect*, by Brian Katcher. Delacorte Books for Young Readers, 2010.

- *Beautiful Music for Ugly Children*, by Kirstin Cronn-Mills. Flux, 2012.

- *Every Day*, by David Levithan. Ember, 2013.

- *Freakboy*, by Kristin Elizabeth Clark. Farrar, Straus and Giroux, 2013.

- *George*, by Alex Gino. Scholastic Press, 2015

- *Gracefully Grayson*, by Ami Polonsky. Disney-Hyperion, 2014.

- *I am J*, by Cris Beam. Little, Brown Books for Young Readers, 2012.

- *Luna*, by Julie Anne Peters. Little, Brown Books for Young Readers, 2006.

- *None of the Above*, by I.W. Gregario. Balzer + Bray, 2015.

- *Parrotfish*, by Ellen Wittlinger. Simon & Schuster Books, 2011.

In addition, I would encourage all teens, and anyone struggling, to check out this book:

- *Hello, Cruel World: 101 Alternatives to Suicide for Teens, Freaks, and Other Outlaws*, by Kate Bornstein. Seven Stories Press, 2006.

Youth Homelessness and Foster Care

1-800-999-9999
The Nine Line
24 hours a day, seven days a week

1-800-231-6946
National Runaway Switchboard
24 hours a day, seven days a week

True Colors Funds, LGBT Homelessness Project https://truecolorsfund.org/ Campaign working to end homelessness for LGBT youth.

Homeless LGBT Youth and LGBT Youth in Foster Care. *Safe Schools Coalition* – http://safeschoolscoalition.org/RG-homeless.html – Resources for people concerned for, or caring for, LGBT youth.

Lynn's Place Guide to Homeless Shelters – http://tglynnsplace.com/ homeless.htm – Most of the shelters listed are LGBT youth friendly or accessible.

Homeless or in Foster Care. Safe Schools Coalition http://safeschoolscoalition.org/youth/homeless-or-in-fostercare.html Resources for LGBTQ homeless youth or youth in foster care.

"Supporting Your LGBTQ Youth: A Guide for Foster Parents." *Child Welfare Information Gateway* – https://www.childwelfare.gov/pubPDFs/ LGBTQyouth.pdf

College and Athletic Resources

Campus Pride Index – https://www.campusprideindex.org/ – National Listing of LGBTQ-Friendly colleges and universities, university speaker's bureau, scholarship listings, and college prep resources for LGBTQ youth.

TONI Project Transgender On-Campus Non-Discrimination Information – http://transstudents.org/ – NCTE is a national social justice organization devoted to ending discrimination and violence against transgender people through education and advocacy on national issues of importance to transgender people.

National Collegiate Athletics Association (NCAA) Inclusion of Transgender Student Athletes – http://www.ncaa.org/sites/default/files/Transgender_Handbook_2011_Final.pdf

"International Olympics Committee Consensus Meeting on Sex Reassignment and Hyperandrogenism" International Olympics Committee, 2015. – http://www.olympic.org/Documents/Commissions_PDFfiles/Medical_commission/2015-11_ioc_consensus_meeting_on_sex_reassignment_and_hyperandrogenism-en.pdf

Parents who Transition

COLAGE (Children of Lesbians and Gays Everywhere http://www.colage.org/ – Support groups, events, publications, and other resources for individuals whose parents are LGBTQ.

Families Like Mine – https://familieslikemine.com/category/transgender/ Stories about, and experiences of, children whose parents have transitioned, on a site that includes children whose parents are LGBT in general.

Family Equality Council – http://www.familyequality.org/ – Events, parenting groups, and diverse resources for LGBTQ parents, ranging from legal issues to school and faith group information.

FYVCTP Tumblr – http://fuckyeaverycutetransparents.tumblr.com/ Links, advice, pictures, videos, and stories about trans people with kids.

Genderqueer and Transgender Parenting Group (GQTGParenting) – http://groups.yahoo.com/group/GQTGParenting/ – Advice and support for trans and genderqueer parents, from other trans and genderqueer parents.

Pregnant Men's Resource Network – https://www.facebook.com/birthingpapas/ – Facebook support group for trans male birth parents.

"Protecting the Rights of Transgender Parents and Their Children: A Guide for Parents and Lawyers", by Leslie Cooper. *American Civil Liberties Union and the National Center for Transgender Equality*, 2013. – https://www.aclu.org/files/assets/aclu-tg_parenting_guide.pdf

Transsexual Parenting Group (TSParenting) – http://groups.yahoo.com/group/TSParenting/ – Support group for transsexual men and women to discuss parenting issues.

Transgender Parents and Parents-To-Be LiveJournal Community http://transparents.livejournal.com/ – Advice, resources, and information for transgender people and their partners who are parents, parents-to-be, or are trying to conceive.

Relationship Resources

Engender Yahoo Group – https://groups.yahoo.com/neo/groups/engender_partners/info/ – For partners, SOFFAs, wives, and girlfriends of transgender and crossdressing people to discuss challenges, understand gender theory, and create community.

Head Over Heels: Wives Who Stay with Cross-Dressers and Transsexuals, by Virginia Erhardt. Routledge, 2006.

"The Invisible Gender Outlaws: The Partners of Transgender People" by Pat Califia. *Sex Changes: Transgender Politics*, edited by Pat Califia. Cleis Press, 2003.

Love, Always: Partners of Trans People on Intimacy, Challenge and Resilience, edited by Jordon Johnson and Becky Garrison. Transgress Press, 2015.

My Husband Betty – http://www.myhusbandbetty.com/ – A blog and resource page from a woman whose husband transitioned into being her wife.

My Husband Betty Community Boards – http://www.myhusbandbetty.com/community/index.php – A discussion forum for understanding and discussing diverse transgender topics, especially within the context of established relationships, hosted by Helen Boyd.

Partners of Transgender People Livejournal Group – http://partners-of-tg.livejournal.com/ – No longer active, but full of information from people telling their stories, and resources.

Trans/Love: Radical Sex, Love & Relationships Beyond the Binary, edited by Morty Diamond. Manic D Press, 2011.

Trans People in Love, edited by Tracie O'Keefe and Katrina Fox. Routledge, 2008.

Trans People's Partnerships: Towards an Ethics of Intimacy, by Tam Sanger. Palgrave Macmillan, 2010.

Intimate Partner Violence

National Domestic Violence Hotline
1-800-799-SAFE (7233)

Gay Men's Domestic Violence Hotline (for all LGBTQ people):
1-800-832-1901

LGBT National Hotline (other issues as well, not just IPV):
1-888-843-4564

Survivor Project – http://survivorproject.org/index.html/ – Resources and support for intersex and trans survivors of domestic and sexual violence.

Amy Sun. "Let's Talk About Domestic Violence in the Trans* Community." *Everyday Feminism,* 25 Mar 2014 – http://everydayfeminism.com/2014/03/domestic-violence-trans-community

Trans Aging Resources

Family Caregiver Alliance – https://www.caregiver.org/lgbt-caregiving-frequently-asked-questions – Information, support, and resources for caregivers of LGBTQ elders.

FORGE Transgender Aging Network – http://forge-forward.org/aging/ Support and projects to improve the lives of current and future trans and SOFFA elders.

"Improving the lives of transgender older adults: Recommendations for policy and practice." *SAGE (Services and Advocacy for GLBT Elders) and the National Center for Transgender Equality (NCTE)*, 2012. – http://www.lgbtagingcenter.org/resources/pdfs/TransAgingPolicyReportFull.pdf

Lesbian, Gay, Bisexual, and Transgender Aging: Research and Clinical Perspectives, edited by Douglas Kimmel, Tara Rose and Steven David. Columbia University Press, 2006.

Lesbian, Gay, Bisexual and Transgender Ageing: Biographical Approaches for Inclusive Care and Support, edited by Richard Ward, Ian Rivers and Mike Sutherland. Jessica Kingsley Publishers, 2012.

The Lives of LGBT Older Adults, edited by Nancy A. Orel and Christine A. Fruhauf. American Psychological Association, 2014.

Midlife and Older LGBT Adults: Knowledge and Affirmative Practice for the Social Services, by Ski Hunter PhD. Haworth Press, 2005.

National Resource Center on LGBT Aging – http://www.lgbtagingcenter.org/ Extensive resources, trainings, events, and information for LGBT elders and their loved ones, family, and allies.

SAGECAP (SAGE Caring and Preparing) – http://www.sageusa.org/ programs/sagecap.cfm – Educational seminars and counseling for caregivers for LGBT individuals.

"Transgender Aging: Aging poses unique challenges for transgender older adults." *SAGE: Services & Advocacy for Gay, Lesbian, Bisexual & Transgender Elders* – http://www.sageusa.org/issues/transgender.cfm

Health Resources

"Finding Insurance for Transgender-Related Healthcare." *Human Rights Campaign*, 8 Jan 2015. – http://www.hrc.org/resources/finding-insurance-for-transgender-related-healthcare

Informed Consent for Access to Trans Health – http://www.icath.org/ Information on the informed consent model of care.

My Trans Health – http://MyTransHealth.com – Connects trans people to doctors who understand the needs and concerns of trans patients.

"Primary Care Protocol for Transgender Patient Care." *Center of Excellence for Transgender Health* – http://www.transhealth.ucsf.edu/

RAD Remedy – http://www.radremedy.org/ – Connecting trans, gender non-conforming, intersex, and queer folks to accurate, safe, respectful, and comprehensive care.

Trans Health – http://Trans-Health.com/ – Articles and resources on diverse trans health issues, and listings of trans-specific clinics across North America.

Transobriety Yahoo Group – https://groups.yahoo.com/neo/groups/transobriety/info – Mailing list to provide support for those, or those who want to be, drug and alcohol free.

TransMedicare – http://transmedicare.com/ – Information for transgender Medicare patients seeking transition-related health care.

Vancouver Coastal Health: Transgender Health Information Program – http://transhealth.vch.ca/ – Clear, varied, and accessible information about trans medical care, social transition, and other support needs for trans and gender nonconforming individuals, as well as their providers.

For Medical Professionals:

In addition to the resources above, there are additional resources with more information of interest to medical professionals. Trans and gender nonconforming individuals may also find some of these of interest, as research and advocacy for one's own care is also important.

Gender Spectrum – https://www.genderspectrum.org/resources/medical-2/– Resources created to assist physicians and nurses who are places in a critically important position in the care of gender-expansive youth

International Journal of Transgenderism – http://www.tandfonline.com/loi/wijt20 – Access current and past issues, or individual articles on transgender medical issues.

The National LGBT Health Education Center – http://www.lgbthealtheducation.org/ – Educational programs, resources, and consultation to health care professionals and organizations, a program of the Fenway Institute.

"Primary Care Protocol for Transgender Patient Care." *Center of Excellence for Transgender Health*, April 2011. – http://www.transhealth.ucsf.edu/trans?page=protocol-00-00

Principles of Transgender Medicine and Surgery, 2nd Edition, edited by Randi Ettner, Stan Monstrey, and Eli Colemen. Routledge, 2016.

Transgender Emergence: Therapeutic Guidelines for Working with Gender Variant People and Their Families, by Arlene Istar Lev. Hawthorn Press, 2004.

"Transgender Health." *American Medical Student Association* – http://www.amsa.org/advocacy/action-committees/gender-sexuality/transgender-health/

"Transgender Health Injection Guide" *Fenway Health*, July 2015. – http://fenwayhealth.org/wp-content/uploads/2015/07/COM-1880-trans-health_injection-guide_small_v2.pdf

TransLine Medical Consultation Service – https://transline.zendesk.com/home/ – This project works free of charge for medical providers, and their website includes protocol, lab and hormone information, patient handouts, sample letters, and more.

World Professional Association for Transgender Health (WPATH) - http://www.wpath.org/ – Membership organization for professionals working with transgender and gender nonconforming individuals, whose site includes rich and extensive resources, including the opportunity to download their Standards of Care (SOC).

Youth Specific:

Social Work Practices with Transgender and Gender Variant Youth, 2nd Edition, by Gerald P. Mallon. Routledge, 2009.

Treating Transgender Children and Adolescents: An Interdisciplinary Discussion, by Jack Drescher and William Byne. Routledge, 2009.

For Mental Health Professionals

Casebook for Counseling Lesbian, Gay, Bisexual, and Transgender Clients and Their Families, edited by Sari H. Doworkin and Mark Pope. American Counseling Association, 2012. – http://www.counseling.org/Publications/FrontMatter/72917-FM.PDF

Counseling LGBTI Clients, by Kevin G. Alderson. Sage Publications, 2012.

Gender Variant Children and Transgender Adolescents, an Issue of Child and Adolescent Psychiatric Clinics of North America, by Richard R. Pleak, MD. Saunders, 2011.

Handbook of Counseling and Psychotherapy for Lesbian, Gay, Bisexual, and Transgender Clients, edited by Kathleen J. Bieschke, Ruperto M. Perez, and Kurt A. DeBord. American Psychological Association, 2006.

Handbook of LGBT-Affirmative Couple and Family Therapy, by Jerry J. Bigner and Joseph J. Wetchler. Routledge, 2012.

The LGBT Casebook, edited by Petros Levounis MD, Jack Drescher MD, and Mary E. Barber MD. American Psychiatric Publishing, 2012.

"Report of the APA Task Force on Gender Identity and Gender Variance." *American Psychological Association,* 2008. – http://www.apa.org/pi/lgbt/resources/policy/gender-identity-report.pdf

Transgender Emergence: Therapeutic Guidelines for Working with Gender-Variant People and Their Families, by Arlene Istar Lev. Routledge, 2004.

Transition and Beyond: Observations on Gender Identity, by Reid Vanderburgh. Odin Ink, 2011.

World Professional Association for Transgender Health (WPATH) - http://www.wpath.org/ – Membership organization for professionals working with transgender and gender nonconforming individuals, whose site includes rich and extensive resources, including the opportunity to download their Standards of Care (SOC).

People of Color Resources

Asian Pacific Islander Queer Women & Transgender Community – http://www.apiqwtc.org/ – Offering networking, support and social opportunities, their website includes resources on coming out for individuals of Asian pacific islander descent.

Black Transmen – http://blacktransmen.org/ – Their site includes information on black trans male pioneers, and has a support network for black trans men. They also produce a transgender advocacy conference.

The Brown Bois Project – http://www.brownboiproject.org/ – This group works across race and gender to end sexism, homophobia, and transphobia while encouraging health forms of masculinity. They do so through advocacy, producing original materials, and organizing events.

Freeing Ourselves: A Guide to Health and Self-Love for Brown Bois, edited by B. Cole and Luna Han. Brown Boi Project, 2011.

INCITE! Women of Color Against Violence – http://www.incite-national.org/ – This nation-wide organization works to end violence against women of color, and trans people of color, while their website has a collection of useful downloads and other resources.

National Black Justice Coalition – http://nbjc.org/
Dedicated to empowering black LGBT people, their site includes essays, downloads and resources on diverse topics, and a useful media center.

National Queer Asian Pacific Islander Alliance – http://www.nqapia.org/
Organization that advocates for LGBT Asian American, South Asian, Southeast Asian and Pacific Islander rights, supports immigration initiatives, and hosts a yearly conference on these issues.

Queer Women of Color Media Wire – http://www.qwoc.org/
News, trends, media, resources, and articles for and about queer women of color across the gender history and presentation spectrum.

Trans People of Color Coalition (TPOCC) – http://transpoc.org/
The national social justice organization that promotes the interests of trans people of color, their website links to their active twitter and Facebook pages.

Translatina Network – http://www.translatinanetwork.org
Based in NYC, they offer resources, support, and information for Latina transwomen at the local and national level.

TransWomen of Color Collective – http://www.twocc.us/
Advocacy organization that does political, social and media appearances, they also offer leadership training and do a variety of restorative justice work.

Legal Resources

American Civil Liberties Union (ACLU) Transgender Information and Rights – https://www.aclu.org/lgbt-rights/ – Breaking down information on LGBT rights by category and sub-category, they also offer an online confidential system for reaching out concerning civil liberties violations.

Audre Lorde Project – http://alp.org/
Though based in New York City, their SafeOUTside antiviolence program, TransJustice events and actions, and work to end employment and immigration discrimination continues to influence the world at large.

Captive Genders: Trans Embodiment and the Prison Industrial Complex, 2nd Edition, edited by Eric A. Stanley and Nat Smith. AK Press, 2015.

Lambda Legal Transgender Resources – http://www.lambdalegal.org/ know-your-rights/transgender – With great FAQs, information, resources, and personal stories of those affected by trans legal issues, they also have regional offices and a legal help desk.

The National Center for Lesbian Rights – http://NCLRights.org The NCLR has a transgender law project, tools custody and workplace issues, and a legal help line.

The National Center for Transgender Equality – http://www. transequality.org/ – One of the best sources online for everything from changing documentation to understanding various legal rights, please pour through all of their links to find information that can help you and your situation, as their available resources are impressive.

The National Gay and Lesbian Task Force – http://www.thetaskforce.org/ A political and social action organization, their #StopTransMurders Project, and Trans/Gender Non-Conforming Justice Project, are doing important work.

Trans Respect Versus Transphobia Worldwide. – Trans Respect – TransRespect.org – Catalogs comparative research data worldwide in an accessible matter concerning legal issues and coordinates the trans murder monitoring project.

Transgender Family Law: A Guide to Effective Advocacy Paperback, edited by Jennifer L. Levi. AuthorHouse, 2012.

The Transgender Gender Variant Intersex Justice Project (TGI Project) Especially useful for trans incarceration issues, police violence, they have a variety of resources for black trans legal and social justice issues, and do work on poverty and other issues of injustice that affect trans people.

The Transgender Law and Policy Institute – http://www.transgenderlaw.org/ Important information and data on non-discrimination and hate crime laws, employment and health care policies, and a rich collection of topic-specific legal resources.

The Transgender Law Center – http://TransgenderLawCenter.org In addition to their wide array of resources for diverse legal issues affecting trans people, they also have resources for attorneys, a legal information helpline, publications available for allies, organizers, and individual trans people finding their way.

The Transgender Legal Defense and Education Fund (TLDEF) – http:// TransgenderLegal.org – Working on test-case legal cases to affect broad trans civil rights issues, TLDEF also runs the Name Change Project which helps those in need do name change services, and partner with law firms to help trans people have legal counsel.

Transgender Persons and the Law Pap/Cdr Edition, by Ally Windsor Howell. American Bar Association, 2014.

Transgender Rights, edited by Paisley Currah, Richard M. Juang and Shannon Price Minter. University of Minnesota Press, 2006.

Workplace and Housing Resources

The Complete Guide to Transgender in the Workplace, by Vanessa Sheridan. ABC-CLIO, 2009.

"Know Your Rights." *Transgender American Veterans Association* – http:// transveteran.org/for-veterans/know-your-rights/

Transgender Economic Empowerment Initiative – http://www.teeisf.org/ The nation's first program designed to help transgender and gender non-conforming people find, and keep, good jobs in safe workplaces.

Transgender American Veterans Association – http://tavausa.org/ –Online resources for veterans, and systems for connecting with providers in the VA system.

Transgender Employment Experiences: Gender Perceptions and the Law, by Kyla Bender-Baird. State University of New York Press, 2011.

The Transgender Housing Network – http://transhousingnetwork.com The THN helps connect trans people in need with safe and supportive places to crash.

Transgender Workplace Diversity: Policy Tools, Training Issues, and Communication Strategies for HR and Legal Professionals, by Jillian T. Weiss. BookSurge, 2007.

"Workplace Gender Transition Guidelines." *Human Rights Campaign* – http://www.hrc.org/resources/workplace-gender-transition-guidelines

Faith Resources

The Center for Lesbian and Gay Studies in Religion and Ministry – (CLGS) http://clgs.org/– Based at the Pacific School of Religion, they host various events for Christian clergy and people of faith, and their website has a variety of downloadable PDFs for creating community, and to spur conversation.

Courage to Love: Liturgies for the Lesbian, Gay, Bisexual, and Transgender Community, by Geoffrey Duncan. Pilgrim Press, 2002.

Hermaphrodeities: The Transgender Spirituality Workbook, by Raven Kaldera. Asphodel Press, 2010.

Institute for Welcoming Resources – http://www.welcomingresources.org/ A resource of the National LGBTQ Task Force, they help Christian and Jewish people find welcoming congregations or seminary programs, offer trainings and events, and have a variety of downloadable resources.

LGBT Religious Archives Network – http://www.lgbtran.org/ This site features an amazing collection of recorded oral histories from faith leaders across the spectrum of spiritual experience, and aims to record LGBT faith and spirituality history.

Omnigender: A Trans-Religious Approach, by Virginia Ramey Mollenkott. Pilgrim Press, 2001.

Transfaith – http://transfaithonline.org News, information, activism, and tools for creating trans day of remembrance events, for people across the spectrum of spirituality and faith.

Trans-gendered: Theology, Ministry, and Communities of Faith, by Justin E. Tanis. Pilgrim Press, 2003.

Transtheology – http://www.transtheology.org/
This open-source project, though academic in nature, is accessible to a broader audience and has information on trans and gender nonconforming experience across faith and spirituality perspectives through history, from atheism and Christianity to Hinduism and Wicca and beyond.

TransTorah – Trans-Torah
Rituals, liturgy, essays, and resources for and about trans and gender expansive experience in Judaism.

Conferences and Events

There are diverse events and gatherings worldwide for, and about, trans and gender diverse individuals. These include LGBT youth camps, academic conferences, community gatherings, medical and mental health trainings, religious events, ally symposiums, and events that cross over between multiple communities. They are large and small, and different events will be of interest to different people. Please see our website for a much more expansive list. Only a handful of national and international events have been included here.

- Creating Change Conference – https://www.creatingchange.org/
  This LGBT activism conference has videos of its keynote, and other resources from the event, online for those who could not attend.

- Fantasia Fair – http://www.fantasiafair.org/
  Includes workshops, presentations, gender presentation training, special events, and couples support.

- Gender Odyssey – http://www.genderodyssey.org/
  Includes workshops, seminars, events, keynotes, a family track, teen programming, and professional training.

- Gender Spectrum Conference - https://www.genderspectrum.org/ quick-links/events/ – Includes workshops, seminars, a professional's symposium, and youth programming.

- National Transgender Health Summit
  This medical professional's event has all of its plenary presentations online for those who could not attend

- Philadelphia Trans Health Conference – https://www.mazzonicenter. org/trans-health – Includes workshops, seminars, events, keynotes, a family track, and medical professional training.

- Southern Comfort Conference – http://southerncomfortconference.org/ Includes workshops, seminars, special events for different age groups, vendor's market, and adult social excursions.

- Transgender Leadership Summit – http://transgenderlawcenter.org/ events/leadershipsummit – Includes workshops and skills training for community members and professionals on diverse topics affecting trans and gender expansive individuals

- Transgender Lives: The Intersection of Health and Law – http:// www.transadvocacy.org/transgender-lives-conference
  This conference is appropriate for community members and allies, as well as legal and health professionals.

- World Professional Association for Transgender Health (WPATH) Symposium - http://www.wpath.org/ – Conference for professionals working with transgender and gender nonconforming individuals.

It is also important to keep in mind the following events, or opportunities for connection and activism, listed in the order of how embedded they are in the trans community experience:

- International Trans Day of Remembrance, November 20th – http://tdor.info/

- Trans Day of Visibility, March 31st – http://www.transvisibility.com/

- Trans Day of Action for Social and Economic Justice –
  http://alp.org/tdoa_pou

- Trans Lobby Day – https://transgenderequality.wordpress.com/tag/
  lobby-day/ (each state organizes this work on different days, find out
  where to get involved near you)

Trans History

Arresting Dress: Cross-Dressing, Law, and Fascination in Nineteenth-Century San Francisco, by Clare Sears. Duke University Press Books, 2014.

"The Female Marine" and Related Works: Narratives of Cross-Dressing and Urban Vice in America's Early Republic, edited by Daniel Cohen. University of Massachusetts Press, 1998.

How Sex Changed: A History of Transsexuality in the United States, by Joanne Meyerowitz. Harvard University Press, 2004.

Transgender History, by Susan Stryker. Seal Press, 2008.

Karn Publications – http://www.karnpublications.com/ – Multiple books on the history of crossdressing and transfeminine edited by Peter Farner

Trans Theory and Academia

Assuming a Body: Transgender and Rhetorics of Materiality, by Gayle Salamon. Columbia University Press, 2010.

decolonizing trans/gender 101, by B. Binaohan. Biyuti publishing, 2014.

Delusions of Gender: How Our Minds, Society, and Neurosexism Create Difference, by Cordelia Fine. W. W. Norton & Company, 2011.

Gender Diversity: Crosscultural Variations, by Serena Nanda. Waveland Press, 1999.

The Lives of Transgender People, by Genny Beemyn and Susan Rankin. Columbia University Press, 2011.

Queer Theory, Gender Theory, by Riki Wilchkins. Riverdale Avenue Books, 2013.

Nobody Passes: Rejecting the Rules of Gender and Conformity, edited by Matt Bernstein Sycamore. Seal Press, 2006.

Normal Life: Administrative Violence, Critical Trans Politics, and the Limits of the Law, by Dean Spade. Duke University Press, 2015.

Sex Changes: Transgender Politics, edited by Patrick Califia. Cleis Press. 2003.

The Riddle of Gender: Science, Activism, and Transgender Rights, by Deborah Rudacille. Pantheon, 2005.

Third Sex, Third Gender: Beyond Sexual Dimorphism in Culture and History, edited by Gilbert Herdt. Zone Books, 1996.

Trans-Academics.org – http://www.trans-academics.org/ – A project of the Association for Gender Research, Education, Academia & Action (AGREAA), this site is full of educational and community resources for individuals with academic interests in issues affecting trans and gender nonconforming people and communities, including a reference library and other research tools.

The Transgender Studies Reader, edited by Susan Stryker and Stephen Whittle. Routledge, 2006.

The Transgender Studies Reader 2, edited by Susan Stryker and Aren Aizura. Routledge, 2013.

Transgender Studies Quarterly (TSQ), edited by Susan Stryker and Paisley Currah – https://www.dukepress.edu/TSQ-Transgender-Studies-Quarterly/

Personal Journeys and Biographies
MtF

- *Hung in the Middle*, by Alana Nicole Sholar. EWH Press, 2012.

- *A Queer and Pleasant Danger: The True Story of a Nice Jewish Boy who Joins the Church of Scientology, and Leaves Twelve Years Later to Become the Lovely Lady She is Today*, by Kate Bornstein. Beacon Press, 2013.

- *Redefining Realness: My Path to Womanhood, Identity, Love & So Much More*, by Janet Mock. Atria Books, 2014.

- *She's Not There: A Life in Two Genders*, by Jennifer Finney Boylan. Broadway Books, 2003.

- *Warrior Princess: A U.S. Navy Seal's Journey to Coming Out Transgender*, by Kristin Beck and Anne Speckhard. Advances Press, 2013.

- *Whipping Girl: A Transsexual Woman on Sexism and the Scapegoating of Femininity*, by Julia Serano. Seal Press, 2007.

FtM

- *As Nature Made Him: The Boy Who Was Raised as a Girl*, by John Colapinto. HarperCollins, 2000.

- *Born on the Edge of Race and Gender: A Voice for Cultural*, by Willy Wilkinson. Hapa Papa Press, 2015.

- *Just Add Hormones: An Insider's Guide to the Transsexual Experience*, by Matt Kailey. Beacon Press, 2005.

- *One in Every Crowd*, by Ivan E. Coyote. Arsenal Pulp Press, 2012.

- *Two Spirits, One Heart: A Mother, Her Transgender Son, and Their Journey to Love and Acceptance*, by Marsha Aizumi and Aiden Aizumi. Magnus, 2013.

- *What Becomes You*, by Aaron Raz Link and Hilda Raz. Bison Books, 2008.

Two Spirit

- *A Two-Spirit Journey: The Autobiography of a Lesbian Ojibwa-Cree Elder,* by Ma-Nee Chacaby and Mary Louisa Plummer. University of Manitoba Press, 2016.

Trans Youth

- *I'm Your Daughter, Too: The True Story of a Mother's Struggle to Accept Her Transsexual Child.* By R. Madison Amato. CreateSpace, 2012.

- *Jazz Mergirl: The True Story of Jazz Jennings, a Transgender Girl Born in a Boy's Body,* edited by Bruce Edlen. CreateSpace, 2015.

- *Mom, I need to be a Girl,* by Just Evelyn. Walter. Trook Publishing, 1998. – available free at http://ai.eecs.umich.edu/people/conway/ TS/Evelyn/Evelyn.html

- *Raising My Rainbow: Adventures in Raising a Fabulous, Gender Creative Son,* by Lori Duron. Broadway Books, 2013.

- Trading Places: When Our Son Became a Daughter—A Mother's Story of a Family's Transition, by Jane Baker. Braefield Press, 2014.

- *Transitions of the Heart: Stories of Love, Struggle and Acceptance by Mothers of Transgender and Gender Variant Children,* edited by Rachel Pepper. Cleis Press, 2012.

Trans Teens

- *Becoming Nicole: The Transformation of an American Family,* by Amy Ellis Nutt. Deckle Edge, 2015.

- *Beyond Magenta: Transgender Teens Speak Out,* by Susan Kuklin. Candlewick, 2015.

- *Some Assembly Required: The Not-So-Secret Life of a Transgender Teen,* by Arin Andrews, 2014.

- *Rethinking Normal: A Memoir in Transition,* by Katie Rain Hill. Simon & Schuster Books for Young Readers, 2015.

Trans Parents:

- *Dress Codes: Of Three Girlhoods–My Mother's, My Father's, and Mine,* by Noelle Howey. Picador USA, 2003.

- *Families Like Mine: Children of Gay Parents Tell It Like It Is,* by Abigail Garner. Harper Collins. 2004.

- *Labor of Love: The Story of One Man's Extraordinary Pregnancy,* by Thomas Beatie. Seal Press, 2008.

- *Stuck in the Middle with You: A Memoir of Parenting in Three Genders,* by Jennifer Finney Boylan. Crown Publishers, 2013.

Relationships

- *My Husband Betty: Love, Sex, and Life with a Crossdresser Paperback,* by Helen Boyd. Seal Press, 2003.

- *She's Not the Man I Married: My Life With a Transgender Husband,* by Helen Boyd. Seal Press, 2007.

Genderqueer

- *Life Songs: A Genderqueer Memoir,* by Audrey MC. Miniminor Press, 2014.

- *Queer and Trans Artists of Color,* edited by Nia King, Terra Mikalson, and Jessica Glennon-Zukoff. CreateSpace, 2014.

- *Nina Here Nor There: My Journey Beyond Gender,* by Nick Krieger, Beacon press, 2011.

- *Troubling the Line: Trans and Genderqueer Poetry and Poetics,* edited by TC Tolbert and Tim Trace Peterson. Nightboat Books, 2013.

Anthologies

- *Finding the Real Me: True Tales of Sex and Gender Diversity*, edited by Tracie O'Keefe and Katrina Fox. Jossey-Bass, 2003.

- *Kicked Out*, edited by Sassafras Lowrey and Jennifer Clare Burke. Homofactus Press, 2010.

- *Sexual Metamorphosis: An Anthology of Transsexual Memoirs*, edited by Jonathan Ames. Vintage, 2005.

- *Trans Forming Families: Real Stories About Transgendered Loved Ones*, 2nd Edition, edited by Mary Boenke. Oak Knoll Press, 2003.

- *Trans/Portraits: Voices from Transgender Communities*, edited by Jackson Wright Shultz. Dartmouth, 2015.

Blogs and Social Media

Ask A Transman – http://askatransguy.tumblr.com/
Trans men answer questions by and about transmen concerning social, legal, and medical transition.

Gender Blogs – http://www.genderblogs.com
A large number of members have shared their thoughts, feelings, and information on everything from relationships and spirituality, to youth and gender-specific issues.

Gendermom – https://gendermom.wordpress.com/ – A mother of a trans daughter reflects on life, answers questions, and hosts a podcast.

Gender Sexuality Support – https://www.instagram.com/gender_sexuality_support/ – Links, inspirational pieces, and questions from teens answered by teens about LGBTQQAII issues

The Intersex Roadshow – http://intersexroadshow.blogspot.com.au/
Information about transgender concepts and issues, with an accompanying Tumblr account.

Safe2Pee – http://safe2pee.org/ – Discussions and information about public restrooms.

Transgender Universe – http://transgenderuniverse.com/ Politics, entertainment, science, and thoughtful articles on trans issues.

TransGriot, Monica Roberts – http://transgriot.blogspot.com/ Top notch news, essays, and material on trans issues.

TransMusePlanet – http://transmuseplanet.blogspot.com/ News, resources, and an associated community for trans and gender nonconforming individuals.

Traversing Gender Facebook Page – https://www.facebook.com/ TraversingGender – Resources, news, project updates, and information for and about trans and gender nonconforming individuals.

Hashtags

On social media, hashtags are an interesting way to look up a variety of posts and resources, as well as share your own material. They can be looked up on Instagram, Twitter, Facebook, Pinterest, and others. Beyond the ones listed below, you can also search based on any of the topics or journeys you have seen listed in this book.

Trans people and issues:

- #trans

- #transgender

- #translivesmatter

- #transphobia

Trans women:

- #GirlsLikeUs

- #mtf

- #transwomen

Trans men:

- #ftm

- #GuysLikeUs

- #transmen

Black trans issues:

- #blacktranslivesmatter

- #transblacklivesmatter

Documentaries:

- *The Aggressives*, 2005.
  A look at women that prefer to dress and act as men, who participate in NYC's predominantly African-American drag balls.

- *Blossoms of Fire*, 2001.
  This film celebrates the extraordinary lives of the Isthmus Zapotecs of southern Oaxaca, Mexico, whose strong work ethic, independence, and culture has resulted in powerful women, the region's progressive politics, and their tolerance of alternative gender roles.

- *Colonel Jin Xing*, 2004.
  The story of Jin Xing who was a male colonel in China's People's Liberation Army, and now is a mother, world class ballerina, actress, and China's most famous modern dancer.

- *Gender Redesigner*, 2007.
  This movie explores the plight of a man who was born into the body of a woman, in an introspective and often funny look at living as a modern transsexual.

- *I Am Jazz: A Family in Transition*, 2011.
  This documentary follows the life of an extraordinary family, and their transgender daughter who has grown up as a trans activist in the media spotlight, Jazz Jennings.

- *Middle Sexes: Redefining He and She*, 2005.
  Examining the diversity of human sexual and gender variance around the globe, this film includes commentary by scientific experts and people who do not conform to a simple male/female binary.

- *Mohammad to Maya*, 2012.
  A look at the spiritual and emotional side of transition through the story of a devout Muslim from India named Mohammed, who was persecuted by her orthodox Muslim family and religious community undergoing sexual reassignment surgery.

- *Out Late*, 2008.
  An intimate look at the lives of five people across North America who chose to come out as lesbian, gay, or transgender after 55, and the choices that brought them there.

- *Paris is Burning*, 1990.
  A chronicle of the 1980s New York drag scene, focusing on balls, voguing, the ambitions, and the lives that gave the era its warmth and vitality.

- *She's a Boy I Knew*, 2007.
  The filmmaker turns her camera on her family and herself for this down-to-earth documentary that follows her transition from male to female over the course of several years.

- *Southern Comfort*, 2001.
  The final year in the life of trans man Robert Eads, who was turned down for treatment of ovarian cancer, and when he did receive it, the cancer was too advanced to save his life.

- *Trans*, 2012.
An up-close and very personal look into the lives, loves, and challenges of trans people of all ages and from all walks of life.

- *Transparent*, 2006.
A documentary about 19 female-to-male transsexuals from 14 different states who have given birth and, in most instances, raised their biological children.

- *Trinidad*, 2008.
Trinidad, Colorado, dubbed the "Sex Change Capital of the World," talks with the trans women there, the doctors who have performed surgeries, and locals as they reflect on it all.

- *Two Spirits*, 2011.
The story of Fred Martinez, a *nádleehí* murdered at age 16.

TV Documentaries:

- *Dateline NBC: Living a Transgender Childhood*, 8 July 2012.

- *20/20: My Secret Life: A Story of Transgender Children*, 27 April 2007.

- *Our America with Lisa Ling: Transgender Lives*, 22 Feb 2011.

- *TransGeneration* (tv miniseries), 2005.

- NBC News: *Life As a 5-Year-Old Transgender Child*, 22 April 2015.

- CBS News: *Born This Way: Stories of Young Transgender Children*, 8 June 2014.

Movies and Television:

- *About Ray*, 2015.
  After Ray decides to transition from female to male, Ray's mother must come to terms with the decision while tracking down Ray's biological father to get his legal consent.

- *Beautiful Boxer*, 2004.
  The story of Muay Thai boxer Parinya Charoenphol, who pursued the sport to pay for his sexual reassignment surgery.

- *Boy Meets Girl*, 2015.
  A funny, tender, sex positive romantic comedy that explores what it means to be a real man or woman, and how important it is to follow your dreams.

- *Boys Don't Cry*, 1999.
  Female born, the young Brandon Teena attempts to find himself and love in Nebraska, though the tale turns dark.

- *The Dutch Girl*, 2016.
  The marriage and work of two Danish artists, Lili and Gerda, evolves as they navigate Lili's groundbreaking journey as a transgender pioneer.

- *Her Story* (TV-2015 debut) http://herstoryshow.com/
  Two trans women in Los Angeles have given up on love, when suddenly chance encounters give them hope, featuring predominantly LGBTQ women, both on-screen, and off.

- *Leave It on the Floor*, 2011.
  A young man finds his footing with a family of choice, set in the Ballroom scene of Los Angeles, with relationship drama and amazing dance sequences.

- *Ma Vie en Rose*, 1997.
  Ludovic is a transgender girl who talks of marrying her neighbor's son, and is confused why everyone is surprised, while her family struggles with her actions and gender.

- *Normal*, 2003.
  A Midwestern husband and father announces his plan to transition, and everyone works to find new footing as she changes life at work, and around those she cares for.

- *Romeos*, 2011.
  A drama centered on the relationship between a young man and his female to male transgender cohort.

- *Tangerine*, 2015.
  A transgender working girl tears through Tinseltown on Christmas Eve searching for the pimp who broke her heart.

- *Tomboy*, 2011.
  A 10-year old transgender boy moves to a new neighborhood with his family, and introduces himself as a boy for the first time to new friends.

- *TransAmerica*, 2005.
  A pre-operative trans woman learns that she fathered a son, now a teenager, and the two of them embark on a long and strange road trip.

- *Transparent* (TV-2014 debut)
  An LA family have their past and future unravel when their father comes out as a trans woman, causing everyone's secrets to spill out.

- *Wild Side*, 2004.
  A trans woman who survives prostituting herself in Paris returns to her family home in the countryside, with her two male lovers, to look after her dying mother.

Author Biography

Lee Harrington is an internationally known sexuality, relationships, and personal authenticity educator. He brings a combination of playful engagement and thoughtful academic dialogue to a broad audience, with the belief that everyone's story matters. An award-winning author and editor on gender, sexual, and sacred experience, his books include "Traversing Gender: Understanding Transgender Journeys," among many other titles. An active contributor to a variety of anthologies, collaborations, and audio projects, he also produces the Passion and Soul podcast. Lee has been blogging online since 1998, and teaching worldwide since 2001. Read more about Lee at PassionAndSoul.com.